CREATING
with OTHERS

CREATING
with OTHERS

The Practice
of Imagination in
Life, Art, and the Workplace

SHAUN McNIFF

SHAMBHALA
Boston & London
2003

Shambhala Publications, Inc.
Horticultural Hall
300 Massachusetts Avenue
Boston, Massachusetts 02115
www.shambhala.com

9 8 7 6 5 4 3 2 1

First Edition

Printed in the United States of America

Designed by Ruth Kolbert

⊛ This edition is printed on acid-free paper that meets the
American National Standards Institute Z39.48 Standard.

Distributed in the United States by Random House, Inc.,
and in Canada by Random House of Canada Ltd

Library of Congress Cataloging-in-Publication Data
McNiff, Shaun.
Creating with others: the practice of imagination in life, art,
and the workplace/Shaun McNiff.—1st ed.
p.   cm.
ISBN 1-57062-966-8 (alk. paper)
1. Creative ability.   2. Creation (Literary, artistic, etc.)
3. Imagination.   4. Social groups.   5. Teams in the workplace.
I. Title.
BF408 .M336   2003
153.3'5—dc21
2003003851

"All streams run into the sea,
yet the sea never overflows;
back to the place from which the streams ran
they return to run again."

—ECCLESIASTES 1:7

". . . a lucid invitation to live and to create,
in the very midst of the desert."

—ALBERT CAMUS,
The Myth of Sisyphus

CONTENTS

ACKNOWLEDGMENTS   xi

"IN THE BEGINNING"   1
    From Solitude to Creating with Others   1
    Creativity Is Everywhere   3
    How to Use This Book   5
    The Workplace Widget   12

1   CREATIVITY IS GETTING
   OUTSIDE YOURSELF   19
    Perceptions Are Doorways to Creation   19
    Marc: I Have to Be Connected to Other People   20
    Support and the Feedback Loop   24
    Eleanor: People Need to Get Away   25

Keep the Space Safe 28

Creative Practice 31

2 SISYPHUS IN THE SLIPSTREAM 37

The Muse Is in the Present Moment 37

Alone and with Others 39

Steve: I Respond in Ways
I Never Knew Were Possible 42

Sharon: There Has to Be a Give-and-Take 43

Assisting Forces 45

The Mental Switch 48

Creative Practice 51

3 FLOW AND SPONTANEITY:
THE MOVEMENT BASIS OF CREATION 55

Creating Outside the Lines 55

In and Out of Contact 56

Interaction Generates Ideas 57

Peter: The Importance of Goals,
Structure, and Rules 59

From One Movement to Another 67

Creative Practice 72

4 GATHERING TOGETHER:
THE INTEGRATING PROCESS
OF IMAGINATION 74

The Mediating Place of Imagination 74

Showing Up and Falling Together 79

Sarah: The Creative Energy of Teams 83

Bill: Being Compelled to Stretch 88

To Imagine Is to Let Go 93

Active Imagination and Creative Problem Solving   99

Creative Practice   110

5   POSITIVE ATTITUDE AND MAKING
THE MOST OF BAD SITUATIONS   115

Simple Acts of Renewal   115

David: Stay Open and Positive   116

Wendy and Luis: Tap into the
Creative Energy and Learn How to Let Go   117

Ida: Falling Apart   123

Vital Communities   127

John: It's an Attitude   128

Creative Practice   136

6   CRITICISM AND TWO VIEWS
OF OPEN SPACE   139

What Are the Goals?   139

Sam: Struggles with Criticism   142

Aesthetic Distance   147

Fallow Periods   150

Karen: The Cultivation of Creative Ecology   151

Paul: No Letting Up   153

Creative Practice   156

7   FLYING SPARKS: RELATIONSHIPS
WITH PEOPLE AND PLACES   163

We Owe Everything to Those Who Shape Us   163

Mary: A Social Basis to Creativity   165

Laura: Different Kinds of Creative Relationships   167

Stan and Leah: Yin and Yang   171

Lucy: Affirming Others   175

Seeing Familiar Places for the First Time 179

*Matthew: Different Environments
  Energize One Another* 181

Creating Is Conversation 186

Creative Practice 189

8 WHAT LEADERS CAN
   AND CANNOT DO 193

Control and Liberation: The Necessary Interplay 193

Witnessing Others 197

*Mike: There Are No Road Maps for the
  Deep Terrain of Creativity* 199

*Shirley: We Need to Delegate More to
  the Environment* 208

*Build a Culture That Supports the
  Creative Process* 214

*Norm: Everyone in the Organization
  Has to Be a Leader* 218

Creative Practice 230

9 CREATING FROM THE HARD PLACES 233

The Creative Process and Healing Are Inseparable 233

The Power of Disturbance 235

*When Existential Discontents
  Grow Out of Proportion* 236

M. L. O'Connor: Art Kept Me Alive 238

*The Transforming Role of Crisis
  and the Healing Power of Community* 243

*Lisa: Making Creative Energy
  as an Artist-in-Residence* 247

Creative Practice 254

INDEX 259

ACKNOWLEDGMENTS

The making of this book was itself a process of creating with others. It is affirming to see how the principles being examined manifested themselves in every phase of the book's construction. I am indebted to colleagues who helped me within individual discussions, interviews, and focus group sessions to explore and understand the process of creativity in relationships, groups, and the workplace.

As I said to my friend Steve Levine, I can't believe that I wrote this book during one of the most demanding winters of my life, and maybe this is what creating with others is all about. Vital and challenging interactions with people energize us and make it possible for individual expressions to flow from a larger interplay of cooperation, even when there appears to be little free time and open space for creation. Crowded, busy, and demanding conditions paradoxically served as the muses for *Creating with Others*.

I give special thanks to my primary collaborators who participated in interviews and allowed me to reshape our conversations into dialogues presented in different sections of the book: Peter

(Hart), Mary Louise O'Connor, Norm (Becker), John (Bigelow), and Laura (Rossi Le). My closest collaborator in this project, as well as my three previous Shambhala books, has been Kendra Crossen Burroughs, who has been an invaluable guide and critic from the conception of the project to its completion. I am also grateful to Jacob Morris for his perceptive work in copyediting the manuscript, and special thanks to Dave O'Neal, Managing Editor, for his guidance and generous attention through the final stages of book production. I am indebted to Kendra, Dave, and all of the Shambhala staff for their support and the aesthetic care given to the publication of my books, all of which makes for one of my best and most sustained creative collaborations.

The following friends and colleagues contributed important thoughts and statements that found their way directly into the text: Judith Butterly, Mark Towner, Catherine Cobb, Tom Redman, Julia Kristeller, Barry Thompson, Paolo Knill, Kelsey McNiff, Susan Koso, Steve Levine, Steve Slocomb, Abigail Bottome, Bob Meahl, Bill Brean, Ian Gardiner, Cathy Malchiodi, Ed Stygar, Bill Harney, Bob McGrath, Vivien Marcow-Speiser, Mark Kuhn, and Lynn Kapitan, the maker of the magical cloak. The process of conversation with my collaborators embodied the subject of creating with others and reinforced for me that the best of creation is always characterized by interplay of some kind and not simply the consequence of one person acting alone. Other characters presented in the book are fictions who embody experiences I have had in creating with others.

Ideas and inspirations emerged from group conversations during or after lectures in Boulder; Houston; Cuyahoga Falls, Ohio; Caldwell, New Jersey; Philadelphia; New York City; Cambridge; Quebec City; Saas Fee, Switzerland; Netanya, Israel; Milwaukee; and other places. I do not know the names of every contributor, but I want to collectively thank the lecture audiences who so freely shared their frustrations and dreams about living more creative lives within the workplace.

"In the
Beginning"

From Solitude to Creating with Others

Most people envision creativity as a solitary and quasi-magical activity in which individuals acting alone make something from nothing. God is portrayed in the Bible as making the world from an abyss. An idea of a desired outcome exists, and God calls light, earth, and living creatures into being with striking immediacy, thus initiating the solitary and directive notion of creation.

Many of us give up on the creative process when we find ourselves unable to bring mental ideas of desired expressions into the world with the same ease attributed to God's creation of the world in Genesis. I remember my frustration as a child when I could not precisely paint the pictures that existed in my mind. Like so many other children, I transferred my interests away from the arts to other things. When I returned to creative activity in college, I became more aware of the give and take that occurs between painters and their materials. My teachers and the other students helped me to stay committed to the process of learning through sustained experimentation with materials and ideas, and careful study of the works of other people.

Everything is shaped from something else and in cooperation with agencies other than ourselves. Life is always created from interplay among different participants who make contact, influence one another, exchange their essential natures, merge, and generate new forms. Yet we still imagine ourselves like the Creator in Genesis, making things from "the void" and according to the dictates of the strategic mind. Creativity does not happen this way for most people. Solitude has a crucial place in creative practice but it is only part of a larger exchange among people, places, and things. Even in our most solitary moments creativity is a group process of interacting forces, images, ideas, and possibilities, all gathering together to make something that is shaped from the unique qualities of their relationship to one another.

We also assume mistakenly that creativity is a gift given to a select few and believe that it exists "inside" people as an attribute of some kind. Creativity is inside and outside us. It might be more accurate to say that creativity is in us and we are in it. Creativity is ubiquitous. It circulates through our environments like the air we breathe. But not everyone uses it. We engage this essential creative energy of life when we join ourselves to its transforming movements through interactions with other things and people.

I am frequently asked whether there is a difference between art and creativity. For me the former is a discipline and the latter is an energy or force. In this book, art is the practice and creativity is the medium. The two will be integrated into the art of leading a more creative life. Any person can do this and do it well.

The contemporary focus on the interplay of body, mind, and spirit reflects a deep yearning for integration in a world where knowledge, professional practice, and even the most intimate qualities of our personal lives have been compartmentalized. We are rediscovering how everything is connected to everything else in a creative ecology where small and large things influence one another. Nothing lives in isolation, and everything that we do has an impact on ourselves as well as the overall environment.

This book will explore the genesis of human creations in a reciprocal world of inspirations and collaborations. The benefits of this way of approaching creativity are many for our personal, family, and community lives. Without rejecting the actions of individual creators working alone, we will discover that even the most solitary forms of creation are based upon relationships of some kind. As we gain a more complete understanding of the interactive basis of creativity, we might even be able to revisit Genesis with the goal of continuing where God left off in creating the world. Communities and relationships committed to the mutual creation of new forms will change the world as we know it.

Creativity Is Everywhere

Have you ever sat alone trying to get started on a project? The experienced creator knows what it is like to spend hours, sometimes days, trying to decide what to do, how to get started. How about the times when you got started and then abandoned the project for any number of reasons—distractions, doubts about its value, a loss of self-confidence, or simply shifting attention to another area of interest.

Compare these indecisive times to occasions when you work with others on a job that needs to be done. There is group energy, a contagion, and a spirit of support among the group members that draws you into the action. You might perform a small role in a project, but what you do is necessary to the creation of something larger than yourself. The collective creation takes shape around you. It also grows inside you, because you feel the effects of what is made and you are influenced by the energy of cooperation.

In a group you might take the risk of giving a suggestion as to how to solve a problem, and someone says, "Great idea," and there is an immediate adoption of the new direction. Everyone begins to focus on what you recommended. There is a sense that people are far more generous and supportive than you expected.

Not all of your ideas are likely to be adopted but you understand that suggestions are simply part of the interactive flow. Sometimes

outrageous or impractical proposals spark other insights and different ways of approaching the problem. One thing is generated from
another and every contribution plays its part in the movement of creation. There is a sense of connectedness and you realize that no one
could do this alone. You get past the feeling that your recommendation must be adopted in order for you to be a valued contributor to
the action. You might even get to the point where you take more
pleasure in affirming and implementing the ideas of others.

It can be wonderful to stand back and reflect on the whole, realizing that your contribution helped make it possible. A sense of creativity pervades the event. From the perspective of these aesthetic
reflections, the challenges, the give and take with others, and even
the unpleasant memories, are necessary to the ultimate completion
of the project. We realize how there was a general sense of purpose,
but otherwise everything took shape in an improvised way in response to whatever presented itself at a particular moment. Within
these group activities, creativity is experienced as a responsive process, as something we do within a particular context where problems
and the expressions of others play an essential role in stimulating our
reactions.

Do you have a vision of creative imagination that involves others
in this way? Perhaps you are one of the many people who see creativity as a special gift given to a select few who exercise their talents
in an individual pursuit. Do you feel that creativity has passed you
by in life?

"I'm not creative," you say to yourself or to others when given opportunities to express yourself. You know that judgments about creativity are highly subjective, but nevertheless you keep yourself
tagged as uncreative.

The large majority of the people that I encounter in my work with
the arts say that they are "not creative." This fairly common self-
perception is ripe for change.

Creativity exists everywhere as potential energy, always inviting
us to participate. Yet most people stand on the sidelines while only a
few participate. The more we watch, the further removed we become. Contemplation without action breeds paralysis. Ours is a culture of onlookers, spectators who are keenly observant and full of

critique but far removed from the action. We think in terms of the "creative few," as contrasted to the rest of us. We have lost the all-encompassing whirl of creative energy that draws everybody and their different gestures into "its" expression. So many of us are afraid to stand out. There is often an absence of creative role models. It is safer to blend in. Creative types are all too often seen as living on the fringes of life and this perception threatens our universal desire to be socially accepted and included.

A change in the general perception of creativity may be the most viable way of expanding participation. Rather than focusing on what you do not have or what you are not capable of doing, concentrate on what is uniquely yours. Find the creative vitality and opportunities in the community where you live, the school you attend, or the place where you work, and do something with it. Creativity is everywhere, ready to be engaged.

How to Use This Book

To realize a more complete creative life with others, it may be necessary for you to experiment with new ways of acting in the world. This book is designed to help you reflect upon your personal relationship with creativity while offering suggestions for practice.

Every conversation I had in researching the book affirmed that an endless stream of ideas can flow from open and passionate dialogue with others. It is my hope that you will continue and further expand this interplay as you respond to this book. I guarantee that your insights and new creative expressions will multiply into possibilities far beyond what can be written in a book or presented at a workshop. I perceive this book as a generator of opportunities, a source of potential energy to be released and carried forward by your responses to the text.

I intend this book to be a consistent and safe space to which you can return again and again to renew your relationship with creation or explore new areas of experience. You can have an individual dialogue with this book or you can involve others.

You might keep a journal of thoughts as you read and try to answer the various questions asked throughout the text. Make your own personal book in response to this one. I present the questions in italics so you can return to them or choose to engage them when you are ready. It may be helpful to record the book page number next to your response to each question in your journal. This simple notation will enable you to maintain a close relationship between the book text and your responses.

If a question or a statement stimulates you in a positive, negative, or puzzling way, simply respond with drawing gestures, collage, or poetic statements in your journal. Most people find that the best way to start is by making simple and spontaneous expressions in whatever media are most appealing and accessible. You will find that expression with creative media will help you approach problems in new ways. They present opportunities for discovery that flow outside the lines of verbal analysis.

Try not to think too much about what you want to do, and avoid mental plans. Just begin to move as naturally as possible with colors, words, lines, shapes or whatever expressive gestures help you to express yourself and record thoughts in your journal. Generally, if you let the image or idea pass unrecorded, it will be gone. Some of the best ideas slip inconspicuously into consciousness. Unless these unexpected arrivals are entertained, they will slip away in the same unobtrusive way they came. There will be dreams and visions that stay forever; but subtle and fleeting insights need to be engaged and held, or they will vanish into the vast undifferentiated flow of life.

Letting go can have many salutary effects. Holding on to experiences, including memories, emotions, and thoughts, often blocks our receptivity to what is happening in the present. As Ecclesiastes 3:6 advises, there is "a time to keep and a time to throw away." The flow of expression requires open channels of communication. We constantly see examples of how organizations and individuals lose relevance and vitality through their inability to maintain creative movement into the future.

Sustained reflection can be distinguished from retentive clinging to an experience. The contemplation of ideas and images can be done in a way that continues and enhances the flow of life. The practice of creative imagination gives attention to what is happening to

6

us without blocking the ongoing movement. So try to avoid excessive fixation on something that is not working properly. Put it aside and move on to something else. You might find that the new engagement will help you resolve the old and persistent problem. Sometimes we find our way to new discoveries simply by moving on and taking new vantage points on an experience or by returning again on another day with an open and receptive mind.

Document your dreams, ideas, feelings, and visions. Try not to be concerned about anything but making contact with the images and sensations you experience in the present moment. Use the journal as a way of becoming more aware of what is happening to you. The practice of creativity reveals that moment-to-moment awareness is the alpha and the omega of imagination, the most necessary condition for discovery and expansion.

Time has to be made for attunement. Yet there is nothing more difficult for many of us than scheduling time for creative reflection and practice. The more involved we are in the world, the more difficult it becomes to devote time to creation. As with any spiritual discipline, making time for practice will in itself bring benefits.

I estimate that the average professional person gives much more time each week to physical exercise than to creative expression. We have discovered that health is significantly affected by how we care for our bodies. Why is it that we have overlooked the way creative energy influences our individual and collective well-being? Can you consider making a small weekly time commitment to creative exercise?

If your time is really constricted, consider how a discipline like creative movement can combine body, mind, and creative spirit. Use your journal to briefly track what the creative practice sessions evoke in you, how your feelings are altered, and whether the experience brings satisfaction. I have predicted that simple outcome studies of how people feel before and after creative activity will provide empirically-minded researchers with the data they need to confirm whether or not art heals and changes moods.

Whenever I view journals made by beginning or experienced creators, I find a great variety of creative expressions: quick sketches, elaborately drawn pictures, axioms, long reflections on a particular theme, descriptions of dreams, notes, ideas for future projects, plus an assortment of images—photographs, artistic images, memorabilia, objects from nature—attached to the pages. Invariably, the spontaneous expressions of the creative imagination exhibit this diversity. Some people might use their journals in a more systematic way to describe dreams or to paint a daily mandala, as C. G. Jung did during a certain period of his life. In this way the journal becomes a primary medium of creative practice.

Use whatever format works best. You might prefer digital media and even explore the creation of collaborative journals online. Just remember that the process of keeping a creative journal in any medium should be focused on regular practice, spontaneity, and openness to whatever is passing through your life in particular moments.

Some might wish to move outside the confines of a journal and respond with spontaneous movement expressions, voice, music, dramatic enactment, ritual acts, sculpture, or other creative constructions. All media are welcomed and you are encouraged to use whatever fits your purpose. New digital technologies (photography, video, multimedia) make it possible for you to incorporate these varied modalities into a single body of work. Use your imagination and find ways to respond that satisfy and extend your expression.

Beginners as well as those who are more experienced with the creative process do not always realize that the practice of creation can take place within these instants and fragments that ultimately come together in ways that are unplanned but surprisingly effective and revealing. The key is getting started and then sustaining practice. Ideas simply emerge from the overall movement and circulation of creative energy. The dynamics of creation taking place within these practice activities can be applied to any realm that values creative insight, from the art studio or science lab to the workplace. What matters most is creative momentum and flow from which outcomes will result.

I was reading a newspaper account about the revival of Sufism in Afghanistan as the society begins to tolerate free expressions. The story described how the participants came together in rituals of free expression that welcome people from outside the established group.

The Sufi group rituals involved spontaneous movement, singing, and percussion. These individual expressions always found their way to a natural unity. The reporter was describing how the melding of parts into a whole results in a deeply moving experience that can only be achieved in community with others.

In my experiments with free creative expression in groups over the past three decades, I have consistently observed the presence of natural integrating force at work within every community. People experiencing this for the first time are typically in awe of how the process gathers together their various contributions and emotions in such a powerful way. Participants discover that if the environment is safe, respectful of differences, protected from the control of dominating persons, and open to the inevitable struggles and conflicts that expression entails, a creative force always moves the group toward integration. We learn to trust the process, which is so much larger than ourselves acting alone. Later sections of this book will show that the individual imagination works in the same way.

Don't be afraid or overly concerned if something in your expression seems out of place, odd, or even disturbing. As with the Sufi group, every action makes a contribution to the whole. The distinct, unusual, and challenging expressions are always the ones that drive the overall system into a new phase of creation.

Read this book with a group of friends and respond to the questions through an interactive e-group. The text is designed to address creating with others through both reflection and practice. Treat it like a course on the role of creativity in your life and use it as an opportunity to actually create with others. You will find that the responses of others will help you clarify and expand your thoughts and actions. Work together as co-researchers and record the responses that are generated. Identify patterns and establish priorities from the data you generate. Empower yourselves as creativity consultants who make observations and recommendations for immediate and long-term changes.

Group work inevitably presents a variety and richness of responses. The diversity of creations and possibilities tends to be the most remarkable outcome of creating with others. This is why I ask questions throughout the book. I want to encourage your infinitely unique expressions. The landscape of creative imagination is vast and beyond the grasp of any one person's description.

The queries addressed to the reader are intended to enlarge the discourse by including your reflections and experiences. They reach out to you *where you are*. In keeping with the responsive nature of the creative imagination, the text is designed to stimulate rather than explain. Approach the queries as invitations to creation, as opportunities to activate creative resources, and as a way of finding your personal links to creativity. The text strives to ask you your own questions, the ones you need to explore in order to understand more about yourself, your history with regard to creativity, and your potential for future creations. This book is concerned with the creativity of consciousness and how you think about things. Every person capable of reading this book has full access to the medium of creation. It is about changing the mind.

I encourage returning over time to the questions that interest you. Whenever I read through the text, the questions constantly evoke new and different thoughts. Watch how your responses change and expand when you revisit a situation.

In keeping with the dynamics of creation I discourage attempts to follow sequential steps and fixed stages of development. You can enter the discourse with creativity at any page of this book or any point in your life. Every moment is an opening to the complete spectrum of possibilities. What matters is the quality of your engagement and that you sustain the discourse. Pick it up at any moment, and see where it takes you.

Work with anything that comes to you outside the context of the questions. If you stay with the process and sincerely open yourself to reflection, your life-long history with creativity will be revealed. This process of self-examination will enable the creative spirit to establish a foothold in your life. It is hoped that the questions, vignettes, and suggestions presented in the text will provoke other possibilities and ideas you may wish to explore. They can serve as sparks igniting your creativity. Approach the practice of creativity with the realization that inspiration and insights typically appear like flashes of light, fleeting and forever changing, just like the creative process itself.

Self-assessment helps us to become more present and aware of the subtle dynamics of everyday life. As we reflect upon our environments and ourselves, we open to the circulation of energy that exists within particular situations. We all know how easy it is to be anesthetized to our surroundings and our own feelings and intuitions. When in single-minded pursuit of a goal, we often fail to notice other things and can quickly lose contact with immediate conditions. Creativity requires perceptual awareness and the ability to see connections between different aspects of experience. Self-assessment gets us involved and enables the process to take hold and do its work.

Reflection on our personal involvement with creativity helps us become more aware of its presence everywhere. Experience constantly affirms that we have to be involved in our own practice in order to be aware of the creative potentiality that moves through every environment. The sections of this book dealing with leadership emphasize how leaders need to find ways to be involved in their own creative practice as a way of establishing environments that liberate and support the creative expression of others. Current leadership training, which does not focus sufficiently on the dynamics of the creative process, will benefit from encouraging leaders and managers to explore their own creativity.

One of the early readers of this book in manuscript form described how people are sometimes reluctant to open themselves to probing questions. She said: "They can lead you in directions that may be difficult and even painful. The questions open you up."

I was concerned that the questions presented throughout the text might be perceived as superficial exercises, and she was saying that open-ended queries could expose the core of a person's life. The questions do provoke and they offer opportunities for readers to appreciate the manifold dimensions of a life situation.

My reader continued: "All of us have different answers based upon our experiences. We see the questions in so many ways. They multiply into wide-ranging things that people recognize in themselves."

Creating with others is forever permeated by surprise. We never know how different people will respond to the same experience, the same text. This is the beauty, the magic, and the sometimes frightening power of opening to our honest responses to life situations.

The Workplace Widget

Rather than selecting painting, creative writing, or dance as the "widget" through which connections are made between ideas and practice, I have focused on something more ubiquitous—the workplace as a center of creation. The widget is defined as a particular situation through which universal dynamics are manifested. There is an assumption that groups of people will act in similar ways whether they are working together to make computer parts, plan a city budget, or produce an art event. The concept of the widget acknowledges the existence of a fundamental process of creation that operates in different life situations.

Although examples are drawn from the arts and other everyday environments, the community of work is the focus through which this examination of creating with others will take place. Illustrations drawn from work demonstrate how creativity, so often viewed as a rarefied and esoteric domain, is essential to everything we do.

Our experiences with jobs, though rarely linked to art, are universal. Readers of creative reflections on archery, tennis, golf, motorcycles, and other subjects have been successful in applying insights from a narrow subject to all of life. Particular activities like changing the oil of a Harley, returning a serve, or lining up a putt make fresh connections to the whole of experience. Even though these subjects are sometimes distant from the common ground of all people, they offer attractive metaphors for the creative process because they connect to everyday experiences. I believe that the experiences that we all share with the workplace can present far more potent metaphors for creativity, largely because we take them for granted and miss the opportunities for creation that they so generously offer.

Using work as the focus of creative practice will be challenging. Obstacles are plentiful, and work is loaded with complex and mixed emotions. Some will argue that the very nature of organizational life, together with its commercial values of productivity, uniformity of quality, hierarchy, control, and the bottom line, is the antithesis of creativity. I agree with these concerns and understand how the idea of viewing work as a place of creation may seem far-fetched to some.

Yet the most valuable quality of the creative process is its ability to place things in new relationships and establish unlikely partnerships: the poison becomes a remedy, and problems are transformed into doorways to new ways of living. The advantage of the workplace widget is that it connects us all. It offers common ground for creating with others.

My reflections on the creative aspects of work are informed by years of experience in leading art studio groups. Beginning with different art therapy and therapeutic community experiments in 1970 and continuing to the studio retreats that I lead today, I have always focused on creating in groups. Making art with others in the studio and the process of creating with others at work share many common features. What we know about creativity in the art studio will be of great help in cultivating a more imaginative atmosphere on the job.

While leading studio groups I have simultaneously held more conventional positions within institutions of higher education. Although both areas have a common commitment to creativity development, the demands of the workplace make assimilation of the creative process a continuous challenge. My years of commitment to the dual worlds of art and work provide a credible platform for exploring their integration. Yet in pursuing a way to enhance creating with others within the workplace, I am still a very humble "seeker." I am not someone who has arrived and who can show others the way.

As I pursue this vision of integration, I find myself talking with others about their ideas, their hopes for a more creative community life, the serious obstacles they face, and the opportunities we have to make changes. Throughout my career researching the creative process, I have never found a topic or problem that generates nearly as much interest among people as how we can make work a more creative, productive, and fulfilling place. Everyone seems to share the desire, but we all have a long list of stories about how the creative imagination has been suppressed in jobs.

We realize that concerns about health and well-being require us to focus more on the pathological aspects of organizational life, those generating the stress that makes people sick. But completely eliminating tension and conflict from the workplace may not only prove impossible; in making such elimination our goal, we may overlook a great source of creative energy. Our afflictions and disturbances, the truly hard places of our lives, have always been sources of creative transformation. These lessons from the most difficult areas, from what Rumi called the bandaged places, suggest that we can always do something with the problems of our lives. Even when trying our best to make work the safest and most benevolent place possible, disturbing conditions are inevitable because they reflect the essential human condition. What matters is what we do with these conditions, how we respond to them and use them as a source of creative inspiration.

I have spent my life walking between the worlds of art and work. In spite of my longing for their complete integration, the two areas maintain considerable polarization. Because of the complete focus in the art studio upon the creative process, it has been relatively easy to create an environment where the imagination can flourish and where people can continuously support one another in perfecting their expression. Work does not offer this complete and supportive focus on creation. It is often a place that stifles, hurts, and breaks people. Maybe that is why it looms as such a large and attractive challenge.

There are many principles that contribute to making the studio a place where creativity can flourish, and they will be discussed in the following pages. The same conditions are generally required to further creativity in the workplace. But the latter setting presents numerous and continual deterrences to creative expression. These very obstacles also present opportunities for a new and enlarged life of the imagination. They are a major frontier for the practice of creativity.

For all its infinite variety, the creative process is governed by certain universal principles. In my focus group meetings and discussions with others, people describe fairly uniform obstacles to the creative process within group life. There is also wide agreement that creativity within organizations is greatly affected by the values and operating styles of leaders. Therefore the subject of leadership, including both effective and pathological elements, will be examined.

I will write about work as the practice of art. If we can simply relax our fixed attitudes about life and open to the common features of all experience, we will see that it is not such a big stretch to equate the two. The core themes related to creative expression in the art studio and creativity in the workplace are the same: safety, creative energy, seeing problems as opportunities, transforming conflict, control versus letting go, problems with ego, fear, affirmation, and so forth. If we accept the possibility that these once antithetical worlds can meet, merge, and transform one another, the path of creation will be cleared and will invite us to proceed.

The path leads to a new vision in which creation happens in relationships, in contrast to the more traditional orientation to creativity as a singular, individual journey. We will open ourselves to the creative forces that exist both within us and out in the world. As artists and leaders we will learn how to create environments in which the natural and life-enhancing forces of creation are free to work their magic.

The solitary aspects of creative contemplation will be embraced as necessary elements in the larger ecology of imagination. But we need to do more within our organizations and community life to embrace creativity as a primary value in relationships with others. I believe that we will achieve a more complete and fulfilling process of creation by joining personal and collective experiences. The need for this integration is greater than ever. Too many people are feeling that their primary human needs are not being met at work, while organizations are only beginning to consciously address ways in which they can foster more creatively fulfilling environments.

Leaders have not been trained to be facilitators of the creative process. They have not been exposed to systematic and effective experience with the depths of creativity. This must change and creativity enhancement has to become a prerequisite for the next generation of leaders. Similarly, artists and creative types have not been educated or prepared to work with other people in a deeply collaborative creative process. I have seen many artists rise to positions of leadership within their particular organization and then exhibit the most restrictive, controlling, and unimaginative ways of doing business with others. There are immense gaps of understanding to be bridged as we begin to explore how creativity and organizational life can become partners, learning from each other. The opportunities and needs cry out for attention and change.

Performing artists, arts educators, and creative arts therapists have all been exposed in their training and practice to the dynamics of creativity in groups and in relationships between people. These disciplines have established a body of knowledge and methods that we can begin to apply in the context of organizational life. As someone who has always had a foot in both the worlds of art and work, I know there are many others who are prepared to bring these domains together in a new way.

Yet those who are trained to use the arts with groups have not typically imagined themselves practicing outside fairly narrow specialist roles in schools, clinics, museums, adult education centers, or other institutions where arts programs are commonly found. At the same time, professional education and leadership training programs have not focused on how to foster creativity in organizational life.

People often assumed that I left creative work when I served as a college provost and as the president of a national professional association. I'd say to them, "No, not at all. I am always trying to expand the work of creation to new and challenging frontiers. The creative imagination has the most to offer us in those places where it is least recognized."

From my experience in working with people throughout the United States, Canada, Israel, and Europe, I know we have the resources and the vision required to bring creativity and work together in a way that will transform them both. However, as with other areas of creative expression, I am not sure that people always have the confidence necessary to achieve this result or the willingness to take the risks required to make it happen.

Those of us who have for many years helped people over the hurdles and through the resistance to their initial creative experiences know that once the work begins, once people make the first movements toward constructing a new culture of creativity, the process will unfold in ways that can never be planned in advance.

Commit yourself and your community to this undertaking, and you will discover how the objects of creation are always at least a step or two ahead of the calculating mind. This ability to surprise and inform experience with outcomes that emerge unexpectedly from your efforts is the very heart of the creative enterprise. Give it a serious and sustained try, and notice how it works. Your life and the lives of those around you will be changed and enriched.

Before shifting to an enlarged view of the creative imagination, we might revisit four misconceptions about creativity. Let us begin by declaring first that creativity is available to every person; second, that this energy exists everywhere in life; third, that when we create, it is always "with others" in some sense; and finally, that we need others in order to fully realize our creative potential.

Creativity is a physical and spiritual energy that spreads to every corner of life, seeking new experiences to be transformed. It is available to all of us at every moment. Everyone has it. Every person is a creator. The difference lies in those who have the desire to cultivate the gift and who choose to look at the world as a creative opportunity.

1

CREATIVITY
IS GETTING
OUTSIDE
YOURSELF

Perceptions Are Doorways to Creation

Some of the most resourceful and imaginative people I know believe that they are not creative. This attitude has its origin in the exclusive identification of creativity with artistic talent, scientific inventiveness, or spontaneous humor. These notions are then reinforced through psychological tests, school experiences, creative stereotypes, bad experiences with the arts, and conscious decisions that people make to avoid creative activities. Our concepts of creation and our self-perceptions are often the major obstacles to leading a more imaginative life.

The most effective deterrent to creativity is the tendency to focus attention on what we do not have or upon what we think we cannot do. Each of us has constant access to the ideas and materials of creation. Perhaps we keep creation at bay to stay clear of the entanglements and commitments that accompany a serious relationship and personal creative discipline. I guarantee that if you focus completely on a conversation with a person, listening more than speaking, you will begin to discover the subtle treasures of human interaction. Similarly, if you attend fully to your creative discipline, your life will be enriched.

Daily life is often experienced with blinders on, confining our vision to narrowly defined goals. We all need objectives, and distractions can be bothersome demons. But there are ways to concentrate while opening to what is outside an immediate frame of reference.

I worked with a group of Boston conceptual artists that made "art ideas." They were more concerned with opening up possibilities for creative life that went beyond making art objects. Their exhibitions urged people to imagine the world differently, to try new ways of acting and looking at their most familiar activities. Every art idea was based on shifts in perception.

Daily routines in the office were imagined as works of art. We found that framing any activity as "art" brought with it an appreciation of the unique aspects of the most mundane activities—sharpening a pencil, speaking on the phone, folding a piece of paper, writing a memo. Creative freedom is determined by how we behold the world. Any one of us can make new things with our perceptions that serve as doorways to the creative imagination. No one is excluded.

People seeking a better life beyond the horizon repeatedly discover the value in what they already have. Saint Augustine articulates this ancient truth when he says that he searched for God in distant parts of the world, only to find God within himself. Looking into the distance for what we desire sometimes takes us away from the unique conditions of our creativity. The search can also bring us home to a better appreciation of our unique resources.

MARC
I Have to Be Connected to Other People

Marc left the workplace in order to make time for personal creation, only to discover that he needed the stimulation of other people. He found that the things that bothered him the most at work were actually vital ingredients of his creative expression.

"It was a big lesson for me," Marc says. "I spent ten years in different jobs after college, with the goal of saving enough money so that I could paint and write full time. The initial discovery was that my creative expressions were not necessarily 'better' than what I did on weekends and at night after work. The first months of my new lifestyle were very relaxing and healthy. I needed to detox from all the stress I carried inside my body. My dreams were vivid, and I became aware of subtle aspects of life that had been lost in the work routine.

"It was very good to get away," Marc continues, "but ironically the biggest revelation was that I need the workplace. After six months of solitary life, I started to envy the people driving to work in the morning. I imagined what they were thinking in their cars, what they did in their offices, how they interacted with other people. They headed toward the highway, and I stayed at home, painting landscapes and writing stories about what I saw every day. My creative work was satisfying, but it lacked a mission, a sense of purpose.

"I was invited by a former colleague to do a brief consultation with a company that was having difficulties with teamwork. I had a reputation as an open guy who gets people talking to each other and finding new ways to solve problems. I see now that my artistic side was finding an outlet at work over the years. The five days I spent with these people as a consultant helped me see that I am at my best when responding to problems and situations. The separation from work taught me the importance of the responsive aspects of creativity. I need to be in an environment that throws challenging pitches at me. Working alone in the studio all of the time isn't for me. I missed the informal conversations, the deadlines, and being part of a collective work effort."

Marc needed to get away from his familiar environment to see it more completely. The break helped him discover his unique creative interests and skills. Immersion in day-to-day work activities can narrow our perspective, shutting out a more complete vision of our lives. Marc's life was turned inside out when he realized that the things he saw as impediments to creativity were actually vital ingredients.

"I was caught in the heroic myth of the artist creating alone, and with complete freedom. I discovered that freedom involves the ability to respond to situations in new ways. I have to be connected to other people in order to exercise creative freedom. There was too much of a void when I was alone; I need stimulation. I also found that I like doing different things at the same time. I'm 'polymorphously perverse'—I thrive on a mix of activities. Total solitude was a bust, an abyss. I went back to work."

Marc also realizes that creative expression is an ongoing challenge. He declares, "Perfect situations don't exist. Please don't think that I am trying to idealize the workplace as an artistic utopia. My time away helped me get a more realistic handle on both creativity and work. I understand how much my sense of creative vitality is stimulated by interactions with others, and I know all too well how jobs can limit my perspective and exhaust me with demands and stress. I don't have any answers or blueprints for others or myself. Yet it feels good to know that there may be creative opportunities where we least expect them."

Do Marc's experiences relate to your own? Have there been times when you left something and then discovered that you needed it? Identify the situations in your life that you find most difficult. Try to turn these irritants inside out and see if they stimulate you in creative ways. How do you respond to them? What would your life be without them?

Marc discovered how groups generate creative energy. The well-functioning group will always be capable of doing things that are not possible for an individual acting alone. We experience our most effective personal levels of creation and performance when interacting with others who stimulate us to reach beyond previous thresholds of experience.

The simple process of expressing ourselves creatively together with people sincerely interested in what we are doing can be strikingly new for many of us. We discover how our views of the world can be turned upside down by environments where others give us supportive and careful attention. These experiences underscore the art of witnessing others within safe settings where helpful feedback enhances creative collaboration. Too often I encounter people in my studio retreats who have never expressed themselves freely without fear of criticism.

If this mutual perspective on creation is useful in our personal lives, imagine how it could transform the way groups, organizations, and countries interact with one another. Our ideas about creativity and imagination have focused largely on individual talent and not enough on the interplay or ecology from which every creative act originates.

> *Compare your experience as an onlooker with situations where you have been immersed in an activity with other people and were able to express yourself spontaneously. Recall a moment when creative insights and helpful ideas came out of you effortlessly and without conscious thought of any kind. Perhaps it was in a group or conversation where you were comfortable and relaxed, where you felt valued by others and in sync with what was happening, and where you let down your guard and became part of the overall flow of energy in the particular situation.*

In these positive scenarios other people paid attention to you, listened to what you said, or watched what you did. You were able to let go of inhibitions and self-consciousness, and contribute to a collective creation that really did depend upon your participation. The flow of experience and the results emerging from these interactions was always a step or two ahead of your thoughts about what you were doing. The momentum of the situation carried you along, and you didn't have time to get caught up in doubts and deliberations about what you should or should not do. You were in a context that presented you with opportunities to act. You accepted the invitation and experienced the responsive nature of creativity.

Support and the Feedback Loop

My years of experience in leading art studios for people from diverse walks of life suggest that the majority believe they live outside the orbit of creativity. Yet in a stimulating workshop environment open to people's unique ways of expressing themselves, participants invariably leave with a sense that anything is possible in their creative expression. Affirmation replaces negation. Serious work within an environment that supports natural and authentic ways of self-expression reveals that participants can express themselves in ways that have an emotional impact on others, can achieve personal satisfaction, and can contribute to the overall creative energy of a group.

When I began to take creative activity seriously, I was in need of support from others, and fortunately I got it. I see now that my teachers had a great influence on what I have done with my life. They could easily have discouraged me from continuing with creative expression. The subtle nods of approval that I received kept me going. Critical comments helped me know when to change direction.

In competitive sports the measures of ability and skill are relatively objective and follow universally accepted standards of excellence. Creative skills are infinitely variable, and yet we assume that they can be measured with the same degree of precision as the speed of a runner or the distance of a javelin throw. Because value judgments and differences in taste figure so largely in the creative realm, we rely upon the affirmations of others.

The feedback loop is crucial to the creative process. Even the most competent creators fear the loss of their gifts and doubt their abilities when they become isolated. It is a rare person who is able to sustain creative work without receiving some kind of affirmation from others. There are artists who keep going without public acclaim. A prominent painter told me that she only needs the sincere interest of one person to stay with her work.

There is also the need to see our creative offspring having some kind of impact on other people. A writer friend died forlorn that his work was never widely read and that he was not able to help others as he had hoped. "I sit here in my study waiting," he said, "and no one comes."

This particular writer did not experience doubts about his gifts. His turmoil resulted from the absence of creative interaction with others and the fear that his efforts were not having an effect on people. Even though his writings were highly regarded by respected critics, he wanted them to play a more useful and transforming role in the world.

If experienced and acclaimed artists have these struggles with the value of their work, it may seem like a daunting task to involve the average person in a serious relationship with the creative process. The marginalizing of artistic experience in our culture makes it even more challenging. Art for art's sake may have significance for an elite few, but it is not in step with our more pragmatic society. If creative expression is to enlarge its place in our communities, there has to be a clear value attached to it. Perhaps it is possible to transcend these obstacles by locating the value and benefits of creativity in group and community life.

ELEANOR
People Need to Get Away

Eleanor is a human resources director in a large organization. She is also a painter. "For most of us creativity and work are completely separate," Eleanor says. "I'm convinced they can be combined. But it's not going to be easy."

"Why?" I ask.

"Primarily because we've got to demonstrate results. Business and the workplace are designed to achieve very specific outcomes."

Even if organizations see the benefits of a more creative workplace, there are operational challenges. "We haven't figured out how to do it," Eleanor asserts. "We don't have successful models of long-standing programs. Right now I am being led by a vision."

I inquire, "What is the primacy obstacle to the implementation of your ideas?"

"It may be the clock," Eleanor replies. "Creative work requires sustained time. At work we are constantly moving from problem to problem. It is challenging to complete tasks and projects by their deadlines, never mind find the time for creative expression."

I ask Eleanor, "How do you concentrate on the creative process when there are so many other things you are expected to do?"

"I try to be realistic about what organizations expect from people while they are on the job," she replies. "I am not going to propose that our lawyers and engineers spend their work hours writing poetry when they have urgent projects to complete. My more idealistic friends might think that I am too rigid, but I believe that engineers are paid to be engineers and lawyers to be lawyers. For me the question is, How can they be more productive engineers and lawyers? I am convinced they will be better at their jobs if the creative process has a larger place in their lives."

"What is your plan for doing this?" I ask.

"I don't have a step-by-step scheme for the workplace," she says. "The dynamics of creativity are too individual and complex for strategic plans."

I ask, "If given free rein to help a company become more creative, what would you do?"

"People have to get away and create in groups," Eleanor responds. "Once we begin to internalize the dynamics of creativity, we will find our individual ways to bring it to work. If the average person has more opportunities for creative expression, we will start to see changes. My vision is based on opening people to creativity. When we can set up the right environments, the process will take care of itself. Creativity is the antithesis of strategic planning. It's all about exposure to stimulating things that infect us with good vibes and imagination.

"I don't have a grand plan for redesigning the workplace," Eleanor admits. "I simply want to involve people in the creative process. If they become infused with this energy, creativity will find its way into their lives. It's more like pollination than structural engineering.

"People need to get away and experience something out of the ordinary," she emphasizes. "Even the most creative people in organizations are restricted by their routines. We have to do completely different things sometimes to discover what we can be."

Many of us spend our days at work responding to necessary tasks. Even at the end of our most productive days, we still feel that there is so much left to do. I describe to Eleanor how I had just returned from a short trip to find hundreds of e-mails. "I stayed late in my office to respond to them all, and the next morning there were twenty-five new ones waiting for me."

Eleanor says, "You have to recognize that the demands will never let up. This is why it is so difficult to create in new ways while at work. In keeping with the classic idea of a retreat, we need to get ourselves into a new environment from time to time, one that presents us with challenges for creative expression. You might be ingeniously creative with your responses to e-mail, but imagine what you can do in a studio that offers more distance from the endless flood of demands and responsibilities."

"And while I am away," I lament, "the e-mails pile up again."

"I never said that creativity is easy," Eleanor says. "E-mail never rests. The needs of the job are unending."

Eleanor feels that any person who becomes involved with creative activity needs attention from others. "I am creating environments where the emphasis is on giving others support for their creative expression," she says. "It's liberating to turn the typical self-centered approach on its head. We've got to receive this support ourselves to see how much others need it."

> *Do you agree with Eleanor's vision? How might you be*
> *affected by a creative retreat? Are there people you know at*
> *work who might change if they had this opportunity? Do*
> *you think that having the time for personal creative*
> *expression might help you be more productive at work, or*
> *do you think that Eleanor is too idealistic?*

People and organizations expend considerable energy in preventing change and imposing their will on others. Some of us try desperately to control our environments, and we hurt ourselves and others in the process.

> *Think of the most controlling person you know, and imagine*
> *how that person might be affected by serious involvement*
> *with the creative process.*

Our experiences with repressive situations can be instructive. Eleanor is altering her life to grasp an opportunity. Eleanor's vision of a more creative workplace has been shaped by the problems she encounters. She knows that she must ultimately demonstrate that the workplace will be more productive if it is more creative. In art groups she sees people growing more vigorous and optimistic as a result of creative expression. As a human resources director, she observes many disenchanted and unhappy workers who see few opportunities to change their conditions. She is convinced that creative expression will ultimately transform work environments.

> *Examine your personal history of creative expression in light of Eleanor's beliefs. To what extent do you rely on support from others when it comes to taking risks and doing something different? Have you received this support in the past? When was the last time you received this support from another person? What person has been most influential in your creative development?*
>
> *Were there times in your life when you stopped creating due to the lack of response from others? What does it take to stay active with the creative process when your expression is not being recognized? Do you see yourself as someone who is sensitive to the needs that others have for support? How effective have you been at supporting others? At work? In your personal relationships? What can you offer others to support their creation? Are you apt to receive more than you give? Give more than you receive? Recall an incident where you were influential in helping another person, and one where you missed the chance to help.*

Keep the Space Safe

If we are inviting people to take risks with their expression, then safety must be a priority. If the environment is relatively free of threats and dangers, it will support the natural and life-enhancing movement of the creative process. People constantly affirm that nothing is more essential in the cultivation of their creative expression than the need for safety. Whether in an art studio or on a job site, we need to feel a certain degree of security if we are to venture into new territory, where the ultimate effectiveness of our performance is uncertain.

Unfair treatment, negative judgment, and unrealistic expectations are universally perceived as major threats to expression. A colleague described to me how fear is the greatest enemy of creativity within organizational life and personal expression. "Fear will kill creativity faster than anything," she said. "Creativity is challenging to nurture and easy to stifle."

Perhaps the most important principle guiding the cultivation of creativity in others is "safety first," and then throughout every phase of creative work. Although many important creative insights occur through our responses to troubling situations, most people choose to work in supportive environments that relax inhibition. We generally perform better when our contributions are considered valuable or even indispensable.

Clear and predictable structure is ironically the best way to promote the expressive freedom of the average person. Like jazz musicians, we need a rhythm from which we can leap into improvisatory forays and then safely return. Creativity takes a material of some kind and places it in a new relationship to something else. Structure liberates so long as it encourages variations of its themes.

Clearing the path for others is the sustained discipline of the leader. In addition to restrictions imposed by others and by organizational structures, we all do things to ourselves that block the free circulation of creative imagination. We need help in clearing the way for creative action; few can do this alone because our personal paths are always part of a larger complex of relationships and demands.

> Reflect upon the past and present environments in which you
> felt most safe. Identify the characteristics that have remained
> the same as well as those that may have changed. Have you
> been able to express yourself freely within environments and
> relationships where you have not felt safe?
>   To what extent are you able to create a sense of security

*and safety within yourself even when the outside environment
is threatening? How important is safety to your expression?
How safe do you think you are in terms of supporting and
affirming the expression of others? List the things you do to
enhance the safety of others together with the things that
might threaten them. What are you willing to change?*

Leaders striving for productivity need to invest time and energy in
being attentive and responsive to the needs of others in their communities. Creative resources are wasted and new problems are created if the person in control is unresponsive to the needs of others.
Insecurity, discomfort, and nonproductive anger can be engendered
by these insensitivities.

Generosity of time and attention has great value in community
life. Even if motivated by complete self-interest, we find that giving
to others benefits both ourselves and the environment as a whole.

*Are you perceived as generous in giving attention to others?
In personal relationships? At work? In other parts of your
life? Are there differences? Why? Recall those situations in
your life where a person you valued paid attention to you.
What was the result? When was the last time this happened?
Reflect upon situations where you wanted attention and did
not receive it. How were you affected? Would your life be
different if you did receive attention in any of these
situations?*

Complete safety in any environment or relationship may hinder
creativity. Risk, conflict, and mistakes are inevitable features of creative exploration and discovery. If we go too far in reducing tension,
we are apt to anesthetize the environment and deny the necessary grit
that underlies creative vitality. Situations that are set up to guarantee
success for everyone are artificial and contrary to nature. Safety when
creating depends on how we treat one another, and ourselves.

CREATIVE PRACTICE

Skill in working with creative energy involves an understanding of its natural flow and circulation as well as the ability to sustain its movement. Like muscles, creative reflexes atrophy when they are not used. Regular exercise of creative energy sustains healthy circulation.

The circulation of creative energy is based upon the simple and fundamental principle of sustained motion whereby one gesture emerges from another. In painting, writing, dance, and music, we must get physical movement started in order to initiate the circulation of energy. Nothing happens in the creative process unless we choose to connect to the energy source moving within ourselves and the environment.

The most basic tenet of creative practice is that positive energy reinforces creativity. For the beginner, creative expression can be like a delicate flower, tender and vulnerable, and easily destroyed. The cultivation of creativity in others is furthered by presenting inspirational ideas and examples that correspond to what people are capable of doing. These suggestions are accompanied by consistent encouragement and the affirmation of expressions, all geared toward building self-confidence.

The fear that we feel when expressing ourselves with other people is an instinctual realization that the energy of creative expression can be easily shut down by negative responses from others. Yet fear is also a natural manifestation of the uncertainty we feel as we prepare to express ourselves creatively. There is always the possibility that the energy will not flow and that the force of creation will abate at a particular moment. Moderate fear before a creative performance is a natural reaction that activates and stirs the creative energies circulating within us. Approach fear as a chemical catalyst, as a sign that the creative moment is important to you and that you desire to express yourself as completely as possible. The fear is tied to a wish to succeed and the very real possibility that this might not happen. We fear humiliation and do not want to appear foolish. A positive environment can minimize the crippling effect of these common and real fears. As with other tensions and conflicts, fear can be engaged as a vital energy to be transformed by the creative process.

⟶ Set up a safe space in which you can begin to explore new ways of expressing yourself. You might be able to make art before you begin your day, during breaks at work, or at the end of the workday. Creative expressions on site at the workplace have the ability to directly engage the energies of the environment. I visited a university technology department where original and long obsolete Macintosh computers were placed on tables and shelves like icons. An artist had taken the inner workings of old computers and fashioned them into elegant assemblage constructions hanging on his walls. Another person made humorous sketches of coworkers and hung them on her walls. Artistic exercises at home or in other places outside the workplace will have different qualities and, as Eleanor suggests, we need to take time to retreat and give sustained attention to creative exercise. Both forms of practice are important and they complement one another.

A safe space requires the presence of people who will give you attention, feedback, and support. These affirming contacts with others often prove more important than establishing ideal physical spaces and time for creation. Safe people are the basis for undertaking an open investigation of the creative process.

⟶ Begin your creative exercise with visual perception. Select an object in your environment and contemplate its physical structure, independent of its uses or previous experiences you have had with it. Look carefully at the object's form, texture, and colors, and the way it reflects light. Examine it from different perspectives and reflect upon how this enlarged perception differs from your usual way of looking at the object.

⟶ Choose a representational painting that you made or one that is hanging in your space. Begin by looking at it in your usual way. Now put aside "narrative interpretations" of the image, the stories that it conveys, and look at it purely in terms of the interaction of colors and shapes. Assess the energetic dynamics of the painting and the degree to which it conveys movement. Envision the painting being made as a series of gestures. Pay attention to these movement qualities as the basis of the final configuration. We are so apt to look at paintings in terms of the messages they convey that we miss the more kinetic and dynamic building blocks.

Record in your journal the observations and discoveries you make from these perceptual exercises. Apply this way of envisioning creation to other aspects of your life. Look at objects, creative works, environments, and workplace projects as synergies of different movements and dynamic energies.

Shift now to simple graphic expressions in your journal or on a sheet of paper. Use movements and gestures with pens, markers, pencils, or other expressive tools to reflect upon and express creative energy. Make use of the widest possible range of basic gestures: scribbles, lines, dots, jabs, flicks, smears, scratches, twitches, sweeps, glides, and anything else that conveys the feelings you are experiencing. Try to stay away from shapes, concepts, and other things that may interfere with the direct expression of emotion through pure movement.

Start by meditating upon the degree to which your life has been characterized by creative expression. Get in touch with your creative history in terms of feelings. Close your eyes and begin to move freely with your art tools, expressing the kinds of energy that best characterize your creative history. Don't worry about the appearance of your expression. Authentic expression of emotion is the goal here, and every person can do this. Be concerned only with conveying feelings, not appearances. Make marks and gestures in a percussive way, as though you are playing an instrument. Pay more attention to the sounds than the visual configurations.

As you begin to feel relaxed with what you are doing, open your eyes and use vision together with movement to express your feelings. Stay with this exercise for at least five minutes to allow the expression to emerge.

Make another of these gesture drawings to express your history with regard to feeling safe and supported in your creative expression. Think about your past experiences with others, ranging from intimate relationships to workplace interactions. Once again begin by reflecting on the subject, and then start to move freely, realizing that it is impossible to fail at this exercise so long as your movements are connected to your feelings. Make a note on the back of each image to identify the date, theme, and feelings you are exploring.

In the final sketch of this series, focus on how you feel right now. Get in touch with your sense of personal vitality and move from this feeling. Reflect upon whether or not your creative energy shifted during the course of doing these exercises, and then express the fluctuations.

If you have fears regarding expression, make contact with them and express their energy without worrying about their visual appearance. Focus on their forcefulness. Also express your aspirations and your hopes for creative expression. Again, try to stay with the process of expressing these feelings for an extended period of time. Let the energy rise and fall and find its way to complete expression.

The purpose of these exercises is the activation and flow of creative energy. We never know what phase of expression will take us to the most significant areas of discovery. Sometimes our level of awareness and satisfaction is consistent from start to finish, and at other times a shift between media or from one exercise to another might open the door to deeper sensibility. The key to discovery in all cases is sustained movement with pauses and periods of reflection that play an important role in the overall circulation of creative expression.

First alone, and then with another person, sit and look carefully at the patterns in the images you made; at the forces they convey; at their various degrees of intensity. Are you satisfied with what you see? What would you like to change? Why? Make another series of sketches or diagrams charting what you would like to see happen.

To what extent do the expressions of these images correlate with your life? Do these exercises with confidence that your life can begin to imitate the art that you make. Record your reflections and discussions in your journal. Respond to your images with brief poetic writings.

⟶ Place the images on a wall or on the floor and respond to what you see in them through body movements. Feel the expressions of the images in your body and act upon them. Work with one image at a time. Respond to the overall configuration of the picture, to details, and to whatever features arouse your feelings and imagination. Expand the expression to include vocal improvisations. If you have the time, make yet another series of pictures expressing the feelings aroused by these expressions with your body.

Responding to an artwork with yet another form of creative expression is a trademark of the work that expressive arts therapist Paolo Knill and I did in developing integrated arts programs in therapy and education. Narratives and stories that we tell about images and other creative expressions are wonderful, but they keep us in the realm of words. Art expressions contain so much more than verbal language. When we respond to an image with movement, voice, and performance, we imagine it further, as C. G. Jung said: we respond to its energy, sometimes augment its expression, and always vitalize the circulation of creativity.

⟶ Have a partner witness your interaction with an image, as described above. Shift roles and invite your partner to respond creatively, with movement and sound, to what you just did. Avoid verbal and narrative responses, trusting that these new ways of responding to images will take you to places that words cannot reach.

⟶ Working together with other people opens up new worlds of expression and discovery. A supportive and attentive partner increases the overall sense of safety, inspiring you to take risks and do new things. There is a contagion of expression when you work freely with a partner. Elements are added that just don't exist in solitary practice.

Even if you practice exercises in an individual way, it can be ener-gizing and inspirational to do this work in the presence of others similarly engaged. Creative practice with others can be likened to meditating in the company of other people, which is quite a different experience from meditating alone.

Many of the practice sessions described in this book are directed toward work with partners and groups. Other suggestions involve individual artistic expressions. Creative practice requires both types of engagement; each has distinct and important features, which we can learn about through comparative reflection. However, we can-not always have the luxury of colleagues, and so many readers of this book will explore the suggested exercises alone.

Creating with others is not just about doing things together in a di-rect way like a team exercise. My experience has indicated that valu-able collegial creations take place simply by being in the presence of other people, practicing parallel expression. We influence and sup-port each other in subtle and indirect ways. Sometimes the mere pres-ence of other people, without attempts to perform in cooperative exercises, can be the most precious incentive to create. We convey in-spiration in unlikely and unplanned ways through example, support, persistence, humor, energy, and all the other factors that can only be accessed through relationships with others.

2

SISYPHUS IN THE SLIPSTREAM

The Muse Is in the Present Moment

In Greek mythology, Sisyphus was a cruel and devious king of Corinth. He disclosed a secret of Zeus and was punished by having to push a large stone up a hill in Hades, only to have it roll back down again. The repetition of this sequence was the eternal fate of Sisyphus. Many people experience the Sisyphean aspect of work each day, with all of their energy expended just keeping up with a workload that never lets up. The demands are perpetual. As soon as one project is completed, two or three more call for attention. There is never closure or a sense of completion.

The artist sometimes feels like Sisyphus, striving to realize creative potential and reach the pinnacle of expression, but never achieving complete satisfaction. Even when artists realize their creative potential, they often feel a compulsion to create again and stay connected to the process of successful expression. The obsessive aspects of creation tie artists to the yoke of endless repetition. This cycle is transcended when the creator does something new, fresh, and unexpected.

Artistic traditions identify the source of inspiration as the "muse," imagined as an inner guide or figure, the beloved, or some other personal character that stirs and guides expression. From the nine muses of Greek mythology who watch over the various arts and sciences to Dante's Beatrice and the beloveds who continue to inspire artists today, the basis of imaginative expression is often located in a relationship with an intimate other. The idea of the muse suggests that the wellspring of creative power is a connection to something other than the self, even in the most solitary process of creative contemplation. Perhaps the power of the muse is its ability to get us out of ourselves, to mobilize all of our resources and concentrate them on service to another person.

In my experience, the muse resides in the particular dynamics of the present moment. I have a tendency to make notes of ideas and observations and keep them in journals and files for future use. These materials are helpful as a way of holding onto insights, but their ultimate value depends upon whether or not they activate and connect to whatever happens to be moving within consciousness at the moment when they are being reviewed.

Similarly, I might put aside pages of notes for a talk or lecture and focus on ideas that emerge from the present moment. The research and note-taking play a role in the overall process of preparation, and the relevant ideas always find their way into the presentation. Access to the flow of creative expression might require putting aside what has been prepared, in order to connect to the currents moving through the immediate environment. These dynamics are located both within the audience and myself. I have learned that I must establish a reciprocal relationship with the other person, audience, or group that carries us all to new places of discovery. When these links are made, the present moment infuses the creative act with energy and momentum.

Alone and with Others

In my creative life, I depend upon a mix between group energy and sustained private contemplation. I may receive inspiration and new insights from my interactions with others, but then I need to be alone in order to amplify and explore them through my particular creative disciplines. Thomas Wolfe described how the artist can be "torn between loneliness and gregariousness." The character George Webber in Wolfe's *You Can't Go Home Again* describes how people involved with creativity require isolation to work but are lost without the "fellowship" that keeps them connected to the "naturalness of life" upon which all creation depends. Referring to the natural interactions with other people, George says: "Every artist feels the need of this world desperately."

A magazine editor described how his creative work with teams of colleagues is complemented by the need for time to work alone. "I'll work in my home office on a project that needs sustained focus," he said, "but the shaping of the magazine and the direction of the company is generated through teamwork." He emphasized the importance of creative teams in contemporary companies.

Depending on their media, some artists require isolation, while others demand interaction. Where most artists need time alone to form creative projects, I know creative people who spend little time in solitary work. They have difficulty with the silence and isolation and need constant contact with others.

The complete solitude some prefer can be an abyss for others. Many of us create when we are busy and fully involved with projects and other people. We need the convergence of energy and experience supplied by daily life. These differences are important to accept, and we have to give ourselves the space to find our particular ways of sustaining the creative process.

> *Examine your history with individual and group creative activities. Have you been involved with both? Are you more comfortable in one area than another? How are you different in the two types of activity? Are there qualities that characterize your work alone and with others?*

Time must be committed if creative insights are to flow naturally from teamwork or solitary reflection. In groups where there is a set schedule of activities, time is less of a challenge. Solitary reflection tends to be characterized by more potential distractions as well as the freedom to do other things. The person working alone has to make a commitment to practice.

The individual creator needs to enter what has become widely known as "the zone." Deep contents will emerge only when the creator's consciousness is in sync with the total environment. We need to let go of other attachments and concerns in order to be completely present to the formative dynamics of the creative process.

The emergence of ideas from creative solitude can be likened to meditation and distance running. But unlike these two disciplines, most people do not make a life commitment to continuous artistic practice. The average person is more likely to have opportunities throughout life to create with others in teams.

Are you more accustomed to creating alone than with others? Have you ever been part of a team of people working together to achieve creative goals? Were there things that you were able to do within the team that you were unable to do alone? What were they?

How would you describe the essential qualities of your solitary creative activities? Have you been able to bring these ways of creating to your work with teams? What are the essential elements of creative teamwork? Can you apply these to your solitary creative activities?

Are there significant differences between your creative experiences when working alone and with others? Where are you more comfortable? More challenged? More creative? What can you change to make your creative life more complete?

Few of us ever achieve the perfect balance between high-quality group and individual creation. A realistic goal for the majority of people is the avoidance of one-sidedness on either extreme. Too much of one thing often generates the need for its complement. I have always been fortunate to be surrounded by creative people in the workplace and in the art studios that I lead. The collective energy and creativity of our work together take me to places I never would have visited without them. "My" discoveries and creations have all been shaped by what I have done with others and what they have given me.

I owe everything to the ideas and common goals established with these teams of people, but I also need to get away on a regular basis. Where some might find solitude daunting, I need it to respond to interactions with people and to make new creations.

Teams of people working together offer something completely different than solitude. They have a chemistry, dynamism, and generative power upon which the most experienced creators depend for new and fresh insights. Most of us need injections of creative and life-affirming energy from teams of people. The input of others sustains us.

Groups of people help me assess current interests, needs, and how people respond to things. They provide a necessary forum in which I can test ideas and determine the extent to which they connect with others. I am always using groups as a place for informal survey research ("What do you think of this?"). I am always trying out ideas with others and using their responses to inform what I am doing. I need affirmations and expressions of interest from others as fuel for the long hours of creative work that I do alone. I have to feel that my creations have value and usefulness to others.

Many of my creative projects have taken shape from discussions with others in which a new direction and priority became apparent. Ideas appear spontaneously through the flow of conversation, and I put them to use. As Oscar Wilde said, "The true artist is known by the use he makes of what he annexes, and he annexes everything."

I have concluded that everything is universal. There are few truly "new" ideas. In this respect we work together with the continuous movement of essential principles, and we keep giving them a different shape or twist based upon our interactions with them. Individuation, the development of the individual from the universal, occurs through how we personally interact with the fundamental process of creativity.

STEVE
I Respond in Ways I Never Knew Were Possible

Steve, a professor, described how he generally comes up with new ideas in quiet contemplation; but while describing his solitary musings, he realized how students in his classes spark new insights. "There are times," he says, "when a student asks the magical question in class, and I respond in ways that I never knew were possible. I say things that I didn't think I could say. I express thoughts and insights that I didn't know I had. In these inspired moments I am certainly more articulate than I view myself as being. I get on a roll. I can't explain why this happens. Something is triggered."

"In my experience," I say to Steve, "these moments are connected to the responsive power of creative expression. Maybe creativity is as much a reaction as an initiative."

Imagine what it would be like if teachers like Steve did not ask questions. If they just continued with their established routines and lectures without opening to the environment. If they were asked questions and did not move in new directions in order to answer them. If the only questions they valued were the ones reinforcing what they currently know and their plans already underway. This happens so often in all aspects of life. People in charge completely control the discourse and make sure it does not depart from what they have decided to do.

To experience the magical moments Steve described, we have to open to what is outside ourselves. Perhaps the magic comes from re-aligning the way familiar things relate to one another. In my close relationships with creative people, I have regularly experienced how the exchange of ideas generates new insights that are invented by the discourse, not by a single person. The source is the interplay of participants.

How do you rate yourself in terms of openness to the ideas of others? Are you someone who grinds away at your own agenda no matter what is happening in your environment?

SHARON
There Has to Be a Give-and-Take

In a focus group discussion on creating with others, Sharon described how she works with a person who is always disrupting group conversations with extraneous statements and who doesn't appear to follow the flow of the group's discussion.

"This man is always confusing us," Sharon reports. "When we tried to figure out what he was doing, we first thought that he was not listening. We concluded that although he is not the best listener, what's really happening is that he can't let go of his idea of what needs to be done. We move on to a new issue, and he is stuck in his agenda. He keeps pushing away at the same thing. I have to admire his tenacity, but it takes a toll on the group.

"Sometimes we have to sacrifice our personal priorities for the benefit of the whole. This man makes me contemplate the difference between those of us who truly hang in there with unpopular positions to help others and those who can't get past their habits of stubbornness and egocentrism, what the psychologists call narcissistic omnipotence. There has to be a give-and-take between taking a lone position and some universal standard of reasonableness. We've got to evaluate what we do according to something outside ourselves."

Recall situations when your insistence and stubbornness was
a drag on the forward momentum of a group. Was it
worthwhile to do this? Did the group benefit? How did it
affect you?

We can all identify moments in our lives, as well as in history, when the lone protestor or visionary, holding out against huge odds, ultimately had a major positive impact on others. The first abolitionists, suffragists, and civil rights leaders identified problems that needed to be addressed, and they stood fast with their visions long before they saw any success. These people were committed to a morality that gave them the strength to persist when others considered their efforts futile. Ultimately their positions grew into a wave of transformation that carried others in its wake. However, if we look back at many of these people, we see that for years they have appeared to be chained like Sisyphus to an impossible task.

There is a man in the city where I live who runs for mayor every year, with no chance of winning. No doubt he enjoys the process, perhaps the attention, and being in the public eye. In this era of carefully coordinated political systems, I admire his willingness to put himself before the public and affirm how every lone citizen can have a voice in the affairs of the city. But this situation contrasts with those who truly suffer for their efforts to bring change, persisting against impossible obstacles. Others might see these efforts as Sisyphean, but they are missing the deeper motivations, which have little to do with personal gain. The novelist Truman Nelson attributed this motivation to what he called revolutionary morality, a passion for justice, and a love for oppressed people.

> *Imagine yourself on the other side of an issue that inspires another person's revolutionary morality. Are you capable of entering into the perspective of another when you represent what that person thinks must be changed? Have you encountered situations like this in your life? What contemporary moral issues can be examined in this way? Will it be helpful to the world if we can simply establish understanding and perhaps empathy for positions and values contrary to our own?*
>
> *Have you ever stood alone in opposition to others on the basis of a moral principle? Were you successful in influencing them? Does it take courage to do this? Simple stubbornness? What factors in your environment make it difficult to go against the prevailing mood? Are there people you know who are especially apt to be contrary in this way? Why do you think they do this? Are you willing to risk sacrificing your own well-being for the sake of others? For an organization? How do you deal with the relationship between risk and self-protection? Have you been able to strike a balance between them?*

In addition to responding more spontaneously to situations, we can do more to take advantage of the energy and stimulation that exist in our environments. When involved in creative projects, I have always been amazed at how helpful my colleagues, neighbors, and family members can be. If I stop, ask a question about something I want to know, then truly listen, it is remarkable what I can learn, even from people with no formal training or expertise in creative work.

I don't spend enough time asking people questions about the things I want to know. When I do ask others for help, sit back, and listen carefully, I note how the other person seems to experience satisfaction. People want to be asked what they think. They want to contribute. The prevalence of top-down organizational structures in the world goes contrary to the dynamics of creation.

Assisting Forces

A friend described to me how his son had taken a new job in a financial management firm where there is a strong commitment to collaboration with others. "He loves the teamwork," my friend says. "The give-and-take really excites him. He worked alone in his previous job, in a cubicle where he was physically separated from people. In the new job they often gather together in common work areas as well as work alone in their offices. He loves it. Everything is based on cooperation. They carry each other in a slipstream."

"Slipstream?" I ask.

"It's what happens when the propeller of a plane or a boat penetrates the resistance of the air or water and creates a wake that carries other things along, like the draft effect in car racing. The slipstream is an assisting force. In racing, the lead car can go faster because the car drafting behind decreases air drag in the rear. They go faster together. The car in front has less drag and the car behind experiences less resistance going forward. Everybody inside the slipstream benefits."

I inquire: "Do you think these principles from physical science apply to what we do in group settings with other people?"

"Absolutely," he replies, "it's all about directing the energy and power of teams in creative ways."

This discussion of the slipstream makes me realize how often we persist in unproductive patterns at work, at home, and with our creative activities. These behaviors thwart the collective momentum of the slipstream. But as I have described, it may be very important to stand against the prevailing currents and advocate a change in direction.

Safe, creative, and productive groups, such as the one at the workplace of my friend's son, are able to respect contrary positions and incorporate their contributions. The person presenting the divergent idea feels respected in these settings; and even if the idea is not adopted, the person has been heard. After a full discussion and analysis of a position that is not adopted, the presenter may not only support the decision of the group but also appreciate the reasons why the idea cannot be adopted. On many occasions I have discovered how "groupthink" has helped me to see that my idea will not work, and I move on to other possibilities with my colleagues.

As I review my history with these situations, I realize that the most important value of group work is sustaining and cultivating the positive momentum of creation. The process of communal creativity that I have observed in my art studio groups carries over into other areas of life and the workplace. If we do not affirm and value the creative expressions of others and the risks they take, these efforts will generally stop. When I look closely at my long friendships, I see these patterns of constant support and acceptance. Personal relationships, too, can be envisioned as moving within a slipstream.

We can learn some major lessons about our creative and uncreative tendencies at home. Let me offer a very simple example. My friend Adam is experiencing some tension with his fifteen-year-old daughter. Like many girls this age, she is finding her father annoying. The tension is being played out around his no longer receiving the hugs that used to be a regular part of their relationship. In relating to his daughter, Adam finds himself reliving his tension with her older sister and his own adolescence. This repetition lends urgency to his attempts to connect with his daughter, thus feeding her desire for distance from him. Adam also has a twelve-year-old daughter, who is still generously giving kisses and hugs. Observing his interaction with her teenage sister, she advised, "Daddy, just walk past her for a few days and don't pay attention to her. Let her have her space, and don't try to talk with her about it. It's all about control."

When we look at this basic family dynamic, we see that Adam's persistence in a behavior annoying to his child is based upon an unwillingness to surrender a point of view. Almost universally such doggedness is bolstered by a rationalization such as, "She's being difficult. Maybe she's just in a bad mood and it'll be better the next time."

Even the closest family relationships need to be continually reshaped. In the struggle for affection with his fifteen-year-old daughter, Adam had a new idea. She was studying at the dining room table, blocking him out with her cassette earphones and not raising her eyes as he walked through the room. He went to the garden and picked a small bouquet of zinnias, dahlias, and nasturtiums and placed them on the table next to her books. She liked it. Adam realized how he had to keep reinventing relationships in order to sustain them.

It is very difficult to let go of habits and familiar ways of getting needs met. Good relationships and teams are able to adapt to constant change. They do whatever has to be done to sustain the positive and creative energy. There is a willingness to let go of personal positions to promote the well-being of the whole. Ineffective teams and bad relationships are locked into fixed positions. They persist in the most negative aspects of Sisyphean effort, stubbornly pushing at obstacles; their attempts result only in a situation that is more resistant to change.

Can you identify with the problems resulting from being locked into fixed positions on issues? Are you stubborn when others protest? Is it difficult for you to change direction and let go of your point of view? Does your resistance make things better? Or does clinging to your perspective isolate you from others? Does it make you feel like Sisyphus?

Recall moments in your life when you felt that a positive group momentum was carrying you. Was there an energy that you and the group created that enabled you to move in new ways and do things that surprised you with their expressive vitality?

Did you ever feel this way when dancing with someone?

*Do you usually lead or follow when dancing? Try acting in a
different way on the dance floor. Reflect upon how your
experience with dance relates to what happens with
coworkers and in other relationships.*

*Consider how controlling or passive you are in various
relationships. If you have experienced the positive
momentum of the slipstream effect, has this been more likely
to occur when you relax control and let yourself be carried
by the forces in your environment?*

The Mental Switch

I notice how the slipstream doesn't work in the simplest interactions of daily life, how a man blocks it by reading the newspaper as his wife tries to talk to him. He then becomes hurt when he feels she is not accessible. It's an endless cycle of control problems, like Sisyphus never breaking through to fulfillment. The transcendence of the negative cycle comes with the realization that creative satisfaction is connected to the slipstream effect, when we see that we are at our best when we open to shared creation with others.

Mark Towner, an art dean, affirmed how powerful the slipstream effect can be within the workplace. "Sometimes I get it from others," he says, "and at other times my own energy can lead the slipstream. Oftentimes it comes out of nowhere, like a wonderful being from above. It's the energy between individuals that generates momentum. I first experienced it in my graduate MFA program. All of the energy coalesced. It was a beautiful experience, almost an ecstatic high. We bounced ideas off one another, and the forward momentum generated new ideas. It's the essence of creativity and what life is about."

"What about poor Sisyphus rolling that rock up a hill every day at work?" I ask. "Do we all have that in us?"

"That element is within us," Mark agrees, "but we mustn't be solely locked into that track. We all find ourselves in that condition at times, and we have to be in it, go with it, feel it, and live it. But never believe that it is our only option."

"If we immerse ourselves in negativity," I reply, "creation stops. Creativity requires an infusion of positive energy."

"Negativity," Mark continues, "can become like the downward pull of quicksand."

I realize in talking to Mark how positive energy in other people inspires me and helps me see that I have to work with whatever the conditions of life may be. It has always been important for me to make a distinction between a negative experience and a negative attitude. The latter, as Mark suggested, can be the most debilitating deterrent to creative momentum. When negative attitudes take over, we truly sink into a quagmire that is very hard to escape.

The atmosphere of negativity can be something as simple as a bad start in a conversation with a new person, or even someone we know well. The negative influence can be difficult to shake. Athletes know this, and they work hard at maintaining self-confidence and a positive attitude. When I hit a bad shot in golf, I am not always successful in letting it go and focusing on the next one with an even temperament. One bad shot can easily immerse me not only in the fears of the moment, but in all of my stored bad feelings from the past.

I just spoke to someone on the phone who caught me at the wrong moment. She was calling to plan a meeting. In retrospect, I should not have taken the call. No matter what I said as the conversation continued, the less-than-positive start permeated the exchange, and we were not able to get past it at that particular time. For the most part, I've learned how to let go of things that are bothering me when someone calls or enters my office. But in this instance I was truly disturbed about something that had happened a few minutes earlier, and I was not effective in putting it aside. The person on the phone had nothing to do with my problem and did not deserve to receive any bad energy from me. This small instance confirmed yet again how negative energy stops the creative process.

Negative experiences happen all the time. They are actually some of the best sources of creative transformation. In the case of my bad phone experience, I accepted responsibility for my bad mood and put an extra bit of positive energy into making the subsequent meeting productive.

Maybe we can even view the Sisyphean tasks in our lives as opportunities for creation. Rather than approach the endless routine as hopeless drudgery, we can embrace it when it happens and perhaps seek out its redeeming or necessary aspects. Who knows what passes through the mind of Sisyphus as he rolls the rock up the hill? Repetition is not always unpleasant; it has its enjoyable aspects. I thought about Sisyphus as I watched students doing reps with weights in a fitness center. There is a place for everything.

I remember John Cage in a lecture/performance at Lesley University saying something like this: "If you are bored with something after two minutes, keep doing it for four minutes. If you stay bored, do it for eight, then sixteen minutes. If still bored, press on to thirty-two minutes, and at that point you might begin to find it fascinating."

Cage's illustration suggests that the mental switch is not necessarily an act of will or intention. It is closer to letting go, to getting beyond mental resistance and judgment. The breakthrough happens when we surrender to doing the activity for its own sake, no matter what it might be. The creative slipstream requires complete involvement in the immediate environment and attention to the present moment. Such immersion in a given context will always transport us to new places shaped by the fusion of the participating forces.

Maybe it is possible for Sisyphus to enter the slipstream with tremendous force and power. I always realize how things that are most contrary to one another have the potential to become very close and vice versa. There is something much greater than the sum of the parts when bitter adversaries become partners in creation. Conversely, close friends and colleagues have much more power to hurt one another and sever all connections than acquaintances. This interplay of contraries can be likened to the transforming interaction of positive and negative currents of electricity. The slipstream's power is based upon using whatever happens to be moving within a particular environment as a source of creative energy and momentum. The effects can be ecstatic, as Mark said earlier, especially when experiences that we see as most restrictive become the source of our satisfying discoveries.

CREATIVE PRACTICE

I was reading a *Boston Globe* story about the sustained excellence of Boston University's hockey program as headed by Coach Jack Parker. One of the players said, "Guys just seem to get better when they get into this atmosphere." The energy, structure, and quality of the program have a clear impact on the individual, who rises to new levels in response to it.

Imagine an environment committed to the excellent practice of something you value. Picture yourself as a part of this context, part of the team fortunate enough to experience superior chemistry. Give the place a name, and describe its qualities in your journal. Imagine yourself entering this environment for the first time. Document both its impact upon you and your potential contribution to it. Notice how you change as a result of being part of the milieu.

Envisioning a supportive environment of this kind can be likened to what athletes do when they visualize images of desired performances. Images act as guides and as sources of energy while the imaginal atmosphere creates a slipstream influencing your activity in the world.

Describe the qualities of this good environment in your journal. Who are the people you want included? Do you need a leader or coach to give overall direction?

Do this exercise with other people, and compare results. See if it is possible to work together in describing the qualities of an ideal environment, and explore whether or not others expand your sense of what is needed. Notice whether or not the process of doing this exercise with other people begins to activate a creative atmosphere that influences you. Does thinking about the environment with others help to make it happen?

This simple exercise has great potential for the workplace. Identify symbols that represent your ideal creative atmosphere, and arrange them into a configuration with your partners.

Also identify the threats to the creative atmosphere, and create symbols for them. Give them a place within your configuration, thus honoring the destructive forces and making yourself more aware of their constant presence.

—— Reflect upon the Sisyphean aspects of your work environment. Identify the area of your greatest frustration; meditate upon it, and exaggerate the problem in your mind. For example, if you experience endless demands upon your time and an unstoppable flood of work in the office, amplify these trends to absurd levels. Maybe humor will enter as you do this, and you will shift out of the victim role. Imagine yourself as Sisyphus deciding that you have to make the most of your condition, saying to yourself: "This is my life. I have to do something with it. It's up to me. Can I begin to enjoy what was originally a source of irritation?"

Write a poetic description of the situation. Make a drawing of it. Enact it through creative movement or performance art. If you are working with another person or in a group, dramatize the situation in a three- to five-minute spontaneous performance in which the others act as witnesses who then give you feedback on how they are affected by your expression.

Instead of trying to escape from the condition or attempting to fix the problem, enter it in a more complete and imaginative way. Accept it, experience its extremes, describe its nuances, and *use it* as a force of creative energy and insight. I trust that as you work with the Sisyphean situation in this way, you will find more innovative ways of relating to it. The irreconcilable problem becomes a source of creative vitality. Since these particular things will always be part of your life, your only option is to change the way you relate to them.

—— Apply the slipstream effect to a problem you are having at work or in your personal life. Rather than struggling to explain the problem or trying to resolve it in a linear or analytic way, prepare yourself to simply contemplate the situation in the most open and expansive way possible, accessing all of your personal resources.

As you sustain your focus on the problem, images, ideas, and feelings will enter your consciousness. Record these insights and sensations in your journal as descriptive notes, poetic images and passages, or graphic expressions and gestures. Welcome all of these responses as assisting forces, and allow them to emerge one after the other without getting attached to any one in particular. I liken this process to placing the images in a cauldron that sustains a steady and low heat. You don't want any individual idea to burn too quickly and disrupt the overall cooking process.

Do this meditation over a period of days, and if you are fortunate enough to recall dreams, record these images through descriptions and drawings. Imagine all of these elements creating a slipstream that will carry you and your problem to a new place. All of the expressions and images will act as assisting forces that work together to enlarge the spectrum of energies, perspectives, and resources available to you. By combining resources and possibilities rather than proceeding alone along a single track, you enhance the power of the overall creative process, which then begins to work autonomously to find a new direction.

Gather together all of the different responses, and reflect upon them all as participants in a diverse group working on your problem. Trust that the interaction of the various elements will always carry you to a new place in relation to the problem.

As you meditate on the different parts and the overall collection of creative responses, relax and use them as stimuli to imagine the problem further. Record your responses. After reflecting upon the various pieces, make another artwork that responds to them all and integrates them into a new synthesis.

This gathering of the different elements of a problem is useful within groups, and it has great potential for the workplace. When faced with a difficult and contentious situation, try to encourage everyone involved to offer suggestions about what is wrong, what is being blocked and missed, and so forth.

Record all of these ideas on a large sheet of paper. Or better yet, encourage people to make images or select small objects that represent facets of the problem; gather all of these things together in a particular place that can function like a magician's cauldron.

As emphasized in the previous exercise, restrain your urge to resolve the problem or impose a particular solution. Let the different facets of the difficulty stay together; try to give them all your full attention, especially the ideas that you oppose. Imagine yourself as the caretaker of this menagerie, as someone committed to honoring and protecting the vitality of each element.

The simple process of symbolically giving every position a place within the whole helps to align their energy in a common direction. Let the positions act on each other, and do your best to let go of all preconceptions. Imagine them all working toward a shared goal. Watch for new ideas and new directions that emerge from the interaction of the whole. Find a new way.

In creative practice I experience the slipstream effect most dramatically in large-group movement activities and vocal improvisations. Moving together with a group of people in a circle, where we make simple gestures like rhythmically raising our hands to the sky, lowering them to the ground, or thrusting them toward the center in unison, affirms the power of the slipstream.

An even more sublime slipstream occurs when making sounds in unison, what musicians call sounding. All individual expressions merge into a whole that dramatically exceeds a mere addition of sounds. The whole creates a very real energy that transports the individual to sublime states where even the most "unmusical" voices contribute to a melodious integration that finds a way to include their contributions to its expression.

Practice sounding and simple group movements with others. Realize that we all need to warm up in order to fully release our vocal or bodily expression. Don't be hard on yourself. Accept whatever sounds or movements emerge, and trust that they will find their way into a collective expression.

If you want to do something very structured as a starting point, simply march together around a large space, stepping in unison, counting your steps together—1, 2, 3, 4—softly yet forcefully. Or practice simple group sounds and movements while standing in place. Focus on the energy and unique qualities of the expressions emerging from what you do together. This is the slipstream. Compare it with how you feel doing these things alone.

3

FLOW AND SPONTANEITY
The Movement Basis of Creation

Creating Outside the Lines

Attempts to describe the psychology of creativity have generally traced a linear development that proceeds from one point to another, according to distinct phases and sequential steps. The following is one such universally discussed model of creativity: incubation, play, gathering, reflection, and consolidation. Such descriptions corral the creative process into fixed concepts and overlook its organic quality; creative expression is closer to the organized chaos of a hurricane, the mysteries of stellar birth and death, even the regular but always modulating experience of breathing than to any predetermined chain of abstractions.

Creativity is an interplay of participants that can be likened to an ecological process. An ongoing movement, it generates outcomes at various moments and intervals shaped by our endlessly variable frames of perception. When we view creativity primarily in terms of the products it generates, we confine ourselves to the perspective of means and ends, actions and goals, and we overlook the more comprehensive and constant movement of creative energy in the world.

Our reflections on creativity in the arts, sciences, and other disciplines have centered largely on the things people create—the observable history of creation. Phases of development certainly exist, but this linear perspective does not necessarily correspond to the movements of nature. Creative energy moves in more complex ways that can be compared to waves, rhythms, stormy outbursts, and tranquil moods.

Do you create in a consistent and step-by-step fashion, or is your creative experience less predictable? How do you go about making something or organizing a project? If you feel that you are not creative, view the way you cook or approach a project as the basis for answering these questions.

Identify the areas in your life where you are totally consistent and areas where you are not. Are certain phases of your creative activity more methodical than others? What aspects of your creative expression are most regular, and where do you experience the greatest variation?

Do creative ideas and insights arrive in a uniform way? Are there things you do that reliably promote creative activity? What are they? Are there qualities of experience that predictably restrict your creativity? What are they?

In and Out of Contact

Creativity is both a physical and a spiritual force; it is transpersonal and transcultural, yet present in all things. It is an eternal movement of nature that passes through people and places, like wind through the trees or the pulsations of a living thing. Creative practice is an integrating process that combines everything from spirituality to engineering.

Artists and other people who have experienced the benefits of creative expression realize how easily they can be lost. The creative person longs to stay in contact with the muse. The experience of the creator can be compared to conversations that stop and start, get stalled and stuck, or flow effortlessly for sustained periods of time. We move in and out of creative grace. The experienced creator knows that what really matters is the energy of creation and being fortunate enough to serve as an agent of its expression. The creative person is not a passive conduit, but a responsive partner who collaborates with the formative energy.

> Have there been periods in your life when you recall losing contact with creative energy and flow? Did you try to regain contact? What did you do? Did it work? Was the creative spirit something that you experienced as beyond your control? Are there aspects of creativity that you can rely upon completely? If so, what are they?
>
> Does creative expression often come upon you by surprise, or is the experience more predictable? Where do you have control? What is beyond your control? To what extent do your most significant creative expressions originate inside or outside the scope of your conscious control?

Interaction Generates Ideas

It can be argued that even the most reclusive artists, Emily Dickinson perhaps being the epitome of this type, require some form of exchange with the world in order to inspire creative expression. Poets routinely describe how ideas and images come upon them in ways that cannot be traced. These descriptions suggest that the contents and formative energies of the creative process are themselves somewhat autonomous and separate from the artist. Therefore, even in the most solitary forms of creation, the artist works together with images, memories, and experiences tied to other people.

There is also general agreement among artists who work in solitude that a routine or discipline of some kind must be established. Artists of all types cite this regular structure of practice as the basis for their work, the soil in which ideas and images grow.

The origins of creative expressions have been debated throughout the history of Western thought. Starting in the twentieth century, the place from which ideas emerge has been called "the unconscious." In earlier times it was known as the imagination. Both the unconscious and the imagination, as described earlier, are realms where experiences, memories, and the energies of the moment meet, mix, and then move spontaneously into consciousness. But the experience of artists, which can be likened to those who practice other physical and spiritual disciplines, suggests that the interplay with environmental factors may have more to do with creative expression than the notion of "releasing" expression from a realm such as the unconscious.

In the context of a regular discipline, interactions with materials and other people generate ideas. Imagination is an interplay between external and internal realms. Whereas the traditional idea of the unconscious suggests the depths of the individual mind as the primary source of creation, my idea of the imagination attributes creative origination to action, mixing, collaboration, communication among participants, and an overall circulation of influences. The Freudian idea of the unconscious overlooks how creations emerge from current physical relationships with materials, ideas, and other people.

When the basis of creativity is perceived as existing in an exchange or discourse between participating elements, conventional ideas of creativity need to be revisited. Creativity, always primarily identified with solitary musings, may be much more of an interactive process, inspired and directed by relationships with others.

In my experience working with groups, and in collaborative projects with other individuals, ideas emerge from communication among the participants. This process is a direct extension and continuation of the exchange that occurs within the imagination of an individual person. When I think alone about a creative project, the different aspects of my experience and imagination work together to generate ideas. In groups, this internal process is stimulated and supported by suggestions and expressions made by other group members.

As jazz musicians say, we bounce off from each other's initiatives. Groups and other individuals also help us to challenge, shape, and correct the raw expressions that emerge from our individual imaginations. Rather than moving from the unconscious to the conscious realm according to linear and predetermined stages, imagination and expression emerge from a complex exchange. Sometimes this interactive process will amplify and expand an idea, and other times it will help us refine or redirect what we are trying to do.

PETER
The Importance of Goals, Structure, and Rules

In the following conversation with Peter, a college administrator who actually enjoys committee work, we explore how the creative process flows within groups, how this fluidity can be enhanced, and how it is obstructed. We also examine how structures and routines support the flow of creation, and we question whether the same methods used by solitary artists also apply to groups.

"I was just working with a very stiff and formal group of people on a project, and humor opened up a creative flow," Peter says.

"You have the trickster gift," I say. "Others may not."

"But there is always someone in a group," he responds, "who is able to come forward in this way to lighten the atmosphere and ignite creative expression. We need to give them the space to do this, rather than restrict spontaneous bursts of inspiration."

"How would you define the creative flow in a group of people?" I ask. "Is it connected to spontaneity?"

"The flow happens when the environment and process are organized but open and safe," Peter muses. "It's creative because everyone is using their own voice and making their own contributions to a common project. We define what we are doing and where we are going, but we have fun doing it. When we are in the flow, the work is generally done quickly and collaboratively with everybody contributing to it."

"Does the flow happen when everyone feels connected?" I inquire. "In my experience, people can block the flow when they are not part of the overall activity. Humor opens people to the unexpected, to things outside their current thoughts. Some surprising ideas emerge, and the new twist opens the heart and makes us laugh."

"For me, humor is crucial to working creatively with others," Peter answers.

"It cuts through barriers that people erect and brings us together on an emotional level," I reply. "Maybe this is why speakers tend to start with humorous statements that help people become aware and receptive. A faculty member was just describing how some level of warmth and intimacy is needed to help people venture out and join the process of collaboration."

"Absolutely," Peter says. "Otherwise everything stays tightly shut. People don't go outside themselves"

"What else contributes to the flow?" I ask.

"We need to have a clearly defined goal and a set of rules that everyone follows."

"There is great truth in the cliché about being on the same page," I respond. "From my earliest work in helping others with the creative process, I have learned that expressive freedom and novelty often depend upon clear structure."

"It is powerful when we can get all of the brains working together, but there has to be a shared agenda and objective," Peter maintains.

"What obstructs the flow of creativity in groups?"

"Nothing stifles the creative process at work more than petty behavior or gossip. It kills the empowering element."

"Why?"

"Negativity and petty complaints break you down," Peter says. "They make you question everything. In a productive group activity like the situation I described earlier, we get outside of ourselves, and there is an elevation of effort. We move beyond the normal constrained sense of work, and we are totally with other people and other minds. Some of my most creative times have happened when I'm in a group that is just jiving as it moves forward."

"Ah," I exclaim. "When the creative process is flowing, we get outside of ourselves. My belief is that creativity is not just inside us. It's outside and in the world all the time. We need to get into 'it.' "

"It's a dynamic place," Peter asserts, "and it feels good to get outside of ourselves."

"Why?"

"I'm not sure," he reflects. "Is it another state of consciousness, like the high experienced when running? Is it a chemical process? What is it that enables us to suddenly feel in sync with other people and processes when we work together? All at once everything moves. Ideas come faster, more clearly. Things fit together and knots are untied. Maybe some of the holes also emerge, things that we have missed. Somebody says, 'Hey you're glossing over this area.' It's easier to accept this comment if you are in a creative process, in a flow. If everyone is working together, if you are on the move, it is much easier to accept criticism."

"Ego doesn't get involved," I say. "We receive the comments as being helpful. Ego, with all of its needs to dominate and control, is the big obstacle to creative flow in groups. There has to be a surrender to common creation, an enthusiasm for it."

"Right. We're all in it together."

"I keep insisting that there is a movement basis to all creative activity, Peter. What you say about the flow and being 'on the move' really supports this idea."

"Yes," he replies, "and the opposite condition is being stuck, frozen, immobile. There isn't much creative flow when this happens. We get locked into ourselves."

I continue: "Artists talk about how the creative process gives them the opportunity to get their emotions outside of themselves and into the world. Maybe the same thing happens in the creative group experiences that you describe. The group enters an art space where everything moves."

"It's like playing music in a group," Peter asserts. "Making music with others empowers me in much the same way as the work situations I have described. I have had experiences jamming on the piano with a bass player and drummer where we achieve the creative flow we have been describing. I have gotten to a point where I am so in sync with the other musicians that the bass player can go off on a riff for twenty-four measures, for three minutes; and I am still hearing my music even though the bass player is going solo; and when it's time to come back in, I know it exactly. It is almost outside of you, going to another emotional and creative level. Communication happens outside the realm of words. The inability of words to capture this experience makes it even more powerful. Now that feels good, real good."

"There is a musical aspect to a group functioning creatively," I say, "a Pythagorean dimension where the spheres are in harmony, where everything fits together, and we get outside of ourselves into something larger. You've described some of the things that support this process—clear leadership and distinct boundaries, as with the making of music."

"There needs to be an accepted protocol and common parameters," Peter says. "In music we need to play in the same key. We keep the same tempo. The protocol is the set of rules according to which you play. The same thing happens in a meeting—clear definitions, respect for each person's ideas and opinions, and never stepping too far beyond the accepted structure of the group. If someone does this, the group can be demolished."

"What threatens the group?"

"When people play by their own set of rules."

"What if you hate the rules?" I ask.

"It may be time to go," Peter suggests. "I really try to respect the outsider, the person who brings a different perspective, but if over time that person keeps breaking the rules, it can be a problem. Every community has a culture of some kind that needs to be acknowledged."

"And in order to be effective, new people in a group or organization need to learn how it works," I reply. "Again we can compare this to music. The group dynamic can be as subtle, as fragile, and yet as powerful as music. For this reason, a person out of sync in a group at work can be as distinct as in a musical performance."

"And people all know!" Peter emphasizes.

"It's like a violin playing out of tune. The group is a musical orchestration."

"An intellectual orchestration," he adds.

"There are profound similarities between art and other life situations," I suggest.

"It is paradoxical," Peter says, "that some of the essential properties of creativity, the things that make creative situations and environments work, are standards, limitations, and what I have called parameters. There is a set of rules that we all accept. If the rules are followed, and if people are engaged, we can enter some extremely creative territory."

"Absolutely," I answer. "Artists describe how they are stimulated by the limitations of a material, what a medium can and cannot do, the containment of the canvas, the range of an instrument, or time constraints. Pushing against these edges and taking them to the limits generates creativity. Limitations, more than vastness, drive creation. Look at how the limitations of black and white film enhance the power of light, shadow, and basic contrast."

"The constructive parameters push creation," Peter responds. "Destructive parameters like negativism and pettiness limit our ability to create, and I try to avoid these situations."

"An artist friend who works in an organization that has a very strong corporate culture described how he learned how to go with the creative flow established by the organizational leadership. Because that flow was so strong, he had to let go of some things that he might instinctively want to do. He didn't compromise principles or go against his moral grain; he just realized that he would be more effective if he stayed within what you have described as the constructive parameters. We need to sacrifice our personal inclinations sometimes for the sake of the movement of the whole. The same thing happens in collaborative artworks. Individuals are always making sacrifices for the overall expression of the piece—the performer whose back is turned, and misses the gestures of another actor; all of the people working backstage. You suggest a generous spirit in group work, going beyond our personal vantage points to something larger that contains us all."

"What about you?" Peter asks. "When you are working with other people, what gets you to feel the flow?"

"When I started my first job as an art therapist in 1970, my group therapy supervisor used to constantly say, 'Never assume that the people gathered together for a group meeting are truly a *group*.' A collection of people might be sitting together in a room, but that doesn't mean they are a group. The supervisor, a Socratic psychiatrist, never defined what it was to be a group, and I am grateful for this. He made it necessary for me to answer the question. I concluded that becoming a group required qualities like cohesion, mutual purpose, support, and attentiveness to individual group members. I have been working with groups ever since, so he must have really gotten to me.

"After all these years, the one thing that keeps deepening my love of groups and their creative potential is the way that people say things or spontaneously express themselves in ways that expand my frame of mind. The creative group, I have learned, is always much more intelligent than a single person acting alone and certainly smarter and more creative than I. The flow of creation and intelligence that I experience in groups is exhilarating."

"Do you have trouble letting go of the authority position?" Peter asks.

"I get my greatest satisfaction when group members generate new insights and wisdom. I see my role as a caretaker of the process, and my sense of pride comes from what we do together. I hope I can step back and let others come forward; yet I am always active in taking care of the overall environment, in helping the collection of individuals be a group. It is amazing how one teacher and one question can shape a life's work."

Peter asks, "I am wondering whether or not the things that we have been describing about group work also apply to individual creative expressions. I try to keep my personal life and work life completely separate, but maybe they are more connected than I realize."

"The need for structure and limits characterizes both individual and group work," I respond. "In my experience, solitary creation has many similarities to the orchestration of different elements that you describe in group work. The various parts of a person's creative expression work together and strive to achieve the same harmony and connectedness that happens when you play with other musicians. And of course the essential flow characterizes all forms of creation. All the rivers of spontaneous expression flow from the same source."

"Is it the same source?" Peter asks. "Do individual and group creativity come from the same place?"

"I'm convinced, Peter, that the source is the same, but I can't say what it is. It's like faith based on deep intuitions. Things that go beyond reason cannot be proven or even described by reason. Origins are always a mystery, metaphysics."

"Try describing it anyway," Peter suggests.

"In my experience, the sources of group creativity have been close to the surface. Ideas and creative transformations are always directly traceable to concrete interactions between people. You say something; I respond to what you say; and then you shift your original position in a way that incorporates what I offered. It's even more complex than this somewhat linear description of the interplay. When this happens in a group or between two people, there are witnesses who observe how the give-and-take between positions occurs and shapes new creations. When we work alone, we don't have these witnesses or the external embodiment of the interaction among positions. But I believe that the same dynamic takes place within us. What is outside is inside, and vice versa.

"The process of creativity has a fundamental consistency. When I paint a picture or write a poem, I see how the different strokes build upon one another. My every action is influenced by my preceding actions. I see this in the most basic expressions of body movement. Gestures grow from one another. No movement is made in isolation.

"So, yes, there is a definite correspondence between the interactive process that occurs in groups and what happens within an individual's expression. The nature of the participants or persons differs. In groups the participants are individuals, and within solitary creation the participants tend to be gestures, ideas, and other aspects of consciousness."

"And do the group creations also include these internal dynamics?" Peter asks. "Does an individual person's memory of a private experience or an image within the personal mind influence the group?"

"Yes, of course," I reply. "As the process is enlarged, all of the elements that exist within solitary creative expression affect the exchanges within groups. It is logical that private reflections have the ability to influence the ongoing expansion of interactions."

"And the large group interactions can all be traced back to what happens in the individual imagination?" Peter inquires.

"Yes, Peter, I am convinced of this. They share the same pulse, the same rhythm, and the same creative energy."

"So the way I feel in sync with other musicians also applies to what is happening with the different energies interacting within myself?" Peter asks.

"Every form of creation involves the essential mixing, interaction, and spontaneity that occurs within the individual imagination." I respond. "How can it be otherwise?"

"I separate," Peter remarks, "and you integrate. You may be right on this one. The working of imagination at the individual and collective levels is different in scale but congruent in form. Our perception of the parts or participants may vary, and we know that perceptions are based upon the vantage points from which we look. Who knows the extent to which the same process of imagination may be operating on micro and macrolevels that we have yet to perceive?"

"The flow process that we experience moves at all levels," I say, "and perhaps connects them all. This philosophizing has a profoundly practical side to it. We tend to put creativity, of all things, into a confined box and perceive it as operating in the most circumscribed ways. Imagine what will happen if we approach creativity as a ubiquitous force that can be likened to universal biological functions like breathing, eating, and procreation. Rather than isolating creativity to rarefied and inaccessible places, we can start to view it as permeating everything we do."

"And how is that practical?" Peter questions.

"Everything we do can offer an invitation to live in a more creative way," I reply. "Imagine that, a future where work and daily living can become frontiers for creative imagination. This might even change the world."

How do you define the experience of creative flow? When was the last time it happened to you? Do you agree that it is necessary to get outside yourself in order to access the powers of creative expression? Is openness a prerequisite to creative expression? Do you agree with Peter's suggestion that rules and safe structures are necessary conditions for creative expression in groups?

Try to recall times when you shut yourself down in relation to other people and your environment. Why did you do this?

Have you observed characteristics of creative collaboration in groups that correspond to your more solitary creative experiences? Compare your creative experiences in groups to

what you have experienced when creating alone. Where have
you been more creative? Are there features common to your
expression in both areas? Identify qualities in one area that
you can bring to the other.

How does the creative process flow when you work alone,
compared to when you work with others? How is it different?
The same? Do you stimulate the creative spontaneity of
others? How do you do this? How have people demonstrated
that they are stimulated by you? What is it that other people
do that enhances the flow of your creative expression?
Obstructs it?

From One Movement to Another

Every form of creation originates in movement. The arts are kinetic activities that are affected by the quality of the movements
from which they emerge. It is helpful to view every aspect of creation
as part of an ongoing flow of movement.

Physical gestures are everywhere in our daily lives. If you watch
people interacting with one another on the street or at home, you
will see creative expression. It happens whenever we lose consciousness of ourselves, act naturally, and allow our physical expressions
to be aligned with inner imaginings. By keeping the focus as simple
as possible, expression is made accessible to everyone.

We don't realize that every movement in a painting, drawing, sculpture, poem, or dance simply emerges from the one that went before it
and then becomes the source of yet another gesture. People need to
learn how to move from within themselves, from their particular place
at the moment. Many find it difficult to act creatively because they try
to do too much and essentially attempt to be in a place other than
where they are. They lose balance and the ability to move with the
forces of the environment that will ultimately support expression.
They expect something other than what they are doing at that particular time, or they think that what they are doing is inadequate. They
become blocked by and caught up in negative and confusing thoughts.

Try the following experiment with creative movement in order to
understand the kinetic basis of creativity.

Make any movement, and let the next one emerge from it. Try to keep moving, don't stop, and trust that a new movement will always come out of the one that went before it. Put everything you have into the movement. Even if you make a slow and delicate gesture with your arm, fill it with all your energy and with total concentration. Identify completely with it. Feel free to repeat movements.

When you stop moving, be aware of your breath, and view the stillness as a pause between movements. Let another gesture come forward and yet another one from it. If you can keep moving in a relaxed way, without thinking about what you are going to do next, the movement will start to direct itself.

The pause is a time of formation and regeneration, during which energy is gathered for the next phase of expression. It is not a time when you want to get caught up in thinking about what you are going to do next. As I tell people in my studios, the only thing you can do wrong is spend your time planning what you are going to do, rather than let the next movements unfold from the place where you are.

In my many years of leading studio groups, I have not deviated far from these simple directions. I do not give people themes to explore or problems to solve, but simply try to give them the opportunity to let expression emerge. Each of us will have a different relationship with the essential movement of creation, and the contents will be infinitely varied. I always encourage people to believe that if they can move freely in a sustained and focused way, while relaxing thoughts about outcomes, important contents will emerge.

"You have to establish your own relationship with the creative movement," I say. I tell them that we are not taking an exercise class where I will teach them how to make specified movements with predictable outcomes.

If people can maintain contact with the essential movement running through them in the present moment, they will engage a creative power with unending variation and vitality. I sometimes frustrate students with my insistence on this simple and constant approach. They often want techniques and gimmicks that they think will somehow further their expertise.

A skilled leader of the creative process knows that only the fundamental movement of life can generate appropriate responses to the complexities and endless variations of the problems we face.

My movement basis of creativity instructions can be likened to the sitting meditation principle of breathing in and breathing out. Our dependence on explanations and formulas for action are frustrated, challenged, and transformed when we learn how attention to the breath can be one of the greatest challenges and opportunities available to us.

When we move freely in artistic expression, there is space provided for the things that need to emerge. Though it is difficult to relax control and believe that essential expressions and messages will be generated, there has to be a trust that this emanation will always happen. If I tell people what to paint in an art studio, I interfere with this process of emanation, which is different for each person.

As people work with this process, they need support. It is easy to become preoccupied and lose contact with sustained movement. The same thing happens in the practice of meditation when we become distracted and disconnected from the breath.

In creative work, the movement is lost when we tighten up and start to think too much about what we are doing. Yet these constrictions of movement are opportunities for regaining spontaneity, as we become aware of them and return once again to free expression. If the creative spirit is not lost, how is it to be regained? My experience indicates that creative expression is actually augmented by an understanding of how it moves in and out of our lives. When I restore full contact with the creative process after losing it for a period of time, my involvement is always intensified by the loss.

This emphasis on movement in creative expression is not new. Goethe said, "In the beginning is the act." Psychoanalysis came into being through free-association processes that mirrored the contemporary techniques of the surrealists. The early art therapists similarly encouraged patients to make random scribbles as the basis for paintings and drawings; and of course the action paintings of Jackson Pollock took kinetic expression to the summit of art history.

In creative writing sessions, "automatic writing" exercises are commonly used to help people write more freely. Rather than stopping to reflect, the person is encouraged to keep the pen in contact with the page so that the words continue to flow. The same kind of activity can be used with drawing, painting, vocal expression, or improvisation with an instrument. These exercises help us get beyond the tendency to plan and control what we are going to do before we do it. If you can surrender to the unplanned movement, it will carry you and the process of expression to new places.

Approach creative movement as a discipline. You need to practice and learn how significant expressions will always emerge from your gestures. Get beyond the voice inside that says, "This is a waste of time. What are you doing moving around without knowing where you are going?"

When this challenge occurs again, welcome the doubting voice as a sign that you are getting close to penetrating the heart of creative movement.

When you reach the state of being moved by a force that is more than your conscious mind acting alone, you have entered the realm of imagination. You become a vehicle for a movement that is larger than what you could envision before making it. Forces within yourself and outside yourself propel your body. As Ahab said in *Moby Dick*, "Is Ahab, Ahab? Is it I, God, or who, that lifts this arm?"

This collaboration with forces outside yourself operates in artistic work with other media, as well as creative problem-solving in groups.

The elemental movements of any person can become truly fascinating when they are made with total concentration and abandon. Rather than judging or rejecting expressions that people make, the skilled teacher introduces other possibilities and builds upon what people are already doing. When a person begins to move in a more relaxed way, the movements not only emerge from one another, but they seem to perfect themselves. The improved quality often comes from within the movement itself.

Simple experiences with movement help us see how we frequently overdo it in other parts of our lives. Those who have encountered the powers and gifts of creativity know firsthand that it is usually the overly controlling mind, excessive effort, and narrow expectations that restrict access to imagination, when what is required is the opposite: a paradoxical discipline of letting go while staying focused and allowing the creation to emerge.

Nothing will happen, however, unless there is sustained movement from one thing to another. The direction is not always clear and the outcome rarely known at the start of an imaginative act. What matters most is the commitment to beginning and the acceptance of what will emerge. As Nietzsche said in *The Genealogy of Morals*, "The action is everything."

Try applying art studio exercises to other aspects of your life. Just as physical movements emerge from one another, new ideas emanate from prior actions. Therefore, exploratory actions are necessary if we are to generate new discoveries. If we stay fixed to our current positions, it is impossible to learn new things.

Brainstorming is a classic exercise for generating creative movement in group problem-solving sessions. As with the psychoanalytic method of free association, people are encouraged to say whatever enters their minds. Self-editing and critical responses from others are discouraged, since they stop the flow of movement and the generation of new ideas from the ones that came before them.

The "blocked" condition when attempting creative activity results from the absence of movement. As Peter said earlier, we become frozen and locked in ourselves. The antidote can be movement for its own sake. Nothing will happen unless you move into action of some kind. When we feel that our creative juices are dried up, or that we have nothing inside ourselves to express, there is a tendency to try and think our way out of the situation, a strategy that only further immobilizes us.

In groups and in organizational life, we often feel that we are working in a vacuum. There is an absence of vital and inspirational interaction with other people. Somebody needs to reach out and make a move toward another person. Movement has to be channeled in a new direction.

In order to move freely with the creative process, space has to be established for this practice. Are you someone who becomes addicted to the things that you complain about? Do you become frustrated with the absence of creative vitality in

your life, but cling to activities and habits that consume all of
your time? Why do you do this? Is it easier than making a
commitment to creativity? Are you more comfortable when
you do not have to take the initiative? Is the familiar more
pleasing than the unknown? Observe the way you pass your
time, and notice how you avoid making space for creation.

CREATIVE PRACTICE

Involve a small group (three to five people) in the process of making sequential marks on a large drawing surface. If you
are engaging a large group of people, break them up into smaller
groups that will work together simultaneously. Use colored markers,
drafting pens, oil pastels, or tempera paints, and ask people to continuously follow one another in making a single mark on the surface.
Encourage people to respond in some way to what others before
them have done. The emergence of the picture will illustrate how different people and their movements build upon one another, shaping
a creation that includes the contributions of each participant and expresses the group's unique synergy.

The exercise can also be done with three-dimensional materials. I
like to work with things from nature such as sticks, grasses, and
other objects. As with the two-dimensional exercise, people are encouraged to build upon one another's actions.

An even simpler group creation involves individuals
taking small stones and arranging them one by one into a configuration of some kind. The constructions that emerge from these interactions vividly convey the spirit of collaborative creation. The physical
markings and expressions designate that something happened
among a group of people at a particular time and place. This simple
affirmation of group creation can generate a sense of wonder in environments where we usually pass days and weeks without a feeling
of ever having created together or having established intimate links
with another person.

You can also apply this movement method to creative writing, where each person builds upon the statements, words, and images of those who went before them.

If you make marks on a surface by yourself, watch how the visual image and its overall expression build upon individual movements. Gestures grow from one another, meet, contrast, and ultimately integrate into the finished object. The art process reveals how individual expressions cannot be separated from the whole, and how the ultimate image is totally dependent upon people taking action of some kind. Everything finds its way into the composition, even if we work in the most spontaneous and unplanned ways.

Reflect upon the completed artworks, and consider whether their visual and kinetic qualities could ever have been planned in advance. Contemplate how specific qualities of the work emerged spontaneously and without directions. Examine how new ideas and creations in other areas of life grow from the simple process of making movements of some kind. Contemplate how the energy within the movement gives shape to new life. Is it necessary to lose yourself within the movement in order to be carried by forces outside yourself? To what extent does immersion in the stream of creative movement depend upon your ability to relax and trust that the unplanned gestures will take you to a new place?

4

GATHERING
TOGETHER

The Integrating Process
of Imagination

The Mediating Place of Imagination

The great contribution of the West to the psychology of creation is the idea of imagination. Between the mid-seventeenth and mid-nineteenth centuries in England and Germany, the imagination was defined by philosophers as an integrating intelligence, "the faculty of faculties," that gathers together different ways of knowing—analysis, aesthetics, sense perception, memory—and mixes them into new discoveries. The imagination was conceived as an "intermediate realm" that "blends" and unifies reason and sensory experience. This mediating place of imagination is strikingly similar to Eastern spiritual disciplines where contradictions are allowed to exist and transform themselves into a greater whole. The creative imagination is an integrating intelligence that has been long overlooked as a priority within educational and social institutions based upon the separation of disciplines and increasing degrees of specialization.

From the European notion of imagination acting as a synthesizing realm to the middle path of Eastern philosophies, we see that creativity is a mediating process that gathers together the polarities of thought and experience. Diverse participants achieve a new synthesis while maintaining their individual identities. Experience indicates that creative vitality actually depends upon the inclusion of contraries, and a certain degree of beneficial strife can force us to move beyond complacent acceptance of current conditions. We struggle with the conflict and oppose it with every fiber of our being, but ultimately recognize its necessity as an agent of change and new life. The most valuable creations often spring from doing what we do not want to do.

In this chapter, we will explore how creative environments at work and in the art studio correspond to the way the imagination works in individual experience. Creative organizations and groups are constructed in ways that support a gathering of perspectives and resources, with the goal of integrating the varied elements into new creations. The practice of imagination orchestrates a community of creation that moves inside and outside the individual person. Each of us is composed of multiple interests and resources that converge within the process of creation. Imagination is the integrator that shapes new forms from the creative mix. Again, the dynamics of the creative imagination within the individual person parallel what happens in a group of people. There is a slipstream within private experience that gathers all of the person's resources into a collective effort.

The creative process also moves between different areas of consciousness. Whereas some have viewed creative expression as originating in a realm called "the unconscious," my experience indicates that creativity is a dynamic movement or process fueled by many different things—actions, perceptions with all the senses, ideas, desires, personal styles, memories, and experiences from the past that exist outside our immediate awareness. Buddhism posits that these past experiences are gathered in our "storehouse consciousness" (in Sanskrit, *alaya-vijnana*), and they are part of the complete interplay of consciousness. The creative process rarely moves from one place to another in a linear way. The inner workings of imagination can be likened to group process and dynamic relations among people, where one thing bounces off another and generates new insights and creations shaped by the mix of participants.

"And what factors support and interrupt this creative interplay?" I am asked. The major hindrance, in my experience, is an overly restrictive control-tower approach to directing everything a person does. I observe this both in individual and group behavior. Individual expression is blocked when we are unable to let go and open to whatever arises in the moment; when we are overly fixated on a routine or a particular way of doing something; when we insist on knowing the outcome before we begin; when we are unable to pursue exploration for its own sake; when we are afraid to make mistakes and therefore stay confined in an unbending routine; when we have a fixed and uncompromising agenda while working with others; and most of all when we block new and unknown elements from gathering together with other aspects of our experience.

These same obstacles to creation are present in groups and organizations, where the most universal deterrent to the interplay of imagination is an overly controlling leader. Sometimes the controlling leader can be highly creative but excludes others in the group or organization from the interplay of creation. Within these "mono-orgs," the creative autocrat might do brilliant things for an establishment while undermining the individual and collective motivation of the community. In contrast, the motivating leader urges others to perform, to try something new, to venture into the unknown and take risks, to accept mistakes and learn from them, to do things in different ways, and to go places where they might be reluctant to go, and he or she always stays committed to the well-being and best interests of the group.

In my relations with creative leaders, there have been many times when I bristled at demands presented to me. They went against my will and my sense of what was important at the time. Life in community, however, often requires that I let go of my personal perspective and implement the initiative of another person or the group.

Ironically, I have had some of my most productive work experiences as a result of doing what I at first did not want to do. This might be as simple as attending a meeting that I wanted to avoid, and having a creative breakthrough in my work as a result of a new dialogue with people.

The tension of resistance often acts as a source of energy, and it helps to refine and hone the ultimate goal. Leaders may similarly benefit from ideas and suggestions that run counter to their visions and plans. Opening to what exists outside our frame of reference is essential to the creative process both in community life and private creative practice. As Heraclitus asserted some twenty-five hundred years ago, the contrast of opposites, at play in a process of exchange and balance, is beneficial to life. Our own egos and habits are often the greatest obstacles to creation. In our individual creative expression, the ego can block access to what lies outside its parameters; and within the realm of leadership, egoism may become a serious pathology. When the leader becomes the alpha and omega of a community or group, and when everything is orchestrated to enhance one person's self-image, the larger and deeper life of the imagination is stopped.

> *Make a list of family and work experiences in which you benefited and learned from doing things that you did not want to do. Did the growth in some way result from opening to ideas outside your immediate frame of reference? Was there a relationship between the degree of tension you experienced and the quality of the outcome? What are some of the things you are most likely to block from entering into your experience? Why? Do these things sometimes make you do things that you do not want to do? How does it feel to successfully complete a project that you initially resisted? Does the initial resistance in any way contribute to the degree of satisfaction experienced at the conclusion?*

These experiences with opposition and resistance indicate that we often block access to the very things needed to shape new creations. All of us have a natural tendency to restrict our personal environments and social gatherings to people and objects that offer familiarity and comfort. We are less likely to welcome what causes tension or goes against our personal point of view.

An international business executive who retired at an early age told me he did not at all miss the interactions with CEOs who interfered with his areas of responsibility. But he did miss the day-to-day interactions with other people at work, the friendships, and the creative decision making and projects they implemented together. "These wonderful aspects of work," he said, "go together with the irritations."

I often wonder whether the creative imagination can function to full capacity in a tension-free environment. Is there is a creative necessity within the things that bother us the most? Can we shift our attitudes toward disturbances and see them as necessary forces in the making of new relationships? Do the irritants bond people together in a shared experience? Do they prepare the way for change and motivate us to do things that we would not normally do?

A secretary described how she left an institution that she loved after working there for over two decades. It was the irritants created by other people that pushed her to move. "Without these problematic relationships," she says, "I never would have left. In retrospect, leaving was important, and it expanded my experience in a major way. Those who bothered me the most were the agents of change. They incited me to move. The change was a risk; but when the opportunity presented itself, I jumped without hesitation."

The practice of creative imagination requires immersion in the process and movement of life, all of life, including what we like and dislike. This flow of living energy is antithetical to the idea of creations springing forth from an unconscious realm. Rather, creation is an activity of consciousness that gathers elements and shapes them into new relationships inside and outside the realm of our awareness.

After a long hiatus from in-depth creative activity, I began a new painting and discovered that things in my immediate environment cohere and undergo a creative integration when I am working with a particular creative goal. As much as I appreciate living with complete openness and receptivity to whatever presents itself at a particular moment, experience teaches me that working toward a creative out-come of some kind triggers the "connecting" function of imagina-tion. There needs to be an objective, a deadline, a vision: something that gathers the varied strands of consciousness, like gravity moving the flow of water in a particular direction. Because rigidly formed ex-pectations limit the formative process, the desired outcome is flexible and open to being shaped by the act of creation.

Showing Up and Falling Together

In order to pick up the communications and opportunities offered by the creative imagination, we have to be "in the game." If we stay on the sidelines, nothing happens— no synchronicities, epiphanies, or creative transformations. As we ponder a problem without a clear resolution and stay open to the environment, our field of conscious-ness is sensitive and open to insights that appear in the expressions of others. The ultimate outcome of the creative process may be far removed from the original intent, but there must be movement of creative energy in a particular direction, any direction, to activate the integrating function of imagination. As energy is applied toward an objective, maintaining an attitude of flexibility, we open channels to other forces in the environment that may augment, contradict, or redirect our initiative.

An artist colleague gives an account of how many of his creative discoveries have occurred because he simply got himself to his studio in the morning. "Showing up," he insists, "is a major part of the cre-ative process. We really have to give more credit to this most basic re-quirement of creativity. Once I get myself to the studio and start working, things always happen. People also need to show up for one another, to be there as sources of support and ideas."

There is probably nothing more fundamental to creative activity than the need to get started with an objective of some kind. The focus might be nothing more than an object of contemplation or rumi-nation. Contemplating the beloved opens lovers to powers of expres-sion and imagining that they never dreamed could exist. It's like exercise: use it or lose it. Practice stimulates the connecting powers of imagination. The linkages of imagination can be likened to free-association. Everything in our particular orbit of activity is drawn into the object of contemplation and used to further the creative connections of imagination.

When I am fully involved with a project, I start the day by working on a certain aspect of the manuscript or painting, and the process of engagement inevitably generates new cycles of creation. It's like a river. The flow has to start moving along a specific path; and then the overall momentum carries the project to completion, spinning off new features from the core energy of the desired outcome.

There is an integrating force in creative work that draws related ideas to our particular purposes. The same process of creative convergence happens in our relationships with other people.

We cooperate with this natural integrating function of imagination by cultivating expansiveness and openness in our individual lives. New insights cannot be expected from a narrow field of experience. The mind is shaped by the company it keeps; therefore I encourage my students to read widely. The creative imagination needs excellent resources and materials in order to do its work.

Creative groups and organizations similarly affirm the varied resources that people bring to the common enterprise. The creative integrations of imagination are driven by the natural interplay of participants. This community of creation with others can also be applied to solitary contemplation. If we approach our time alone as an opportunity to be together with all of the things that exist within the present moment, the integrating process of creation will flourish. This is perhaps connected to what the Buddha was suggesting when he discouraged fixations on wanting what we do not have. As always, everything depends upon how we view a situation.

> *Identify the different ingredients that mix together to form the blend of your creative life. What qualities do you see as truly unique? What qualities do you share with other people?*
>
> *Have you experienced peak moments of creativity? Were there environmental factors that contributed to your creative vitality? Reflect upon the nature of your relationships with other people during periods when you were most creative.*

How might they have influenced you? Did the physical environment affect you? Can you say that your greatest moments of creative vitality originated from within yourself? From environmental conditions? From the interaction between yourself and the environment? What conditions of life have had the greatest impact on your expression?

Have there been times in your creative practice when everything fell together effortlessly? Why do you think this happened? I am sure you can remember times when you tried to create and nothing worked. Artists frequently describe being "stuck" and unable to generate new material. The state of "stuckness" is similar to the Sisyphean condition described earlier, when we feel trapped in one place and keep pushing away at obstacles without progressing. Have you experienced this condition? What are the causes? Perhaps it has something to do with being locked into an idea or position, unable to let it go and move on to another focus. Maybe all of us have to go through these difficulties as part of creative practice. What do you think?

Sometimes even good ideas have to be let go, because others will not support them. This happens frequently in groups and communities when leaders try to move people to new positions and meet entrenched opposition. It may be better to let go of a good cause or idea and move on to another initiative, another way of ultimately arriving at a more creative life within the group. Workers within organizations frequently have to let go of ideas that leaders will not adopt or positions that go against those of leaders. There is great truth to the adage that we have to choose our battles; when our principles and integrity demand that we go against a particular position, we should carefully consider where and when our fight will make a difference.

I have found that working in groups frequently requires letting go of a personal position in order to support the movement of the whole. The same dynamic occurs within the individual imagination. In my work teaching artists and writers, I have observed how people hang on to things and have great difficulty letting go. The practice of creation develops the ability to make decisions about what to keep and what to let go. This is among the most difficult parts of creative activity and group work.

We all know people who never let go, never forget, never forgive, hang on to everything, and stay rigidly attached to past positions. There is a part like that in all of us. What a burden it is to carry these things with us all the time. If we lighten our loads and cultivate spaciousness within ourselves, the creative process will have far greater room to grow. Letting go of fixations demonstrates willingness to move on to something new. Fixity is the antithesis of creativity.

> *It can benefit us all to examine those areas in our lives where we stubbornly hang onto fixed positions. What aspects of your life are characterized by an unwillingness to change? What is the basis of this need to stay the same? Do you hold grudges, nurse resentments, and replay disappointments from the past so that they are with you all the time? In what way has carrying these setbacks for so long turned them into self-fulfilling prophecies? Do the negative things you carry benefit you or others in any way?*
>
> *Letting go may at times require us to physically separate from particular work or community environments. Can you recall moments in your life when a change of surroundings brought a sense of renewal and fresh opportunity?*

I have always been attracted to work environments charged with creative momentum. Even when making major cuts in programs and redefining the focus of an organization, it is possible to direct energy in an optimistic way. This occurs when groups of people work together in realizing goals and when leaders affirm the abilities and contributions of each community member. Threats to well-being can actually serve as effective ways of regaining creative impetus.

SARAH
The Creative Energy of Teams

Groups and organizations can generate something similar to the slipstream draft that we discussed earlier. Like a group of racers, people at work can be carried effortlessly along a common course.

Sarah works as a graphic designer in an advertising firm. She describes how her coworkers inspire one another: "I am part of a small team that includes myself as the visual designer, a writer, and a business coordinator. Although we bring different skills to our projects, it is remarkable how much overlap there is. We cross over constantly, and I have learned that sometimes people from other disciplines can see things in my designs that I overlook. There is a certain freshness and openness that comes with beginner's mind. I also find it invigorating to work with text and to help our business coordinator convey an idea to a client. Once you get a taste of this collaborative environment, it's hard to think of working alone again."

"Has your experience with teams always been positive?" I ask.

Sarah answers, "Everything depends upon chemistry among the group members and the overall environment of the organization. Things are great with my present team, and the company is enlightened. It hasn't always been that way. Bad vibes between team members can be torturous."

"What causes the bad vibes?"

"Ego, negativism, the inability to let things go and meld into a common effort that carries everything along," she replies. "Positive energy in the team transports me into creative action even when I am down. I might go to work feeling sluggish and unmotivated, not wanting to be there at all; but then the momentum of the team starts to work on me. It's like running or bike racing: I have to move with the pack; the team takes on a life of its own. As I let go of my preoccupations, I become part of something outside myself that fills me with its creative energy. It is very good medicine. Our team is keenly aware of this momentum factor. We have all taken our turns being restored by the group effort. Each of us has acted as the 'good shepherd' for another, renewing creative energy when someone slips into a dark valley. It's all about supportive relationships. They carry us through difficulties. We complement one another. It's almost like an ecosystem where subtle adjustments are constantly being made to sustain cooperation."

"The effective team has a creative intelligence," I say, "often surpassing what a person can do alone."

"This definitely applies to momentum," Sarah continues. "I am one of those people who has a difficult time getting started. This doesn't happen within the team. I become part of a creative movement that gathers me into its energy. I am fortunate to have been in this environment for so many years. The teamwork has enabled me to do things that I would never have dared working alone. Our interactions, and the things that arise unexpectedly from them, have also taught me many things about the creative process."

"For example?" I ask.

"The most important thing I have learned is that we can never do enough careful listening to what others have to say," Sarah replies. "As we listen attentively, we can ask one another questions or make comments that clarify an idea or help it to unfold more completely. Listening to others also helps us listen more carefully to ourselves; we can transfer the same responsiveness to our individual efforts."

"This listening process sounds active," I say.

"It is," Sarah declares. "It can be the most vigorous part of the work."

"I call it the 'responding' intelligence of creativity."

"We've got to pay close attention to each other," Sarah responds, "if we are going to create as a team. It is divine when the process is thriving."

"*Participation mystique?*" I ask. "We lose our self-consciousness and act like early peoples who did not detach themselves from their perceptions and surroundings. Everything is part of a living whole. We experience a spiritual feeling of transcending our personal selves when we are immersed in a group effort."

"Yes," Sarah says, "it is a gift when work furthers our spiritual lives."

"But there are probably few people," I respond, "who see working with others as a creative ideal. Most of us with creative interests long for more time alone, in order to reflect, gather our experiences, and do something creative with them."

"I just wrote a poem for my daughter on her sixteenth birthday," Sarah explained. "It has been over a year since I wrote a poem, and the experience reminded me how this form of creative expression demands sustained private concentration. But I also saw that as I reflected alone on my relationship to my daughter, connections to other things began to emerge. I was struck by the way poetic contemplation enabled me to relate more deeply with my daughter. Although I was completely alone, she was intensely present; and the process of making the poem allowed me to collect my most intimate feelings about my daughter and shape them into a new creation. And when I gave her the poem, this opened yet another dimension of relationship."

"So poetry suggests," I question, "that it may be necessary to be alone and reflective if we want to relate more deeply to others and to our experience?"

"Yes," Sarah replies, "we are always moving between these states, from solitude to being with others. And when we are alone, we can make intimate contact with others."

"Maybe the effective and creative relationships," I propose, "are the ones that allow us to move between these realms."

"Yes," Sarah agrees. "This ability to move freely between solitude and active contact with others may be the key to both successful personal relationships and to creating at work. In both areas I have seen how being locked into one domain alone can be stifling."

"In my experience," I emphasize, "solitude is hard to come by at work. I might have moments to myself; but there is always the phone, the next meeting or appointment, the e-mail, the papers waiting. However, I must admit that highly focused meetings and discussions with other people sometimes penetrate to the same depth of concentration and achieve the same state of imaginative integration that I experience when working alone on a creative project. I see that I just have to bring this attitude to my engagements with others. Maybe the most unlikely places are the ones that have the most potential for a new life of creation."

"My private experience with writing poetry makes me realize that others are always with us," Sarah replies. "When I was describing the importance of listening to people in a complete way, I was probably getting at how our relationships with others can penetrate to this place of intense connection that you describe. In these moments of creative fusion, we bring together the best aspects of being by ourselves and being with others. Maybe this is part of the mystery of creation. The two are always present. When we are alone, others can be intimately present; and when we create effectively with others, there is space for solitude."

"I've been called a Pollyanna," I admit, "when I describe the potential of creating with others. There is a deep suspicion about the collective realm. I think it's because so many of us are tied to the yoke of work, school, and family obligations, and we long for the freedom to be alone with ourselves."

"You're right," Sarah affirms. "I have the same needs."

"Time alone," I state, "has become a precious commodity for many of us today. Whereas time with others, at work and everywhere else in our lives, is readily available and taken for granted. The average person probably doesn't approach relationships with colleagues as potentially having the creative momentum you described earlier. I can't tell you how many days of my life have been spent longing for creative freedom; all that time I ignored potentially creative relationships with the people who were right at hand."

"It's all about taking advantage of what we have," Sarah responds. "Wanting something other than what exists disconnects us from the vital elements of creation."

"This is living beyond the horizon, rather than in the present condition of things," I reflect. "Yet yearning certainly has a place in creative imagination. Desire can be a way of penetrating to the core of our present condition."

"I think you may be right," Sarah replies. "We have to find ways for our longings and our present conditions to work together. The same goes for solitude and creative relationships with others. They can be partners."

"We all tend to struggle," I say, "with the challenges presented by empty space. I wonder if creative satisfaction exists in a middle realm somewhere between solitude and connection. Too much of either can create an imbalance. Even though people at work complain about not having enough free time, they still want more attention from others. Solitude has its frightening side."

"But when you get all the attention, there are the demands that go with it," Sarah acknowledges. "People then want to be invisible. Maybe it's all about imbalance, too much of one thing."

"In my early forties, Sarah, I stopped being a dean because there were things that wore me down. After a period of rest and transition, I started to miss the things that bothered me the most. Life certainly has its perverse nature. Maybe these apparently opposing conditions desperately need one another."

"Everything connects," Sarah says. "I recall reading something in Sufi philosophy about the reciprocal nature of things that appear to oppose one another—how the material and spiritual worlds rely on one another for their definition. It's esoteric but really fundamental."

"The things that bug us define us," I respond. "The most private inner experiences team up with what we know from the external world. There is a partnership among the different dimensions of experience. Imagination puts these things together in new ways. We see something that interests us and imagine it further. It's impossible to imagine unless we take something from our lives in the world and transform it through our solitary musings."

Do you have enough time in your life for solitary reflection? Are you comfortable with solitude, or does it frighten you? Why do you feel this way? Is there anything you would like to change about your approach to solitude? Are you able to find peace and stillness when you are working together with others?

I find that some of my most restful moments occur when I am working with a group of people. In many situations other people enhance inner reflection. This happens in church, and it occurs in my experience with studio groups. The energy of the other people triggers contemplative reflection and helps us look more deeply into ourselves. We find ourselves through others; and, as Sarah suggested when describing the poem she wrote to her daughter, we get closer to others through our private reflections.

BILL
Being Compelled to Stretch

Bill, a high school English teacher and published fiction writer in his mid-fifties, sometimes worries about not yearning for anything in particular. "Is my life so complete," he wonders, "that there is nothing left to desire? Or I have lost my edge? Have I become mature, and thus satisfied with the things I have and the people around me? My longing tends to be focused on having more time for creation, for perfecting my expression. Yet I feel that the things I have right now are very complete and without them my life would be less interesting."

"What would you change in your life?" I ask. "How would you make it different?" "The only thing I'd like to have is more time to write," Bill responds. "But I don't want to give up my life with the students and the summer work I do running a sailing program. All of these things have an important place in my life. I've learned that I have to be with people and involved with group efforts. I've concluded that these community activities are more important than being free all of the time to pursue my writing. I can only go so far writing about my private meditations. I need to be in a real world that places demands on me. The challenges bring things out of me that I did not know existed. I also write better when I work from real life situations and actual interactions that I've had with people."

"But you do long for a certain degree of solitude?" I question.

"Yes," Bill says. "But not too much of it. I have learned how much I need my working relationships with other people, and I believe that they can be more difficult to achieve than solitude. I have been fortunate to be involved with creative and intelligent groups of people. The problem is that work is so all-encompassing that it is hard to find or make time for my private expression. It's not easy to completely shift gears for short periods of time. So I tend to stay in the routines of my life."

Bill's experience affirms how the creative imagination needs a mix of different experiences. Again, the aspects of our lives that present the greatest challenges to our creative expression may be the factors that we need the most. Like Bill, I have found that the time and energy given to my work in organizations make it difficult and sometimes impossible to find time for private creative expression.

I say to Bill, "As much as I might try to minimize pressures at work and constraints on my private expression, they keep me in real and reciprocal relations with other people. The unlikely and unexpected influences from outside my current frame of reference always contribute the most to the creative expansion of whatever I happen to be doing. They flush me from the cover of habit and the status quo. The challenges I face at work make me enlarge my perspective on life. I have to do things that I would not choose to do and deal with people and points of view that are clearly alien to my personal orbit of interests."

"Yes," Bill replies. "I am indebted to people and situations that compel me to stretch and adjust. I am a creature of habit, and I gravitate toward things that I know and enjoy. Group work makes it necessary to broaden my understanding of situations."

"And don't you think that these group experiences paradoxically define our most individual qualities?" I ask. "Maybe imagination is where the extremes of the particular and the universal meet."

"In my creative work," Bill responds, "I strive to engage those experiences that are unique and distinctly my own. Ironically, these very individual and sometimes peculiar things have the most appeal to others."

"They evoke," I say, "a corresponding sensitivity to our own lives."

Bill elaborates: "This is the way imagination works, through connections among very personal and particular experiences and images. The wider the spectrum of resources, the richer the ultimate blend will be. We cannot have imagination without very concrete experiences, like Einstein's observation of poles from a moving train. What he saw at that particular time was connected to the physics problem he was trying to solve."

"Imagine what might have happened," I observe, "if he did not take that train ride."

"Yes, I've often wondered to what extent discoveries are tied to a particular set of circumstances. Was that specific train ride essential, or could another experience have triggered the insight?"

"We'll never know. But it is certain that life experiences inform creation."

"And in literature," Bill continues, "the details of Kafka's office experiences are transformed into some of his greatest writing. We create from the terrain that we know. When I read his office descriptions, it triggers my own imagination. It's a sort of creative contagion. One image sparks another. The process can't be planned. That's the beauty and mystery of imagination."

"But work," I say, "is all about plans, prescriptions, strategies, and expectations. How can this environment further imagination?"

"Good point," Bill answers. "I think it has to do with extremes and contradictions. In my work as a teacher, there are expectations that specific outcomes will be achieved. The pressure has been increased in recent years. I'm expected to teach very concrete and universal skills, to be at school at set times, to complete certain areas of teaching within established intervals, to meet standards established by external groups, and so forth. I have an advantage in that the creative imagination is part of the material I teach in both literature and writing classes. But much of what I have to do at school can be compared to what any other worker is 'required' to perform.

"Sounds dismal, doesn't it? But, strangely enough, I am inspired by how the most creative and imaginative events in my work typically happen in response to these limits and within the mandatory relationships I have with people."

I grimace. "The imagination is truly perverse."

"It is paradoxical how limits can provoke the enlargement of creativity," Bill responds. "To access our powers of responsiveness, we need to meet a certain degree of resistance. We all have problems and difficult situations in our lives, and we struggle with them. This is where the energy is and where the major transformations can take place. Kafka, a law school graduate and office worker, used detailed descriptions of and fantastic musings about the labyrinthine bureaucracies he knew and loathed, to evoke a universal experience of psychological alienation. The imagination did something with his upheaval."

"And when you get discouraged at work, how do you deal with it?" I ask.

"I think about artists like Kafka and the painter Edvard Munch who did such remarkable things with their difficult experiences," Bill relates. "I realize that there was not much joy in either of their lives. They suffered terribly from emotional unrest, but they did something with it. If they can make art from the darkest places of experience, I can do something creative with my modest discontents."

"Kafka described how there was an intense world within his mind and that he would be 'torn to pieces' if he didn't express it," I reply. "And he felt that he'd rather be torn to pieces 'a thousand times' than keep this tumultuous realm locked inside himself. Munch said, 'Illness, insanity, and death are the black angels that kept watch over my cradle and accompanied me all my life.' They were both haunted by neurotic obsessions throughout their lives. Kafka suffered from tuberculosis and died young. Munch lived to be eighty but was plagued by physical illnesses in addition to his emotional problems. Like Van Gogh, they really suffered; but there was an accompanying passion and strength that generated brilliant creative achievements. Their lives are significant for those of us who study creativity and emotional unrest."

"Creative expression does offer a lifeline," Bill says, "for people suffering from intense disturbances."

"I agree with your feeling that these great artists, who lived tormented lives, demonstrate how we can do something creative with our less severe complaints and existential discomforts."

"In my simple way," Bill continues, "I keep going back to work as a way of participating in the world and contributing. Perhaps there is something healthy in this. We complain about work and don't see the medicine in it."

"I've often thought that daily interaction with other people and collaborative creation keep me grounded in the world," I acknowledge, "and guard against an isolation that may become alienating."

"On a selfish level," Bill replies, "I've learned that I need these experiences in order to produce expressions that resonate with others. I'm definitely a hunter-gatherer type who takes what life gives me. This is how my imagination works. Maybe others are more capable of cultivating creativity exclusively within the confines of their private lives. Not I."

"You move between worlds," I comment.

"Perhaps that is what I do. I need to be challenged in different ways. Teaching is hard and sometimes tedious because there is repetition year after year; but there is so much energy at school, so many opportunities to shape the world in positive ways. My experiences at work open me to the larger network of creative imagination. Otherwise I'm too much with myself. I need engagements with other people and the ideas they generate. This larger life of the imagination exists out there in the world, and it is something that I bring back to my solitary creation."

> *Where do you experience the most tedium in your life? Have you ever thought of how these difficult experiences may contribute to your creative imagination?*

One of the best ways of dealing with tiresome experiences at work is to use your imagination as a way of establishing compassion for other people who are experiencing similar feelings now and in the past. The imagination has always been viewed as the chief way of empathizing with others. This is why literal-minded people are so far removed from the life of imagination. They are unable to open to how others see the world, and they operate within a circumscribed set of procedures.

> *Instead of avoiding contact with the wearisome aspects of your life, engage these areas as materials for creation and for the expansion of your knowledge. Try to consider the energy that is shared by all of the people in the world who are struggling with these difficult conditions. What images come to mind as you reflect on this universal situation? Does the condition shift from being a passive burden to a source of vital action?*

This small experiment with tedium demonstrates what can happen when you change your perspective on a problem, when you explore the positive energy that exists within difficult situations, and most of all when you shift your attitude from passive victimization to active transformation and creation. We might not be able to change or alter the limitations of our lives, circumstances shared by most people in the world, but by accepting who we are and what we must do, we can certainly change how we think about our lives. Imagination is the tool for remaking everything.

To Imagine Is to Let Go

The creative act is based upon the paradoxical ability to stay focused on what is happening, while letting go of the need to control outcomes. It is important to build confidence at the start that the complexities will ultimately cohere if we allow the creative process to do its work. However, people desiring predictable results and security seek linear, step-by-step guides and find it difficult to surrender to the unexpected. They grasp the controls with white knuckles and leave little space for free movements of imagination.

To imagine is to let go. Yet in creative expression there is a need to stay focused on a particular thing in order to travel deeply and expansively without attachment. Establishing a focal point for creative contemplation helps a person direct energy in a particular direction and avoid becoming scattered. Jumping quickly from one thing to another and trying to do too many things at once makes our perceptions aimless and superficial. Yet we don't want to cling to an object so tightly that we block the movements of imagination that emerge naturally from contemplation.

As we contemplate a particular thing, one image connects to another in a flow of creation. This reflective process corresponds to the movements of art making, as described in the previous section.

Concentration on a particular image, object, experience, or feeling is the entry to creative exploration. Select a focal point as a beginning, and do your best to banish thoughts about what you hope to achieve. Choose anything—an image from a dream, another person, an object, a memory, or a feeling.

Jung advised, when describing his method of "active imagination," that goals should not be "too fixed." He discovered that when we concentrate on any image in a sustained and complete way, "turning it over and over," something significant always emerges from the engagement. Jung wrote in a 1947 letter to a Mr. O., "You must carefully avoid impatient jumping from one subject to another. Hold fast to the one image you have chosen, and wait until it changes by itself."

Practice teaches that creative experiences happen through a partnership between our efforts and our objects of contemplation. We have to learn how to let the process happen as we participate fully.

As you concentrate on the object of your reflection, look closely at its physical qualities. Complete attentiveness to a particular aspect of the object, situation, or feeling becomes an opening to new discoveries that flow naturally from the relationship you have established. The object becomes your partner and you realize that creating with others also applies to physical things.

As James Joyce writes in *Ulysses*, "Any object, intensely regarded, may be a gate of access to the incorruptible eon of the gods." The object of contemplation gives life back to us through its expression, intensified and focused by the energy and attention that we give to it. Potential objects for creative meditation are as diverse as life itself. I have always preferred to meditate upon the most ordinary, overlooked, and troublesome things in my life. The soul, Jung believed, is found in the most insignificant things. Creative perception helps us appreciate every aspect of our lives. Meditation on ordinary things not only opens the paths of creative imagination but also gives new meaning to the physical world.

Longing for the ideal that may exist within the mind's eye can block access to the concrete things that present themselves to us for creative transformation. Nothing will happen unless you let go of your preoccupations and give all of yourself to the process of contemplation. Creative ideas and images emerge from the connections made between yourself and the object of your contemplation.

Practice letting go by contemplating virtually anything; if concentration is sustained, the object of concentration will begin to change. Avoid *trying* to turn it into something else. Just concentrate on the particular object and watch how it is transformed. It is important to give full attention to the object; this way of looking fills the object with life and transformative power. Reciprocal relations characterize every aspect of creative imagination.

Letting go does not require abandoning our commitments. We can meditate on a situation with the goal of discovering solutions to problems, new ways of relating to situations, and ideas for further creative expression. Encourage a series of possibilities to emerge from this method of reflection. The creative imagination will develop options like a group of consultants.

Most people find it challenging to set aside personal ideas and plans in order to encourage and adopt alternatives suggested by others. We are all prone to become overly attached to our creations and strategies, and we see them as extensions of ourselves. This fixation on personal positions can freeze the process of creative discovery.

As you reflect upon an object or situation, try to distance yourself from commitments. Let the possibilities emerge, and do your best not to become attached to any one in particular. Rather, find a way to record your ideas and images, either through notes or tape recordings, so you will be able to return to them later for further consideration. When pursuing the process of creative meditation, you want to give all of your energy to sustaining the stream of images and possibilities. Stay focused on the overall process, but don't become overly attached to a particular object.

The discipline of imagination involves a simultaneous ability to "hold fast" and "let go." Some might call this a creative interplay between the conscious and the unconscious mind, whereas I view it as a partnership between two elements of consciousness: focus and surrender. Through the application of sustained attention, problematic situations invariably shift and offer new insights into themselves. Total attention becomes a means of letting go.

My twelve-year-old daughter began to speak to me when I was immersed in a project. I looked up at her a bit confused, as I was caught somewhere between her statement and my reverie. She smiled at me and said, "Don't worry, Daddy. I know what it's like to be on the train of thought."

I realized that her rewording of the familiar expression "having a train of thought" to actually "being on a train of thought" is closer to the experience of fully letting go.

We enter a vehicle of transport that carries us and makes contact with places that are not otherwise accessible.

The practice of imagination is grounded in the understanding that there are intelligences outside the realm of the reasoning mind acting by itself. Simple creative activities open new doors on reality if they are taken seriously. Insights into persistent problems often appear spontaneously through elementary exercises in an unfamiliar realm of expression. The activity, just like a city that we visit for the first time, establishes the basis for fresh connections between experiences. For instance, a person might gain a new perspective on a challenging group by arranging stones in sand to express relationships and degrees of closeness among group members.

When you let go, things happen. But there are also the realities of preparation and active engagement with whatever is taking place. Creative meditation in this respect corresponds to our earlier discussion of leadership. The creative process, like the leader, responds as much as it initiates. Both maintain a consciousness of readiness and seize opportunities emerging from the interplay of participants. "Genius," Michelangelo reportedly said, "comes to the prepared mind."

I repeatedly find that relaxation, openness, and confidence are three elements that characterize successful expression. These qualities are cultivated through experience and constant practice. After preparing to give a lecture or performance, I must put aside my preparations and open to the forces moving through the immediate environment.

The fullness of "preparation" shifts to the emptiness and receptivity of "presence." The embrace of one does not exclude the other. The two act as partners in creation.

When I write a poem, it is usually in response to an experience. As I meditate on a subject, which might be a person or a feeling, an image emerges; and then another arrives in response to it, and then another, typically in a flow of impressions. After letting whatever comes forth take its place on the page, I go back and trim the words down to an essential statement. I write my poems in the same way that I make a painting or write a book.

The different parts shape one other; and when I return to work on a project, the next phase of movement is likewise activated and informed by responses to what was created before.

The finished poem is a distillation of the words, feelings, and images generated by the movements occurring as I reflect on my experience with the subject. From the total spectrum of sensations, I extract images that evoke the whole. Poetry offers a way of cutting to the marrow of life.

In order to start the creative process, I need to get the flow of ideas moving and recorded in some way. Strong feelings, problems, or desires are always excellent sources of creative flow. This is why artists worry when they become too neutral or complacent in their lives. Tension of some kind is a reliable source of creative movement.

Try using the situations that disturb you the most at work, at home, or in life in general as objects of creative meditation. The simple act of engaging these strong negatives as a potential source of creative transformation will begin to change their place in your life. Don't be surprised if you find this difficult to do. Negative feelings and judgments often give us a sense of power that we may be reluctant to renounce.

Our disturbances define us as much as our longings. Have you ever perceived yourself as a victim? Is there a power of some kind contained in this attitude? Perhaps it protects you from taking action and responsibility, from moving into a new role or position that will stretch who you are and what you can do in the world.

Who are you without the things you despise? Can you forgive the sources of your discontent and embrace them as a wellspring of creative imagination? Identify your most painful betrayal. Do you still cling to it in some way? Why? Is it sometimes easier to stay in the victim role? Change and creative transformation of your betrayal may demand more from you.

Are you able to thrive within an environment offering nothing but creative opportunity? Do your discontents

*protect you from the crucible of creative action and the
changes that it will bring to your life? Will the positive
embrace of your disturbances reveal the part you play in
their formation?*

Creative problem-solving methods similarly encourage a steady
focus on an issue needing resolution. For example, participants may
brainstorm possible responses, as I described in the preceding chapter. Free association is encouraged, and every response, however out-
landish, is welcomed. Analogies to other aspects of life are invited,
and it is frequently discovered that something far removed from the
immediate situation may offer innovative ways of reframing the
problem.

"Spreading out" is helpful, rather than consistently approaching
the problem in the same direction, banging away at it and trying to
bring change through sheer force of will. The issues are restated
from varied vantage points, and sometimes a simple adjustment in
how the difficulty is articulated helps dissolve the most intractable
obstacles.

While concentrating on a particular issue, the creative problem
solver freely explores and plays with the widest possible range of solutions. This ability to stay focused while enlarging opportunities
contrasts with the condition of becoming fragmented and scattered.

Invariably, one thing leads to another, and the most insignificant
of details may be the source of insight upon which a new strategy is
constructed. Sustained commitment to the process of exploration
and faith in its ability to further discovery are the principal requirements for successful outcomes.

Whether practicing creative problem-solving activities alone or
leading others, it is essential to focus on sustaining the movement of
ideas. As we discussed in the previous section, new insights emerge
from the overall flow of expression. Stay loose yet totally focused,
and you will find that your most relaxed efforts are the source of
your greatest creations. The creative process lives at the heart of
paradox, on the edge of holding fast and letting go.

Active Imagination and Creative Problem Solving

Many creative problem-solving techniques make use of our ability to generate new ideas by contemplating randomly chosen objects. Scientific discoveries repeatedly demonstrate that epiphanies can emerge from the contemplation of objects with no apparent relationship to the problem at hand. Einstein's observation of telephone poles from a moving train and Newton's falling apple are among the best-known examples of how sensory experiences outside the lines of a particular pattern of thought offer new insights. The logical mind is adept at perfecting ideas once they have arrived, but it is not very effective in creating totally new outlooks.

The history of discovery reveals that "receptivity" to the sometimes surprising and even intrusive thoughts from outside the existing frame of reference is a fundamental characteristic of the creative thinker. Although stubborn persistence and bold initiatives may often be essential to the practice of imagination, creative discoveries are more likely to happen spontaneously when we are relaxed, receptive, and not overly concerned with a particular goal or objective.

Chance and unexpected openings are more likely to characterize creative discovery than planned outcomes, making it necessary for the creative person to have the flexibility and vision required to seize opportunities. Looking deeply and carefully is a way of activating the potential energy that exists in every situation. We establish a space that welcomes the free interplay of possibilities. As we attend to an object, we give it vitality and the ability to act upon us.

The active imagination methods developed by C. G. Jung early in the twentieth century continue to have great relevance to creative discovery and problem solving. The practice of active imagination, as distinguished from the more passive or involuntary imaginings of the unconscious mind, is based upon what Jung called the objective dynamics of the creative process. Where Freud's "unconscious" images were used as subject matter for what he considered to be the higher functions of analytic problem solving, Jung approached the imagination as an integrative intelligence capable of transforming mental conflicts.

"Active imagination" can be defined as consciously applying the imagination to the process of deepening our understanding of a situation or problem. Jung describes how we can respond to dreams and troubling experiences by engaging with the arts and other methods of creative reflection in order to "imagine them further" and shift our relation to them. The imagination finds its way through complicated situations in ways that cannot be realized through the conscious mind.

Active imagination can be practiced with any experience as the object of reflection. When practicing active imagination, your mind should be relaxed and open, allowing you to enter a meditative or altered state wherein your perceptions are attuned to the object of contemplation and open to its expressions.

A person begins the process of active imagination by selecting an image, usually a detail from within the total configuration, and watching it change. For example, a person working with a painting might begin with a particular tree within a landscape, or a color or shape within a nonrepresentational picture. The same principle can be applied to a scene from waking life, focusing for example on the person in a group situation who did not speak during a conflict, or on the painting hanging on the wall of the room where the meeting took place. Everything depends, Jung felt, upon how we look at things. He discovered that sustained attention animates an image, which in turn will give energy back to the perceiver. He likened this effect to magic and enchantment, and realized that if a person could become immersed in the object of contemplation, it would speak and generate expressive powers. The image "begins to stir," Jung said, in response to the attention we give it. Through the energy of this exchange, the object of contemplation moves to a new place. It comes to life as we watch it. As with any other meditative discipline, the quality of reflection will determine the outcomes.

Jung encouraged people to paint, mold with clay, write, and move their bodies in response to changes in the images they contemplated. Even the most purely contemplative forms of imagination generate contents that will more fully reveal themselves through further expression. The materials of artistic expression give tangible form to inner imaginings; and, as Jung said, the hand may be capable of solving problems that defy the mind.

Jung used active imagination to achieve a new synthesis between conflicting and fixed attitudes. In keeping with the history of creative transformation, he found that logical thinking was incapable of generating "a third thing, in which the opposites can unite."

Throughout his lifelong experimentation with active imagination, Jung returned to the simple method of sustained concentration upon the details of an image and letting the process of discovery emerge from it. He experienced the psyche as a "self-regulating system" and felt that we must be able to "let things happen" within it.

Because logical problem-solving methods keep us engrossed in the polarities of positions, Jung believed that the big problems of life are essentially insoluble. Rather than attempt to "fix" the irreconcilable opposites, we create different ways of relating to them and may even make good use of the tension they generate. In active imagination, the polarized situations are personified. They are allowed to describe themselves, to speak for themselves. As we imagine images further, and in greater detail, they become more complex and pliable. The imaginative process transforms fixed ideas and offers opportunities to respond to old problems in new ways. The nemesis becomes a partner in creation and maybe even a valued part of our lives.

The creative imagination is less likely to "solve" persisting problems than it is to generate new attitudes toward them and ways of living creatively with conflicts. It is generally much easier to accept the persistence of problems when we realize that they can become sources of creative transformation. In this way the transforming dynamics of creation correspond to the process of healing. The poet Rilke, explaining the necessary place of negative experiences in the creative process, said he was afraid that if his devils left him, so would his angels.

I repeatedly see in my work with creative expression how people limit discovery by quickly defining what an image means. Clever attempts to immediately label and fix a problem will often interrupt the intelligence of imagination. To resist change, we defend ourselves against insights that conflict with our current frame of reference; we often accomplish this by jumping to conclusions about what is occurring in a particular situation. Staying in control through aggressive intervention is deemed more valuable than allowing the condition to reveal itself more completely.

We get in the way of the creative imagination and stop the process of discovery with explanations. The mind moves into an entirely different zone where it is less open and amenable to influences and insights. "If you label me," Martin Buber declared, "you negate me." Jung similarly felt that the mystery and depth of an image disappears, "flies away," when it is explained. Explanation is one of the most effective tools the ego uses to maintain its seeming control of a situation.

Attempts to quickly fix a problem through explanation are often motivated by a sincere desire to ease discomfort and tension. As described earlier, most people have difficulty realizing that bad situations can be openings to creative discovery. The disturbing situation is typically caused by blocked energy that is unable to move forward. The problem can be viewed as an opportunity for conflicting forces to be engaged in a new way. I constantly find that the most disturbing situations have the most to offer, perhaps because they bring to our attention circumstances that cry out for change.

We practice letting the image "cook" gradually, without pressure to reach quick conclusions. Imagination is "applied" to an image or problematic situation, and different interpretations are generated. As one possibility leads to another, people realize that every situation is likely to generate numerous options.

Repeatedly I see how people instinctively seek out explanations as illusory ways of controlling and neutralizing the tension, what psychologist Leon Festinger called the "cognitive dissonance," of unknown or vexing situations.

> Do you find it difficult to withhold judgment when faced
> with a problematic situation or conflict? Do you jump to
> quick conclusions based solely upon your point of view,
> without inviting the input of others? Why? Is it because you
> feel threatened and feel the need to protect yourself? Does
> this reaction always help? Has it caused further problems for

you? Have you found that over time your first responses will often change? Is this a result of looking at the issue or problem in a more comprehensive way? When you speak to other people and receive their perspectives, does it help you to think more expansively about what is happening?

Next time this happens, see if you are able to withhold judgment for a while. Imagine yourself walking around the problem, as if it were an object, a person, or a place. Look at it from as many perspectives as you can.

In my experience, the most reliable method for expanding perception is the simple process of observing something standing before us and describing what we see. I first began to do this when responding to artworks in my group studios. When people in groups are encouraged to describe the physical qualities of what they see before them, there is an immediate sense of how we generally make fast and limiting interpretations of experiences; in so doing, we avoid the many other things conveyed in the purely physical and perceptual realms. If we want to look more deeply and imaginatively, we need to become aware of what the object or the experience "says" about itself. Put a lid on what you have to say about it, and discover what it conveys to you.

In the practice of active imagination, Jung encourages the person to "relativize the ego position," to see our self-centered way of looking at an experience as only one of many possibilities. There is a freedom and a new sense of possibility when we realize how our perceptions of threats and problems may be flawed and limited. When a disagreeable situation is reframed as a drama involving different elements, we are able to look at it far more objectively. The troubling characters or images become essential to the enactment when we relax our natural tendency to personalize everything within a problem. The self that views the situation and reacts emotionally to its provocations is only one of many participants in a larger process of creation.

If you are like most people, you probably react instinctively to upsetting situations from a personal perspective. The first response is typically emotional, and then perhaps you start to think more objectively about what has happened. It may be helpful for you to recognize the part of yourself that jumps quickly when threatened or upset. This part or perspective is usually distinct from the one that begins to think through a situation in a more rational way, but both tend to look from the perspective of what psychologists call the ego position. Active imagination encourages you to look from other points of view, to gather a more complete sense of what is happening in a situation, and to expand your options for dealing with it.

When someone does something that troubles you, try to observe the incident from that person's perspective. Are you capable of this empathy? You don't have to accept the other's perspective, but this exercise may help you to better understand him or her. Put your ego aside and try to enlarge your sense of what is happening to you.

If there are other people involved, look from their perspectives. Treat your ego as one of many characters contributing to this incident. This is difficult to do if the situation is hurtful. You can also look at the problem from the perspective of your hurt feelings. Distinguishing your emotions from your reasoning mind might help you see more.

If the conflict took place next to an inanimate object like the water cooler in a hallway, in a car, or next to a rock, personify the thing and imagine the scene from its perspective. Years of experience with active imagination within my studio workshops suggests that looking at a problem from another point of view than our own eases pressure and helps us gain a more creative understanding of what actually happened and what we can do about it.

Crazy as it may seem, this poetic process of personifying things and beings increases, in number and quality, the creative resources you bring to bear on a problematic situation. The process of imagining the situation from the viewpoint of a most unlikely observer generally adds a strikingly different and fresh way of approaching a challenging issue. The surprisingly creative responses tend to have a positive and energizing impact on everyone involved. They take us outside our habitual scripts and predictable responses.

The reality of any life situation is so much larger than the angle from which "the ego" perceives it. In dreams the ego position is typically the "I" who is watching, experiencing emotions, and acting in the guise of the dreamer. However, all of the characters, objects, and settings of the dream are participants in a formative drama taking place within ourselves. This same dynamic characterizes behavior in organizations and within our personal actions. We become so attached to our opinions that we miss the larger interplay of forces working within an environment.

When we identify with only one character and view a situation exclusively from its perspective, we limit the possibilities for understanding. We quickly judge and interpret disquieting conditions from the habitual perspective of the ego, which is offended, annoyed, or threatened. This reflex reaction is triggered largely by the hold that the conflict has on us. If the process is not altered in some way, the conflict will amplify.

People are startled when asked to view their dreams from the point of view of the frightening figures chasing them or the disgusting actions that a person might be performing. This shift sometimes feels like establishing compassion or empathy for a criminal who does horrible things. In order to expand consciousness, it is necessary to see how we view these characters literally versus imaginatively. In the case of dreams, the imaginative perspective is the more realistic one, since it reflects the overall context of the dream. The literal view is a reflection of a realm where people who threaten you might really do you harm. The person in your dream who hurts you may be trying to help, to show you where you hurt.

Fritz Perls, the originator of Gestalt dreamwork, and others have popularized Jung's basic premise that all of the characters in our dreams are expressions of our psychic lives. Every one of us is a complex of inner group dynamics and dramatic characters living lives within our lives. The figures that we repress, fear, and overlook are always the ones that offer the greatest opportunities for expanding consciousness. "Dream figures," I say to my students, "are your intimates. They never come to harm you. The disturbing ones are trying to get your attention. They up the ante the more you avoid them."

Dreams often come to help us resolve our most vexing problems. They display an intuitive brilliance that is inaccessible to the reasoning mind. The dream about brutality and carnage may be telling you that you really are upset about something in your life, while during the day you pass the time thinking everything is just great. Dreams help us pay attention to experiences that we normally overlook.

Remember, be wary of taking the dream literally; relativize the ego position of the dream; view the first narrative you tell as only the first perspective on the dream; retell it from different perspectives; view every character and feeling in the dream as an ally, as an essential player in the overall effort.

Have you ever been consumed by your habitual reactions to problems? Have you felt trapped, with no means to get beyond these reactions? If you were able to transcend these negative responses, what enabled you to do this? Did it have something to do with shifting your perspective on the situation? Is it hard for you to alter your point of view? Why? Do you know other people who are adept at changing their responses to situations, who surprise you with their flexibility? What enables them to do this? Does it have something to do with moderating their egos?

Viewed from within the process of creative transformation, a conflict arouses energy and ultimately our attention by its increasing pressure. "Have another look at me," it says. "Take advantage of the upheaval I cause, and use me to reorganize the way you approach these situations."

Active imagination encourages the person to put aside the ego position and concentrate upon another figure in the drama, to imagine the scene from its perspective, to enlarge its participation through further reflection. Shifts might be made by enacting other characters in the scene, encouraging interaction between different figures, paying attention to small and overlooked details that sometimes have the ability to change everything. This method, developed within the context of individual therapeutic treatment, has enormous potential as a mode of discovery within organizations where people are commonly locked into fixed perspectives, habitual patterns, and egocentric worldviews.

*When was the last time you were in a group where you really
disagreed with another person or felt that you were
misunderstood or misrepresented by someone? Imagine a
meeting where the leader encourages you to present the
problem from the perspective of the person with whom you
may be in conflict. This exercise may be annoying if you
really feel strongly about a situation, but it is guaranteed to
test your empathy and expand your understanding of the
various perspectives that contribute to the problem.*

Leaders who cannot look at problems from different perspectives
are guaranteed to encounter conflict. They don't have to agree with
everyone's point of view, but they will be better informed and able to
make decisions when they are open to the entire context. People are
more able to accept unpleasant decisions when they feel that their
point of view have been recognized and understood.

Your individual responses to conflicts and problems are more
likely to be effective and creative when you are able to view the situation from a variety of perspectives. You don't have to place the burden on yourself to make all of the concessions or changes; but when
you gain a better understanding of the whole, you are more apt to respond in a reasonable way. Purely emotional reactions as well as
one-sided personal positions are always less productive in solving
problems. Active imagination enables you to gather a much larger
sense of what is happening and what you can do.

It might be helpful to "bracket" the ego perspective as you look at
a problem. This is a technique used by the philosopher Edmund
Husserl and the discipline of phenomenology to suspend the usual
way of reacting to an experience, so that we can look more completely at "the things themselves" and reflect upon our dialogue with
them. Bracketing doesn't deny the place of the ego and its judgments.
It just puts the ego off to the side for a while and gives it a rest, some
time on the bench so that other players can get involved and help you
see things in a more comprehensive way. If you can bracket the ego
for a while, you might begin to approach your circumstances from
less familiar and more challenging vantage points.

Is there a person or area in your personal life or at work that you find difficult to accept? Is it possible to look from the perspective of this person or problem? Does anything shift inside you as you do this? Imagine this person or point of view reflecting upon you. What is he/she/it thinking?

Relativizing the ego is perhaps the most challenging and productive feature of active imagination. We repeatedly experience how our ego's needs, fears, and hasty judgments block and stop the process of creation. Our self-centered and protective attitudes can also shield us from looking at the challenging aspects of a problem, at what we might be doing to make a situation difficult.

Sometimes the ego needs to be directly challenged and thrown off-balance, when it becomes too dominant or infringes on the positions of others. It is a very good sign if you can take these jarring experiences in stride, if you can catch your breath when knocked off balance and regain your composure while staying open to whatever is happening. People who are masterful at maintaining their balance when challenged by others often have an ability to laugh at themselves; thus they make the ego much less of a target or an obstacle that has to be reduced or eliminated.

Are you easily thrown off balance when your ego is threatened? Are you able to imagine yourself in a transparent or selfless way, in order to gain an understanding of what is happening around you? Or are you only able to look at situations from your own perspective? If your ego-centered view is the only way you can see the world, you are guaranteed to feel very threatened when it is challenged.

Try relaxing your ego, and develop different ways of looking at situations. It might be helpful to create a humorous alter ego who sees things from a completely new angle. Look at conditions from the perspective of this irreverent trickster. Poke fun at your usual way at responding to tensions.

Imagine yourself in circumstances where your physical balance is precarious. Envision yourself losing balance and

*falling. Let yourself fall without fearing that anything harmful
will happen to you. What does your trickster think about the
fallen condition? Do you fall into anything new? What kind
of person is unable to fall? Does the ability to fall effectively
enable you to regain your balance more effectively?*

One of my graduate students who was studying body movement
taught me these lessons about the connections between the physical
act of falling and the larger process of letting go of ego controls. Creativity demands a certain degree of flexibility. Just as a dominant ego
creates problems within the creative process and within ourselves, it
can cause havoc within organizational and community life. There is
a lack of balance, a swelling of energy in only one direction, which
restricts the natural circulation of creative energy among all of the
participants in an activity or enterprise. In our individual and group
experiences, the ego is only one character, albeit an important one, in
a more comprehensive drama. We need to find ways to broaden understanding without completely dismissing the ego from the scene.
Active imagination instills an appreciation for the fecundity of insights that the creative process is able to generate when it contem-
plates a particular situation.

*Do the active imagination activities that I have described
apply to your experience of different points of view within
groups of people? You undoubtedly know people in your
workplace who play the role of trickster. How do they
relieve pressure and create balance for the group as a
whole? Do they take you outside the literal point of view
on problems and bring a lightness of humor and absurdity?*

*Maybe the tricksters exaggerate conflicts to such a degree
that they become outrageous. Do they help put problems in
a proper perspective in terms of what you value in life?*

*Try to develop this same ability within yourself when you
are feeling stuck, angry, or fed up with a situation. Maybe it
will help to simply change your perspective and your attitude
toward the problem. Cultivate your trickster as a guide to
what really matters.*

As sages of both East and West have realized, the creative flow of life involves everything in the world. Positive and negative feelings are poles within this all-inclusive movement. When we become attached to only one part of the interplay, the flow is encumbered and blocked. Conflict can be viewed as an effort by the creative process to free itself and regain a fluidity of movement. There is always something good in struggle, something that is trying to break free, and something that strives to correct itself. As we move beyond the need to attach ourselves to one particular side of a conflict, we may even start to enjoy the ability of problems to show us a more creative and productive way through life.

CREATIVE PRACTICE

Sarah demonstrates how solitary poetic reflection can open new worlds of understanding and deepen our connection to people and places. Select a person, and take time to contemplate that person's qualities through poetic images. As an image enters your mind, describe it tersely. Don't worry about how the different aspects of your reflections connect to one another. Fragments and glimpses of your relationship with the person are welcomed. Focus only on recording sensations and insights.

Observe how you begin to connect to the person in new and deeper ways through the varied images; how you engage the person through the heart rather than the habitual mind; how the unique spirit of the person is gathered in your images; how the creative imagination carries your relationship to a different place.

After spending time allowing images to emerge, begin to organize the different pieces into an overall composition, in which the lines and fragments connect to one another in whatever way suits your purpose. Take liberties with normal speech patterns, and focus more on weaving your reflections into a portrait that conveys the essence of the other person.

Continue this poetic exercise with other people, places, and memories. You will discover how writing poetry enables you to establish deeper connections to the significant figures and elements of your life. Discover how poetic reflections on others help you learn more about yourself.

~~~~ As Bill suggests, art experiences offer many opportunities to explore how limitations expand and stretch our creative expression. Use a black felt-tip pen, and make drawings with nothing but small straight lines of the same length: one-half inch, one inch, two inches. You might explore making minimalist drawings with a small number of marks and others with hundreds, even thousands. Try to stay with the same size mark throughout each drawing, and let your imagination go in terms of the various ways this one gesture can be made and combined with others. Use different-sized markers from fine to thick, but limit yourself to one kind of tool with each drawing. The limitations of the gestures will encourage you to invent new ways of using them. Repetition can be liberating.

The simple haiku poetic structure similarly expands expression. There are endless ways in which you can limit the means of expression in different media and discover how minimal resources can carry you to new places within the life of imagination. In my studio practice I constantly see how a simple focus generates a greater depth of expression. The simpler the deeper, I say to my groups.

~~~~ Practice the middle way described in this chapter by allowing your contrary feelings about a situation or a problem to exist together. Make journal entries and pictures where you include your opposing feelings as necessary building blocks. Just express these positions without any attempt to reconcile them. See them as participants in something larger than themselves. Do this exercise without any expectation that things will change. Simply recognizing all of the participants establishes the middle way, and who knows where it will take you.

~~~~ We have described many of the essential methods of active imagination in this chapter. Identify a problem or issue that you

would like to explore in greater depth. Reflect upon the theme and try to separate it from yourself. As you begin to view it as an autonomous entity, you will find new ways of relating to it. Put aside and bracket the usual way you relate to this problem. Try to establish a partnership with the problem that will generate a process of reciprocal creation.

Personify the problem, relax your preconceptions, and let it introduce itself to you as though you are engaging it for the first time.

In the beginning most people hesitate to do this because it feels like madness. "This is crazy," they insist. "Things and situations don't talk."

I reply, "This is precisely why this practice has such great value. It turns your world around."

Poets approach rocks, trees, and memories as sentient beings who speak through them. If you feel threatened by letting things speak, act like a poet. Practice personifying as a way of furthering your insight into difficult situations. Allow the problem to express itself. Approach it from multiple vantage points, and encourage different parts of the overall theme to express themselves to you. Record these imaginal dialogues in your journal directly, or speak into a tape recorder and transcribe them afterwards.

You will find that expanding perspectives on the problem will help you to change your relationship to it. Try not to fix the problem or resolve it in any way. Use it as a source of expression and imagination. Your understanding and empathy will be enhanced by giving voice to the different aspects of it, the varied characters, and all of the emotions it arouses in you.

Do your best to "relativize" and bracket your usual feelings about the situation. Try to let the different qualities of the situation speak for themselves. Encourage "them" to describe what they are doing, why they are acting in certain ways, what they hope to see happen, and what they think of you. Invite them to explain why you might be responding to them in particular ways and to evaluate your interactions with them. Imagine the problem as a group dynamic, as a "complex" of participating forces. By shifting the way the problem expresses itself, we change our relationship to it. We become more flexible and creative in responding to the situation. These methods of active imagination, originally developed in depth psychology, have great potential for helping us deal with problems in family life and the workplace.

If you prefer not to work with an emotional theme or problem, just select any object within your environment as a focus of contemplation. The self is enhanced by getting outside of itself, by opening to larger perspectives on experience. If you can articulate and accept the positions that you oppose strongly within close family and work relationships, you may find new and more effective ways of operating in relationship to them. Try to get beyond how they hurt or upset you and find how you can act more creatively in relation to them.

⟶ You can practice active imagination alone or with others. Working together with a partner can be a great advantage. As a general rule, we tend to go further and penetrate deeper when working with another person. Simply acting as a witness is an important mode of support. The interest and attention of another person encourages us to say more, to go further in exploring the different aspects of a situation, and to stay with the process of imagination.

The witness might ask questions or make comments that stimulate insight. After speaking from the perspective of a troubling situation, or that of a person you are in conflict with, you might ask your partner to do the same, to take a turn at contributing to the discourse of imagination.

A partner might suggest that you address different aspects of a situation and point out details that might need attention. You might be asked to examine something you overlooked or something you avoid. These requests energize the ongoing dialogue and take it further. They enhance imagination. Most importantly, a partner can assist us in reflecting more completely on what we have done in a session and how it relates to our lives.

⟶ Readers interested in learning more about C. G. Jung's work with active imagination can consult *Jung on Active Imagina-*

tion, edited by Joan Chodorow (Princeton, N.J.: Princeton University Press, 1997). For a more in-depth description of imaginal dialogue, see my book *Art as Medicine* (Boston: Shambhala Publications, 1992).

5

POSITIVE ATTITUDE AND MAKING THE MOST OF BAD SITUATIONS

Simple Acts of Renewal

My mentor Truman Nelson described how important the process of renewal was in his daily life. "So many people live single-octave lives," he said. "The repetition of what they do sounds like *ping, ping, ping* on a piano. I want to live a chordal life with variations and depth." He went on to describe how his creative method is based upon continuous renewal and the regeneration of vitality every day.

"I experience renewal in the most unlikely things," Truman declared, "like filling the car with a new tank of gas. Nature is constantly renewing and refreshing herself, and I try to live in sync with this process. I need to refresh, recharge, and appreciate the simple things happening around me."

Truman was constantly inventive, finding sources of creative stimulation in his interactions with other people and the environment.

Impoverished situations would yield riches when transformed by his perceptions. He taught me how negativity is a morass from which there is no return. We have all experienced the destructive pull of negativity in the workplace, when people begin to get down on each other and the overall environment. The creative process is forever optimistic, even when situations are permeated by conflict and tension. The creative person or group asks: What can I do with this stuff? How can I use the energy more productively? How do I achieve renewal?

DAVID
Stay Open and Positive

In my work community there is a person who stands out for his ability to always focus on the good in people. No matter how seriously another person may have mistreated him, he responds by reflecting upon the person's positive traits. David is a normal person who gets angry, but he ultimately shifts to seeing the strengths in the other person. The community tends to watch with amazement as he performs this alchemy. David is a happy person, and perhaps this is his way of making sure destructive and poisonous negative energies and stresses do not rule his life. He definitely challenges the rest of us to become more like him. I notice how he stimulates renewal in himself and others when he shifts into this positive embrace of whatever is happening to him.

I don't see David as a powerless victim. On the contrary, his ability to stay positive in the face of adversity is an inspiration. The spirit of his simple affirmations spreads quietly yet potently throughout our community.

David said to me once, "Negative energy will make you sick. It grows fast by feeding upon itself. I try to stay positive because it makes me feel better. I'm sensitive to stress. The hurtful actions of another person have a double whammy if I hang on to them. I have to get rid of the stuff. It's toxic waste. If I try to give it back to the person who gave it to me, I'm caught in it and can't get free. It's got to go somewhere, so I take it and put it into my inner compost pile, where it makes good things grow. It's the only way to purge and go on with life. Every day is a challenge to stay open and positive. Open, open, open, I say. I can never open enough. Life is always challenging me with setbacks and tensions."

David inspires many other people with his generous spirit. Each of us might reflect upon the extent to which we are a source of renewal for others. Do we generate optimism and creative energy in our relationships, or do we feed the currents of negativism?

WENDY AND LUIS
Tap into the Creative Energy and Learn How to Let Go

It is interesting to consider how we might help generate renewal in others in subtle ways that are outside our awareness. Simply paying attention to people, saying good morning, listening to others, and supporting them in difficult times may be the most potent and reliable sources of renewal in relationships.

Wendy, a business executive, described a period when she was feeling discouraged and disconnected from her work. The data indicated that she had just completed her best year ever, but her boss was constantly finding fault in her performance. She was struggling every morning to "recharge the batteries" and get reconnected with the passion for her job. The phone rang early one morning at her office; she was reluctant to answer, but she did. It was a friend who called to say hello. The simple energy of a friendly good morning from a close colleague, and a few affirming words, generated a sense of renewal.

"I don't think it was anything in particular that my friend did," Wendy says, "but the tone of her voice reflected the energy of deeply valued friendship. I realized that I have to reconnect with her and find some time to be together. The energy of friendship and appreciation somehow puts life into perspective. It's all about the passion of life. I need to step back, reflect, and make positives out of negative situations."

When Wendy passed the story along to me, I was feeling a similar lack of direction. As she described her experience, I was inspired. There was a circulation of positive and life-affirming energy from one person to another. Depressing life situations often come from losing perspective on the whole of our lives. We become overly focused on an upsetting situation and get caught in negativity.

Perhaps these powerful transformations aroused by simple insights can only happen when we are down. The simple act of touching base with another person on the phone can put everything in life into proper perspective. The same thing happens when we take a few minutes to look at the landscape or the garden and keep negativity at bay.

Wendy continues, "We all have to keep an eye on the 'me, me, me' complex. Self-absorption needs to be balanced with attentiveness to what's happening outside. I learned early on how important it is to pay attention to people when they call on me in an unplanned way at my office. At first I became irritated when interrupted; then I realized how much time I wasted being upset and how this condition left relationship wounds that took even more effort to remedy. I shifted my frame of mind to viewing the unexpected visitor or problem as an opportunity for me to give something back to life. This 'generosity' of my attention and time was actually more effective and efficient than my self-protective tactics."

"Why?"

"Because giving complete attention to another person is cleaner. It's just right and 'it works,' as artists say. The larger composition of the interpersonal exchange is more aesthetically pleasing. There is a sense of satisfaction that enables us to move more completely into the next phase of whatever we are doing."

I respond, "Simone Weil said that the most difficult thing is to look at another person, ask how things are going, and then truly listen. I've learned that renewal is always available when I have a satisfying conversation with the person down the hall. I call this person, whoever he or she might be that day, the Buddha in the office. The older I get, the more I recognize how much better I feel when I listen and give the other person the chance to be seen and heard. There is an infusion of energy and grace in a good conversation, an awakening. It puts a new gloss on the day. I get a jump start when I am down."

"That's what the brief talk with my friend did for me," Wendy realizes. "What makes that experience so remarkable is that I was really upset, and the conversation completely lifted the cloud."

Luis, who manages information systems, met with Wendy and me in a focus group to discuss creativity in the workplace. "I am renewed," Luis says, "by immersing myself in the company of new people and new ideas. It is very easy to dwell on the negative energies that surround us on a daily basis, and this promotes self-absorption. It has something to do with self-worth. It's the only way some people can share emotions. Maybe talking about negative things bolsters people's self-worth in some desperate way and gives them a sense of control and power."

"But doesn't the expression of negative feelings play a necessary function?" I ask. "Can the positive exist without the negative? Don't they need each other just as people do?"

"Yes," Luis responds, "the negative is part of the charge and countercharge of life's energy. We also have to discharge pent-up and troublesome feelings. If I can share the disconcerting thought with somebody within a safe relationship, I am less likely to go down that road. If I don't purge some of these things, I'll go out of my mind. Ultimately the switch has to be turned back to constructive energy."

"How do you turn the switch?" I ask.

"I love the environment and the people in my workplace," Luis says. "But the place can sometimes get me down. How do I break out of it? I try to tap into the creative energy of life. It's always there, ready to be utilized."

Luis continues, "I've learned the most about positive energy from ordinary life situations. I was in Bermuda and had to get to an early-morning meeting. As I approached my motorbike, wearing a suit, I saw that the seat was covered with dew. There were two hotel workers sitting nearby, and I frantically asked them for a towel. They looked at me, smiled, and said, 'Good morning.' They said it twice, perhaps realizing that I needed to get a message. It was powerful. Those fellows put everything into perspective. I'll never forget it. It's not a person's standing in life or within an organization that is the basis of wisdom and authority. Those two men just sat back and smiled at me. They helped me reflect and understand what's really important in life."

Both Luis and Wendy keep returning to the importance of a

positive attitude toward their relationships with work and other people. They describe how the inevitable bad situations must be placed in proper perspective within the whole of life.

"I try to view rough situations as teachers and guides," Wendy says. "They show us where we need to go, what we need to correct, and what aspects of our community life might need more attention. They reveal how we lose perspective.

"You need leaders with strong positive energy who demonstrate how to learn from problems and how to put them to good use. This transformation of difficulties also prevents pessimism from over-whelming a community. When leaders go completely negative, there can be a very threatening imbalance. If bad situations are used by leadership as ways to control others, we've got problems."

"Yes," Luis interjects, "using negative things as a way to gain power over others usually backfires, because a group cannot go forward without positive and creative energy. People who dwell on negative things live in a vicious cycle of gloom."

"Why do you think they do this?" I ask.

"Fear of the new is at the core of it," he answers. "It's a way of maintaining power and control over the immediate environment. We have all seen how negative people surround themselves with others who share the same energy; it is self-perpetuating. It gives them a sense of control and purpose in a larger organizational structure where they have little power. They reject the new and the unfamiliar."

"This type of person rarely says hello to somebody new," Wendy says. "Luis, your Bermuda story makes me wonder whether we give up some control when we say good morning and open to another. Maybe we lose some control over our environments when we open ourselves to others. Constantly negative people haven't learned how to open themselves up. For many people it's scary to say good morning to someone they don't know."

"The person immersed in the negative can't 'travel' in either a figurative or literal way," Luis answers. "They can't leave their controlled and self-perpetuating worlds. My father gave me one of my biggest life lessons at a time when I was trying to control everything. I was very successful at managing every nuance of my environment, but he saw that I was too uptight. He just said to me one day, 'Luis, learn to let go.' Guess his timing was perfect, because it hit me like a whack from a big Zen stick. He turned my world upside down."

"Why is it so hard for others to make these changes?" I ask Luis.

"I can only answer from my own experience," he responds. "Perhaps I was stronger and less self-absorbed when he said this to me. I was probably ripe for change. If he had said the same thing a year earlier, it would not have registered at all. I was ready to look at myself. I may have felt more confident and less threatened. I guess it was time to look at my imperfections."

"Do you know many people who can look at themselves in this way?" I inquire.

"Unfortunately," Luis answers, "I find it unusual. Few of us can practice meta-cognition. Even though I did it in the moment that I described, I still constantly fall in and out of grace. I am a guarded person, and I protect my personal realm. I guess I continue to keep it largely to myself. It's all about control and safety."

"We all need what the therapists call defenses," I say.

"But there is such rejuvenation in doing something brand-new. I went to the funeral of a friend's father; it was powerful for me in a negative way, because it was sad moment. It was a Jewish service, and I know little about the religion. I was inspired watching a child describe his grandfather, listening to a man sing—everything was new. The freshness is renewing. Even something painful and sorrowful can be rich and rewarding, depending on your perspective. It was fascinating to observe my own behavior. I took a hard look at myself. The whole experience was powerful, because I released some controls. I let myself go. I opened up, let myself cry, released the illusion of power. I realized that I can't be helpful to others unless I observe my own behavior."

"I sometimes think that we have to know and even celebrate our pathologies, acknowledge them, and laugh at ourselves," I reply. "The more we deny our shadows, the more powerful they become. I was starting to complain about my work environment to a friend who doesn't believe in negativity. He didn't respond to me at all, and I read his silence as a suggestion that I was going in the wrong direction. I caught myself and became aware of how depressing and futile it can be to complain. I experienced this meta-cognition that you describe."

Luis nods. "Not many people I know can really sit back and give themselves a good hard look or truly observe their own behavior."

"It's especially hard to look at ourselves in difficult circumstances, where ego is threatened."

"In high school," Luis says, "we all had to go through almost prescribed negative experiences in order to grow. We had to look at our imperfections. Later in life most of us settle into some established mode of control over our environments, and the growth stops. We stop looking at ourselves."

"Yes," I say, "often I think that the bad experiences are necessary elements of growth. We have to go through them and use them in order to have the perspective on the whole of life that Wendy describes. The rough times, like bad dreams, wake us up. They demand our attention. I have to ask, 'What's happening here? What can I do about it?'"

Wendy and Luis affirm that we are renewed and expanded by opening to others and looking honestly at ourselves. Listening to them, I realized how familiar their discoveries were to me. Yet it became clear that telling an old story in a completely fresh way, with new people, brings new energy. One of our greatest powers involves the ability to take a bad experience and fashion it into a life-affirming expression. Nothing recharges our emotions more than drawing sustenance from adversity. Turning difficulties inside out does not require us to dismiss their pathogenic qualities. Rather, creative transformation highlights and embraces problems, using them as sources of positive and life-enhancing energy.

No doubt all of us have considerable experience with the destructive powers of negative thinking. But at the same time we have to acknowledge that there are places in our lives and relationships with others where an awareness of harmful situations is essential. The inability to acknowledge problematic elements in our lives can become detrimental to our overall well-being.

Can you recall situations when you denied troubling conditions? What were the consequences of your denial? Were there times when it was beneficial to yourself and others to overlook problems?

There have no doubt been other times in our experience when we have been able to reap strength and creative energy from confronting and transforming bad conditions. How willing have you been in your personal life to openly confront negative conditions? Are you more or less inclined to do the same at work? Does your willingness to address problems depend upon particular circumstances? Are you more likely to act if there is a likelihood of success? Are you the type of person who does or does not look carefully at possible outcomes and consequences before acting? Are there advantages to cautious examination of possible results? Or does this type of scrutiny hamper your spontaneity and ability to act forcefully?

Have there been times in your life when, as in Luis's case, your awareness of a negative state has helped you examine what you might need to change? Hitting the bottom can often be an awakening experience. We can no longer hide behind illusions, and we must look at the forces within our environment and ourselves that cause harm. Have negative experiences helped you to grow and to create? Has the embrace of the difficult situation generated new energy in your life?

Think about those people in your work environment who dwell on the negative. Are they happy? Would you like to be like them? What kind of effect do they have on you?

I predict that if you identify the happy and creative people in your life, you will see that they have an inherently positive outlook on experience. They accept the conditions of their lives, and they do something with them.

IDA
Falling Apart

Ida, a teacher, listened as I spoke to Wendy and Luis. She says, "It's too simplistic to say that the worst problems at work or in a person's life can be resolved by thinking about them in a different way. You can't control everything. It's not just a matter of turning on the positive-thinking switch. Problems at work, in families, and within ourselves are complex and often beyond the reach of mental adjustments. You're adding another burden on a person when you say, 'It's up to you to see the good in bad situations.' "

"I don't want to sound like Norman Vincent Peale," I say to her. "My sense of positive transformation is about doing something with the problems, rather than being trapped in them."

"What if you can't do anything?" she asks.

"Sometimes things have to fall apart."

"And we have to learn how to let this happen," Ida says, "rather than doing ourselves in, trying to make something work that doesn't have a chance. Do you see what I mean here? It's not just a matter of thinking positively about bad stuff. Some things are just bad through and through, and all the good thoughts in the world will never change them."

"This is helpful," I respond, "because you make me realize that consciousness does not necessarily change rough situations or control them in any way. It's about how we respond to them, what we do with them: Do we become victims or do we find a way to keep going with our lives? I don't want to be accused of being overly earnest. Horrible things happen all the time. Maybe parts of the workplace are beyond redemption. Maybe they are there to sustain necessary pathologies and negative forces in our lives. Perhaps we should accept the inevitability of human pathology in the workplace and do more to examine our lives from the perspectives of frailty, vulnerability, and imperfection. We may expect too much from one another and deny our neediness. The depths of expression may be more connected to the sick and problematic places than the healthy ones."

"And don't always rush in to fix them," Ida emphasizes. "We have to accept some problems and not always try to make them positive."

"I am working with a doctoral student right now who tempers my optimism with her excruciatingly precise documentation of the ills of organizational life," I say. "I also see them too often. You're not going to like what I am saying, but the very worst situations often change us the most and bring out the best in people. Being positive is about persisting with a belief in life. Sometimes things have to be shattered, completely broken, in order to generate new creation.

Falling apart has an important place in the creative process. My college art professor responded to my art and healing work with fascination by describing how his art tore him apart, and in my typical way I said that healing often requires this. Sometimes the biggest edifices that we construct, our deepest attachments, our most ingrained self-images, are what most completely block the way to creative discovery. This is what the Buddha was probably getting at when he spoke of letting everything go. It's frightening."

"There you go with your positive spin," Ida argues. "Maybe we are just different in the way we view the world. I am more negative and guarded. I've been hurt, and I put a lot of energy into protecting myself. I can't just say good-bye to my fears by thinking about them in different ways."

"Didn't I say that it's frightening?"

"You did," Ida acknowledges. "I missed this chink in the optimism. Positive thinking feels like armor to me, a denial of the conditions of life. Maybe we are both afraid."

"This is perhaps what people mean when they say that creativity requires risk," I respond. "The really big changes can be terrifying, and so we don't move."

"And positive thinking becomes denial," Ida says. "We convince ourselves that there is something worthwhile in a bad situation, or we justify the flawed patterns in our lives or the unhealthy ways we are living."

"It's complex," I respond. "Like any other good and strong medicine, consciousness can be misused. When things beyond our control completely fall apart, hopefully bad things, we get some help from the external environment. We have no choice about moving on. It's the lingering indecision that takes a toll on us: whether to stay or leave, whether to risk or lie back, whether to act or do nothing. The decisions are even harder when we know there will be uncertainty and consequences; when what we do might make things fall apart. Uncertainty and discomfort don't charge me up. But they can persist in a way that ultimately makes me act. They eat away at my complacency. So, disturbing and frightening things can motivate us. They deliver a charge."

"This sounds more realistic," Ida responds. "This positive-thinking business and making the most of things can sometimes come across like one of those smiley-face buttons."

"My ideas about creative transformation," I respond, "have been shaped by people who do something positive with the worst situations in life. We see it in history, and I experience it in art. There are people who come up against the toughest things life can throw at them, and they do something creative with it. An artist friend of mind was afflicted with polio as an adolescent and spent a year lying in bed. He began to make art at that time and then went on to a distinguished career in art. Friedrich Nietzsche persistently stressed how we need to do something creative with our problems and gain strength from them. In *The Birth of Tragedy* he says that the 're-deeming vision' of life always grows from suffering. So I am not denying the pain. It's a matter of how we respond to it."

How capable are you of making the most of challenging situations? Do you feel that you have the ability or the power needed to change things that may not be right in your life? Do you have a clear sense of what you will do differently if these problematic things are gone? Is it better to continue making the most of imperfect situations than risking the abyss of having nothing at all? Do you have faith that new opportunities will develop if you let go completely?

When was the last time you were motivated to act by a bad situation? What were the results? Did things get worse or better? The risks are generally higher for us when we challenge the forces that have the greatest control over our lives. This is because our lives are likely to change.

Reflect upon the things that control you the most and cause the greatest frustration. Do you really want them to change? Have difficult situations ever furthered your creative expression? Are you able to be recharged by them?

Vital Communities

I've learned from art studio groups that one of the leader's primary responsibilities is the cultivation and mobilization of positive energy. The same principle applies to experiences at work. If a person feels completely negative about an organization, it's time to move on to something else. No matter how justified someone may feel in having a particular point of view, the thoroughly negative perspective is toxic and all-consuming. When we focus only on what is wrong in an environment and what we do not like, the negativity multiplies and permeates everything we do. The same applies to positive energy. Feelings are susceptible to extreme amplification within both the individual person and throughout our environment. We regularly see how emotions affect performance in team sports. Leaders must then develop abilities to channel the energy of feelings.

Peter Drucker, the celebrated management theorist, observed in *Post-Capitalist Society* and other works that a positive sense of community and responsibility at all levels are essential ingredients of successful organizations. Managers of such organizations, according to Drucker, practice an "integrating process" that generates "dynamic, life-giving" elements in every workplace. In these vital communities, people feel fortunate to be involved and identify strongly with the mission and purpose of the organization.

When individual and collective values are integrated on a deep level, there is an activation of creative energy that spreads and circulates through every corner of the workplace. Macro- and micro-processes are pervaded by a sense of creative vitality. The things we do at work take on a sense of importance for ourselves and for the world. Enthusiasm in the workplace and the art studio comes from fulfillment of the longing for vital connection to things outside us. We contribute to something that matters. These gatherings of people generate a distinct spirit of enthusiasm.

Creative energy manifests in the "aura" of the environment—the distinct atmosphere, quality, and "air" of place. It has a contagious effect on people. When we walk into an environment, we know immediately whether or not this energy is present. Most of us need communities as sources of motivation and vitality; and in keeping

with the basic movements of energy in nature, people charge one another in positive and negative ways.

> *Are there qualities in your workplace that generate this life-*
> *giving energy? Where have you felt this sense of creative*
> *vitality most intensely? What are the qualities of an*
> *environment that arouse your enthusiasm? Are there places*
> *where you want to be on a regular basis? Places*
> *you avoid? What is it about these environments that appeals*
> *to you? Offends you? Is there anything you can*
> *do to enhance the creative vitality of your workplace?*

JOHN
It's an Attitude

John worked as the head of a division in the office of a state attorney general. He loved his work and spoke to me about the qualities that appealed to him.

"It was the freedom that the top person gave to everyone to do
what they are best at, as fully as possible, without interference,"
John says. "He empowered people to identify and develop their individual interests and abilities. The creative atmosphere was driven
by the attitude from the top."

"People say that the existence of a creative atmosphere depends
on leaders," I respond.

"Always," John affirms. "You can transform the mood and the attitude of an organization overnight by changing the message and the
direction from the top. In the attorney general's office, everyone was
encouraged, and the atmosphere was positive for sharing information and ideas across different work units. If a person in one area had
a good idea, the message from the top was to get it around to others
who can use it. The top person devolved power and responsibility in
a nonlinear way; thus, everyone in the organization accepted that it
was part of their role to have the freedom and responsibility to come
up with creative ideas for their own job, the office as a whole, their
division, and their bureau. They weren't told, 'Just do your job and
keep quiet.'

"You can't run military and other command-and-control organizations, where there is an absolute need to follow orders, in this way. But in most other work situations, this is the way to go. I have never seen anything more effective than this model. People get excited, they are more productive and creative, and they work more. They are made to feel that they are essential to moving the organization forward. This was a social and political organization, but these principles apply to any work situation."

"It boils down to how you treat people," I say. "Creativity in groups requires freedom and sustained affirmation."

"People want to feel that they are individually appreciated, rather than being cogs in the wheels of production," John continues. "When people feel that they can contribute creatively, they get fired up about themselves. They feel that their spirit and intelligence are valued and being put to use. The command-and-control organization substitutes duty for country and flag. That is a huge motivating force. Duty goes a long way."

"Others apply this to regular organizations," I say.

"The Japanese have done this," John replies.

"But duty as a motivator has limits," I answer. "And in my experience, duty veers toward guilt. People say to themselves, 'I should be doing these extra things because others are doing them.' More and more time on the job becomes part of the expectation and culture of the organization, and people have to set boundaries or else become swallowed."

"These expectations tend to be set by people at the top," John responds. "Certain types can never demand enough from people."

"There is an aggrandizement of the leader," I say, "rather than a lively distribution of autonomous activity and responsibility. These top-heavy structures arrest creativity. Instead of taking initiative, people begin to see their role as submitting to authority."

"You want to make work fun, creative, and interesting for people," John maintains. "But the 'work as enjoyment' idea can be overstated. It is not a panacea."

"But it's true," I reply, "that we are more productive and creative when we like what we are doing and want to do it."

"Absolutely," John says. "It's an attitude that we are describing. If you can infuse the organization with the attitude, then you change the whole structure and direction by getting individuals to act as if their imaginations are necessary."

"What do you see as the main threat to this positive attitude?" I ask.

"I am particularly sensitive to top-down, command-and-control environments. I'd be a terrible career soldier. I could do it for a short time. Duty is not enough for me. The lack of personal and individual freedom is the main negative for me. I hate having people tell me what to do."

"Do you think the average person feels this way?"

"The average person doesn't hate it as much as I do," John replies. "But average people also benefit tremendously from having the feeling of individual creativity and the realization that they can contribute to the positive movement of an organization."

I add, "Carl Rogers, a founder of humanistic psychology whose thinking influenced my early work with groups, felt that healthy groups will always find their way to effectiveness if given freedom, guidance, and support. I, too, have found that the creative process of people working together is generally more effective than directives from management. Uncertainty as well as freedom are certain to bring conflict and tension, but creativity requires a certain amount of friction."

"We work better," John insists, "when we are not bossed around and when we are free to do our thing."

"And free to make mistakes," I say, "and learn from them."

"Exactly," John agrees. "Many people are so afraid to make mistakes that they don't venture into the unknown. There are some who do well in the command-and-control structures, and we need them. They feel the need for strong direction from an external authority. There's room for all kinds. But most structures today are not hierarchical. When we were kids, everything was command-and-control. All corporations were run that way."

"What's changed?"

"There has been an evolution of leadership models," John replies.

"That's true," I say. "Our generation has seen the shortcomings of the linear and authoritarian models. We've been stifled by them. Leaders want freedom themselves and take the risk of giving it to others."

"Yes," John asserts, "it takes a very secure person to let people have their freedom. The message has to be driven down through the organization in order to work. I tried to do this when I was running a small organization, but in retrospect I probably didn't encourage as much freedom in sharing information as I could have. It's better to err on the side of sharing more information, but sometimes it's difficult to keep that perspective in practice. We are happy at work when we are allowed to do our jobs."

"It's not easy to let go," I say. "If we are responsible for the ultimate outcomes, it can be a challenge to give over more control to the people who work for us, to trust that a group will be more productive if they are free to work in a more autonomous way."

"It is," John says, "and I could have done better in some situations. My experience as a member of a creative community led by a gifted person convinced me that this is the way to motivate a group of talented people and to achieve excellence."

"Group creativity operates in a complex way," I say. "People have to be given the freedom to find their most effective ways of connecting to the purpose of the organization. We can't all be expected to act in the same way."

"Yes," John says, "a good work environment is complex in a positive way. Everything is constantly changing and presenting new challenges. I have a friend who sold his accounting business and retired. He said, 'I had to go back to work and use my brain.' He was also less tense when working."

"That's interesting," I say, "because most people associate tension with work."

John remarks, "Maybe because they haven't had the opportunity to see what it's like to be completely on their own."

"Negative work relationships can also be a source of great anxiety," I add.

"It's very simple," John replies. "For me there are three things that prevent anxiety: creative work, helping others, and communing with nature. It's almost impossible to be anxious if you are doing these three things."

"And does a positive work environment offer these three things?" I ask.

"It does," John says.

"The idea of communing with nature at work might be a stretch for people who commute and work in offices," I reply. "The presence of windows and plants and being able to freely decorate an office area introduce aesthetic elements to the physical space. But most of us probably don't see work relationships as immersion in nature. We might think of work outings and softball games in this way."

"Interacting with people in an affirming way is communing with nature," John says. "There can be a sense of wholeness, even aesthetic beauty, in how people deal with each other in an office. We need a balance between inside and outside relationships with nature, but most of us overlook the opportunities to commune with people at work."

"That's a fresh twist," I say, "to perceive work as an immersion in nature. We are so prone to feel restricted and cooped up at work. Everything depends upon how you look at things."

"Again, it's an attitude," John remarks.

The way we feel about things and perceive experiences is a very real source of vitality and quality in daily life. The most important steps we can take in the expansion of creativity are to change our personal attitudes toward the creative process and to participate in it. Once we realize that everything depends upon how we perceive experiences, the source of creative power moves closer to us.

Try to apply this aesthetic perception to your work environment. When was the last time you perceived beauty at the office? We've all no doubt perceived beauty in other people; but how often do we notice the aesthetic qualities of a meeting, a telephone conversation, a person or a group of people handling themselves in a difficult situation, the placement of objects on a desk, the composition of papers lying on a table, or the gestures and facial expressions of two people interacting?

Our perceptions have the power to change any aspect of life. The shifts in attitude can be subtle and do not have to require major changes.

Identify the qualities of your work environment that are the most consistent sources of positive energy and feelings. What is it that most frequently distracts your attention at work? What experiences are most likely to arouse your negative feelings? Why? What do you usually do when this happens? Are you effective in your response? Can you try responding differently?

Make a list of the things in your work environment that generate positive energy. Do the same with those things that provoke negative emotions. Do other people share your observations? What can you do to change the environment? Will there be changes if you simply respond differently to problems? Try to look more deeply at situations. Look into them with curiosity rather than judgment.

People often feel that work is superficial, that nothing ever happens there of great aesthetic significance. Superficial and clichéd expressions are defined by the absence of individual uniqueness. Maybe this lack of depth has more to do with how we are looking at our environments and treating them. We may be missing opportunities to perceive, document, and celebrate the uniqueness of other people, of ourselves, and of the things we do together.

In what areas do you feel the least creative at work? Why? Is there anything you can do to change the conditions? Do you have any desire to change? My experience has always suggested that what seems furthest away from creation has the greatest potential to renew creative vitality. Take a few minutes to reflect upon where you are most spontaneous, open, and relaxed. Is it possible to transfer the way you act in these realms to the areas where you feel uncreative?

I believe that the energy of creativity is something that runs through us like a vitalizing river. It finds its way to different objects of expression, but we make the mistake of limiting the scope of its activity. The creative energy that characterizes our most passionate and free expression can cross over to other domains of experience.

We simply have to re-vision ourselves in more generous and perceptive ways.

> *Identify your qualities that are most idiosyncratic and
> unique. Is it possible to view them as indications of your
> creative expression? Are you hard on yourself? Is it possible
> that the way you view yourself is the primary obstacle to
> expanding your creative life?*

Our personal creative expression will be enhanced if we look
more expansively at the possibilities offered by situations, relationships, and problems. We tend to think about experiences as extensions of ourselves and ignore their autonomous nature. When you
face a challenging situation, consider how you can further *its* (rather
than *your*) creative possibilities. Moving beyond an exclusive focus
on the self furthers the circulation of creative energy. By becoming
more attentive to the aesthetic qualities and expressions of environments and things other than ourselves, we transcend the limits of
habitual perception; and if we can view the world from their perspectives, the portals of creative imagination will be opened wide.

If we look only at ourselves in efforts to expand creativity, we will
always return to familiar inhibitions and attitudes about who we are
and what we can do. Stepping outside of ourselves, we will discover
the creative energy that moves through environments and within relationships. As demonstrated in the section on active imagination,
objects, places, and physical experiences can also be viewed as "others" with whom we create. The shift away from self-perception as
the locus of creation gets the energy moving.

When we adjust our focus away from ourselves, we realize that individuals participate in the creative energy that moves within life situations. It is liberating to see that it may be egocentric to view
creativity as something that exists exclusively within us. We can
lighten the loads we carry in our bags of negative self-images. Just as
the mystic experiences the destruction of the false self in order to
achieve a sense of oneness with the larger source of life, we let go of
self-centered views of creation in order to embrace the creative opportunities presented by each moment.

Think of a time in your life when you felt creative. Were you alone or with others? Under what conditions do your best insights and ideas happen?

Try to identify the aspects of your workplace that are causing you the most difficulty and that generate the most angst. Think about them in new ways. Stretch your imagination, and identify how these problems can contribute to your life. Most of all, try to get beyond your routine view of the problems. Look at them with a positive attitude, as opportunities for change and new learning.

Establishing this affirming empathy for disturbing situations is not easy to do. Get in touch with the energy they generate, and don't worry if it is loaded with conflict. Anger and discontent are potent fuels for creative transformation. If you can just begin to approach these difficult situations from new perspectives, you are well on the way to creative transformation.

Missed opportunities can teach us how to be more creative in our relations with the world. They help us to be attentive to openings that present themselves in our lives. Never again, the creator says, will I miss a chance to act in response to a creative prospect. I have a friend who made a career of real estate investment as a result of his intense regret over not having bought a promising property. Our past failures in giving attention to others may guide the way we express ourselves today in close relationships.

Negative experiences with others have as much to do with the formation of our creative lives as the good ones do. Everything makes its contribution to our personal ecology. The determining factor is our willingness both to open to the complete range of our lives and to put our resources to use.

Have there been missed opportunities that helped to shape your life in creative ways? Have things that you have not done motivated what you now do in your life?

We need a larger and more inclusive concept of creativity that takes us to a new place in the life of creative imagination. We need an idea that is capable of including everybody and everything in the world, good and bad, exciting and boring. Creativity integrates the totality of our lives. It is a basic energy that exists in nature as a universally accessible resource. Since we are all part of nature, we have the ability to participate in the creative process. No person or place is excluded. Everything depends upon how we view what life offers us at each moment.

CREATIVE PRACTICE

Set up an environment for practice based upon unconditional support. If you are working with others, make a commitment to complete safety when it comes to responding to one another's expressions. This unconditionally positive environment will allow you to take risks in your expression that may not have been previously possible.

Within this positive environment, approach a fear with the goal of presenting it to yourself and others as an objective phenomenon. Try to engage the fear as a fact, as something autonomous, and do your best to separate your feelings from it. See if your relationship to the fear begins to change if you are able to externalize it through creative expression. Try painting, writing, or moving in response to the fear. What happens when you use the fear as the basis for making an artistic object?

Establishing this aesthetic distance in an environment where you will not be judged helps you openly engage what you fear. See if simply being together with the fear in this way takes you to a new place in your relationship to it.

Within your safe space, identify three or four things that disturb you on a regular basis. Work with each of these tensions in the following way:

Begin by reflecting on the problem, and consider how you can take what bothers and afflicts you and make it into a source of inspiration. Record these reflections in your journal.

Practice the art of reversing the energy of your feelings. Consider how you can use the energy rather than be discouraged by it. For example, many people are afraid of performing in front of large crowds; they become intimidated and experience stage fright. Successful performers in athletics and the arts learn how to "feed off the energy of the crowd." As the artist is apt to say, "I love the energy. I love the audience."

If you fear expressing yourself in front of people, imagine them as helpers and as a source of creative energy. Envision their power passing into you. We are so liable to think about how we appear before the audience that we miss what they have to offer us. Apply this reversal of the flow of energy to other life situations. Consider how difficulties and challenges can be engaged as sources of energy. Imagine your discontents as helpers. Make brief reflections in your journal about what they are capable of giving you.

Something magical often happens when you engage disturbances and fears in three-dimensional media. I worked with a woman in an art studio who was tormented by a recurring dream in which threatening figures attacked her. She made a series of paintings of the ominous figures and then felt that she needed to express her fears in three dimensions. She went on to make masks representing the three different figures that assaulted her in the dream world.

Giving physical form to the fears helped lessen the panic she felt when confronted by threatening figures. But it was not until the woman engaged in an improvisational performance, in which she wore the masks, that her relationship to the figures was transformed. Once behind the masks, she discovered that she was able to express powerful emotions that she formerly perceived as attacking her.

The dramatic enactment completely reversed her relationship to the fears. She experienced them as sources of creative energy. Everything was flipped when she got behind the masks. She became one with them, as opposed to experiencing the frightening forces as something outside herself. Through the different phases of the art experience, the projection of power and control onto the dream figures was withdrawn and they were integrated into the woman's expression.

This example is deceptively simple. We have to learn how to use the energy of our fears to our advantage, to invert negative and threatening emotions into positive and life-affirming energies. Everything depends on what we do with the problems, how we engage them as sources of creative expression.

Make a mask of a disturbing figure or feeling with papier-mâché, out of a paper bag, or by simply drawing on a white paper plate. Get behind the mask, express the energy of the fear through dramatic enactment, and watch how your relationship to the disturbance shifts. Make another mask expressing your feelings about the original disturbance after your enactment. How do they differ? How can you use them both?

You need the whole gamut of energies, the creative mix of positive and negative forces. Keep the different masks as Janus figures that express the positive and negative aspects of these situations, and consider both expressions as your allies.

In Gloucester, Massachusetts, where I live, there is an arts center for young people called Artspace, where a unique creative environment has been constructed with the goal of making the milieu an inspirational agent of change. Shep Abbott, the director of the center, believes that the space acts upon people and must be given credit for what "it" does. The environment builds self-confidence and has a distinctly positive impact on the expression of participants. When someone excels within this environment, Shep believes that the space is an active contributor to the success.

Describe your ideal creative space in your journal. Work together with others to identify what you need most from an environment when it comes to creative expression. Imagine what it would be like if a space for creation were established in your workplace. How would you respond to the sound of drums or a piano improvisation as you walked down a corridor at work? If you looked into an art room, smelled paint, and saw people working on creative projects? Experiment with the possibility that a space can act upon people in creative ways.

6

CRITICISM
AND TWO VIEWS
OF OPEN SPACE

What Are the Goals?

Herman Melville stopped writing for more than thirty years after his masterpiece *Moby Dick* was sharply criticized by his contemporaries and his subsequent writings failed to receive a positive response. After this long hiatus, during his last years, Melville wrote *Billy Budd*, one of the world's finest short stories; it was not published until many years after Melville died, a forgotten artist.

Great artists experience the same doubts and frustrations with the creative process as the average person. The intensity of the artist's difficulties is often greater because much more can be at stake. Yet people from every sphere of life find the process of giving and receiving criticism to be one of the most sensitive and challenging aspects of interacting with others. Both history and our contemporary lives are generously populated with strong, dominant people who chafe at the slightest criticism and have the means to construct their environments so as to prevent it. The average person does not always have the same ability to be insulated from critical judgment, and it can be argued that this vulnerable condition may have its positive features in the development of character and morality.

Artists and others who present their creative expressions to the world have virtually no insulation from the free expression of critics. The process of making judgments can often be harsh and direct, with very little consideration given to how the person receiving the information will be affected. The critics of *Moby Dick* wanted to convey what they thought about the book, and they were probably not at all concerned with how their expressions affected Melville; or perhaps they were motivated by a desire to disparage and hurt.

There is no question that the overall cultivation of the creative process must enable people to freely evaluate creative expressions with complete independence from concerns about the feelings of the people who made them. In addition to identifying works that receive universal affirmations of quality, the free exercise of critical judgment reveals the range of perspectives that people bring to the assessment of value. As the philosopher Hans-Georg Gadamer suggested, these biased viewpoints are our individual openings to the perception of the world.

I am not criticizing the critics of Melville or questioning whether or not they should have published their harsh judgments. The sometimes cruel and hurtful expression of viewpoints has its place within the creative process. However, I do feel that this type of criticism does not suit every instance where people communicate with others about the value and qualities of expressions.

There are many situations in which we are as concerned about the well-being of the person making the expression as we are about the assessment of the object. And there are yet other educational, therapeutic, and healing environments where we are more concerned with the person than the object, realizing of course that the ultimate quality of the object might in fact have a profoundly positive effect on the person making it.

Art critics, art historians, and educators who are helping people understand creative expressions, as well as scientists and business people, often engage in activities where there is a primary loyalty to the assessment and understanding of objects as things unto themselves. Phenomena are compared critically to one another with the goal of understanding their natures and unique qualities.

These distinctions among the varied purposes of art are rarely made in our public discussions about the creative process. There is an all too common tendency to speak in absolute language when talking about creativity, to presume that a perspective on one aspect of the overall process applies to all situations.

Just as the reality of the world requires an embrace of the many functions of art, the same sensitivity to differences applies to how we approach critical responses to the creative expressions of other people. If our goal is to nurture creative expression in others, we might not wish to take on the posture of the art critic, whose primary loyalty is to the integrity of the object. As I help people to express themselves more effectively, I do not necessarily overlook an honest assessment of the object; but my primary focus is on the person.

My approach to someone at work, unlike my attitude toward someone with whom I am working in a studio, may not always be exclusively committed to the well-being of that person. I also have a duty to consider the overall good of the organization or the community. But even when working toward the success of the collective enterprise or in pursuit of profits, it may benefit all to adopt an approach to criticism that takes the feelings of the individual into consideration. My experience also suggests that when I honestly focus on the well-being of the person, the organization also benefits.

We know from experience that certain ways of giving criticism work and others do not. Therefore, if our goal is to motivate people, to help them become more creative and more productive, we need to think seriously about how we give criticism.

SAM
Struggles with Criticism

Sam works in a business setting as a senior manager. He is responsible for the performance of a number of different teams within his division. "I've always struggled with giving and taking criticism," Sam says. "It has never come easy to me. Perhaps my discomfort comes from an awareness of how it hurts people. There are times when people are open and truly want to hear my critical response to what they are doing, but it's not common. It's fascinating how open attitudes toward criticism typically produce positive results, but most people guard against being subjected to the opinions of others."

"How does criticism produce positive results?" I ask.

"It gives a more complete perspective on situations and actions," Sam responds. "Most important, this information can help us change and be more effective. The critic helps us see things that we do not see, that we can't see without help. But it can be rough and painful. The critic can stir up things that we repress and keep at a distance because we are not able to look at them. We have to get beyond our fears and realize that we can benefit from a more complete view of who we are and what we do."

"How does a person begin to do this?" I ask.

"We have to step back and look at situations from a more objective and problem-solving perspective," Sam replies. "I try to approach myself as just another player in an overall interaction of forces and avoid self-absorbed positions. I focus on how I can hurt myself by being closed and overly protective. I relax my ego and let go of tendencies to control the situation."

"Do you actually think about these things as you are acting in a situation?"

"I do when I am being effective," Sam says. "When I feel blocked with other people, or when I am uncomfortable or defensive, I am usually not aware of how I am protecting myself from criticism. I have learned the hard way. The atmosphere is much more fluid and relaxed when we are open to each other in this sincere way."

"What has been hard?"

"Blocks in communication that hurt relationships and prevent success."

"And what happens when things are working better?" I ask.

"There is a sense that what really matters is solving the problem, and we don't worry about who gets the credit. There is a liberating feeling when this happens. I do everything I can to develop this spirit of collaborative problem solving with people in my company, and I've had mixed success. It feels sometimes like I am working against human nature."

"Why?"

"Because most people guard against criticism."

"Are they equally guarded in giving criticism to others?" I ask.

"I haven't thought about that before," Sam admits. "Throughout my career I've worked for a number of tough bosses who freely gave punitive criticism of others. I've always abhorred this. I get upset when it is directed at me, and I don't like to see others around me be the recipients of it. One of the most upsetting features of this type of criticism is the way other people in the organization or group go along with it, because they either fear the person in control or they know that they cannot do anything about it. Everything then goes underground. I watch how the anger grows and how it is repressed but always channeled indirectly to other nonproductive outlets. When someone is the recipient of harsh criticism, they may immediately stop doing something or change the particular behavior being criticized; so there are immediate results that some may see as reinforcing the effectiveness of this way of relating to people. This then breeds a continuous cycle of punitive criticism. But I see how the changes are motivated by fear and powerlessness and how people store up their anger at the harsh critic, and this resentment is rarely put to positive use. It's not a good long-term way of dealing with people."

"And how does it affect creativity?" I ask.

"It wipes it out," Sam asserts. "Creativity requires risk taking and sometimes going contrary to habitual and accepted behavior. When we are being controlled by a punitive and powerful critic, we are forced to do what that person wants; so we are always looking at the world from that perspective, as opposed to thinking in terms of creative possibilities that lie outside the lines of what we are currently doing."

"I know what you are describing," I grimace. "We tend to attribute this kind of behavior to historical tyrants, but it is all too close to home. I've probably given my own share of harsh criticism to others."

"Your comments help me understand my struggle with criticism," Sam says. "I may be so afraid of being hurtful and punitive with others that I have not learned how to criticize in an effective and natural way. I go out of my way to generate a positive and supportive atmosphere, but there has to be realistic criticism or else we are working within an illusion."

"What are some of the problems you have faced when addressing critical comments to others?" I ask.

"Too often I see that many people just cannot listen to criticism," Sam responds. "I make sure that the top people in my division have this ability. They have to be able to listen to my critical comments, and they become skilled in learning how to convey their criticisms of me. I need to hear what people think, and I realize that their opinions might differ from mine. I also have enough experience to know that I will be wrong at times and that if we are going to be successful, I might need to change the way I am thinking about a situation.

"But let's be honest. I respond better to some ways of being criticized than others; so my team leaders can probably tell you some interesting stories about how they have learned to deal with this."

"What sets you off?" I ask.

"Just yesterday I got annoyed at one of my directors for saying something in a way that always provokes a negative emotional response from me. He was blaming the organization for everything that is wrong and not being specific about the nature of the particular problem. I thought: 'My goodness, you know it always upsets me when you do this. So why do you do it?'"

"We are apt to become more annoyed with these unchanging patterns of communication than with direct criticisms," I say.

"The experience made me aware of how we have to find ways of talking critically about things that keep us in sync," Sam continues. "The director said that he has to be free to express himself, and I agreed. But I emphasized that there are certain ways of saying things that will generate a better outcome. It's an ongoing exchange of honest communication and understanding. It's a subtle dance because there is so much tenderness and vulnerability on all sides of the criticism process."

"But there are some people within every organization," I say, "who just can't open to giving or receiving criticism."

"Yes," Sam responds, "that's what I have discovered. Some get along by acting in ways that never offend others, by avoiding conflict and playing it safe, and not taking risks of any kind. Others are less successful in evading conflict and the inevitable criticism that they cannot tolerate. They sink deeper into trouble, and they might be let go by the organization; or they move on to something else."

"It's rare to find a person who is completely comfortable," I say, "in openly accepting criticism."

"I agree," Sam affirms. "I am certainly not one of these people. But I've learned that I need to listen to critical comments. Good, intelligent, and sincere criticism always helps me. If I want to be effective, I have to listen to what people think. I can't live in a self-fabricated bubble. At some point it will burst."

"It's probably just as challenging," I say, "to give sincere and honest criticism."

"You are right," Sam declares. "I often ask myself: Am I giving criticism because I am competing with this person in some way? Is there an ego agenda operating here—mine or the other person's? Why am I really offering this criticism? Because the other person provokes me? Am I being critical because I am having a bad day? Because I am frustrated?

"It's very important to be clean and clear when giving criticism. At times I have been critical of someone's work and then realized that my feelings about other things in our relationship were playing into what I was doing. These other agendas can really complicate and confuse the process. Giving criticism is not easy to do. I guess this is why I have always struggled with it. Maybe the difficulty is inevitable."

"The problems you experience with criticism might be ways of keeping you conscious and engaged," I suggest.

"Perhaps," Sam concludes. "It's never going to be cut-and-dried and simple to do. It is a constant challenge to present criticism as a sincere effort to describe what I see happening in a situation and with the ultimate goal of helping other people become more effective."

Recall a time when you received harsh criticism from another person for something that you did or a risk that you took. How did the response affect you? Has criticism ever motivated you? Has it helped you express yourself more effectively? Has the criticism influenced your self-confidence? I imagine that you have experienced different kinds of criticism from people during your life. What type of criticism do you find helpful? Hurtful?

We all know people who cannot take suggestions or supportive criticisms without becoming defensive. In contrast, there are others who welcome every helpful suggestion.

The former type is tightly guarded and impenetrable during evaluations with supervisors, quick to deflect the slightest criticism. The atmosphere feels closed, and there is an absence of flow. Communication is forced. I try to put these people in charge of their own evaluations, and I then assess how accurately they are able to look at themselves.

When people are open, relaxed, and flexible in assessing themselves, the spirit of mutual learning pervades the supervisory relationship; and supervisors are more likely to become invested in the person's learning and success.

Perhaps because they listen to nothing but their driving visions, people who cannot take criticism of any kind are sometimes able to undertake impossible tasks and daunting challenges. Even the most collegial leaders have to go it alone from time to time and block out criticism from others. But a completely closed attitude toward criticism is not amenable to long-term success. There has to be room in our perceptions of ourselves for critical things.

Bring to mind an incident or period in your life when you were able to persist in your creative expression, follow a

vision, or take a challenging course while being confronted
by serious obstacles. What was it that sustained you?
     Can you recall a particular instance when you were able
to open yourself to criticism after a sustained period of being
reluctant to receive it? What was the outcome?

In my experience, the complete denial of criticism is an expression of fear. A shaky self-image does everything it can to avoid hearing what others think. There needs to be a balance with criticism so that we learn how to listen to and consider what others suggest without giving away control or becoming paralyzed by self-doubt.

When the critic is trying to overpower or dominate another person, the process is seriously flawed. Judgment replaces criticism, and the channels of communication are blocked. The process of assessment is flawed when there is an assumption that one person's perspective is supreme. These criticisms say more about the critic than about the work being reviewed.

Successful criticism depends largely on two things: the person's desire to improve and the critic's sincere motivation to be helpful.

Aesthetic Distance

Approach criticism as a practice that seeks to determine what is happening in a particular situation. When we look at an art object or a problem at work with the goal of expressing what we see, rather than what we think or feel, the process becomes clearer.

If you are in a position to evaluate another person's work, you might ask: What works well? Is there something that needs to be altered? Are you achieving the desired outcome?

Focusing on particular phenomena, rather than coming on strong with our personal opinions, helps to prevent the recipient of criticism from feeling attacked and to defuse any defensive reactions. Effective criticism is characterized by an ability to separate from the object of reflection, whether it is personal behavior or something we make. Both the critic and the person being criticized need to maintain this aesthetic distance.

Experience indicates that those who kindle and help support the creative expression of others have gifts for empathy, listening, looking, and giving feedback in ways that enhance expression. One of my graduate students, who is also an experienced theater director, researched this theme of artistic feedback. He explored how harmful and cruel a critical response can be when it is informed primarily by the bias and point of view of the person giving a response. From his work in theater training, he observed how some people became inhibited and ineffective when the responses they received from authority figures and peers were not motivated by a desire to clearly articulate what might be happening in a particular circumstance.

In my studio groups, we work at describing what we see in a purely structural and physical way and what we feel in response to an image or performance. We make a real effort to reinforce that all of these responses are based upon the perceptions of the person offering the feedback. Sensitive attempts to help the creators see their work in a more comprehensive way are clearly distinguished from responses that only express the judgment of another person. These methods developed in group art studios can be applied to the workplace.

Judgments tend to be inflexible, whereas the aesthetic responses that I have described are more fluid and suggestive. The latter responses offer points of view within an overall context where the primary value is placed upon being attentive to the expressions of others, rather than passing judgment. The person whose work is being reviewed is provided with the observations of others and is then free to determine how to use them.

Within close and safe relationships, we can often forgo these sensitivities of engagement and tell each other frankly and bluntly what we feel. When I trust a colleague's judgment about something I am doing, I will say: "Does it work? Do you like it? Should I change this or that? Where do you think I should go from here?"

I am especially reliant upon strong and clear feedback, whereas I know many others who do not want it. When others suggest adjustments or alternative ideas, some people become distracted and lose their sense of inner direction.

*Do you welcome critical feedback or find it difficult? Are
there times when you want it and other times when you do
not? What accounts for the differences?*

Generally those who desire to perfect their expressive skills are
eager to receive critiques from people they respect. The most valued
and effective teachers are the ones who can help us assess our work
more accurately. Criticism is never easy. It is always sensitive. Opening to a severe critique of our personal expression can be extremely
challenging. But if a person is not able to do this, it is unlikely that a
sustained discipline of creative practice will emerge. Creativity, as
well as leadership, requires the ability to digest and incorporate what
we may not want to hear about ourselves.

In my work in higher education, I observe how excellent teachers
are open to evaluations of their work. They have a clinical interest in
what works and does not work for people. Rather than perceiving
critical feedback as reflecting directly on them, excellent teachers
view negative assessments as information that helps them determine
how to teach more effectively.

Every creative discipline is a crucible in which advancement is
based upon the dissolution of certain self-perceptions. The wise and
experienced creator realizes that certain ineffective habits must be let
go in order to perfect expression. However, people find it very difficult to honestly evaluate their weaknesses. Perhaps persistence
against difficult odds requires a large measure of denial.

*Reflect upon those problems and tensions in your life that
stimulated or forced you to make major changes. Have there
been many of these situations in your life? Do you appreciate
their positive impact, or do you still look at them in a
negative way? Have your major learning experiences resulted
from positive and/or negative experiences?*

*Do you find it difficult to say critical things to another
person? Are you afraid to give critical feedback? Are there
times when it is better to refrain from giving honest criticism?
What kinds of conditions might justify this restraint? Are*

*there times when avoiding criticism might have negative
consequences? What might these be? How honest are you in
assessing your own strengths and weaknesses?*

*Do you seek out criticism from others? Why? Reflect
upon those people in your life whose critical comments you
welcomed and those whose feedback you avoided. What
accounts for this? List the criticisms you received from
others that you recall most vividly. Determine the points that
have merit. Which of these has had the most formative
impact on your life? Why?*

Small criticisms are obviously easier to take than devastating ones
that strike to the core of our self-worth. The ridicule of Melville's
most ambitious book must have been torturous. Yet something creative ultimately came from the experience.

Maybe Melville needed to take an extended break. What could
possibly have followed the ambition and depth of *Moby Dick*? Is it
possible that the long hiatus had a positive effect on the compact
form of *Billy Budd*?

Everything we do finds its way into creative expression, and ultimately the quality of expression depends upon contributions from
the complete spectrum of our experience. Criticism, as difficult as it
can be to receive, is a necessary element of creative success. The most
challenging areas of creativity are always the frontiers of new growth.

Fallow Periods

Melville's long period of creative hibernation between *Moby Dick*
and *Billy Budd* attests to how dormant times provide opportunities
for regeneration. Like other forces in nature, creativity needs to re-
constitute itself and draw sustenance from the environment.

During the period when he did not write fiction, Melville no
doubt maintained his connections to the creative process. When we
focus only on tangible outcomes, we can obscure the way in which
creativity operates in all aspects of our daily lives.

The average person may have more in common with an artist like
Melville than we realize. We stop creating in a conscious way, or

never get started, when we are no longer motivated by internal and external sources. Although there are those who are able to go it alone against the greatest of odds and still keep creating without support from others, these cases are unusual. Most of us need support of some kind in order to persist.

Have you experienced the type of hiatus Melville had in his creative expression? What were the causes? Recall the longest gap you have had in your creative expression. What was it like when you started again? Did the suspension have a positive or negative effect on your expression?

There are also many instances where people sever contact with a creative discipline and never return. Melville's long break is unusual, and it is even more remarkable that he was able to return with such precision and brilliance. The more typical pattern of the creative hiatus involves shorter timeframes. To achieve renewal and inspiration through new experiences, artists and writers throughout history have traveled. When we find ourselves repeating methods in a tired way, it may be time to take a break and do something else. However, there are artists who work compulsively every day, driven by a fear that they will lose contact with their creative powers if they stop creating.

How do you manage the balance between regular practice and time away for the purpose of renewal?

In the following workplace scenarios, Karen and Paul present two very different ways of dealing with open space.

KAREN
The Cultivation of Creative Ecology

Karen, a management consultant, describes how the pressure of going immediately from job to job interferes with her ability to thoroughly evaluate situations and access new ideas.

"If the work is too automatic," she describes, "I find myself repeating the same things. When anything becomes mechanical, I am less open to the unique qualities of the situation. I try to take breaks between assignments, do something completely different, and use other sensitivities. I call it the cultivation of creative ecology.

"These 'unrelated' things that I do always find their way into my consultation work. Something that might appear totally disconnected, like the way my neighbor keeps her garden, can help me re-vision a problem that a client is having. The work environment might be getting too deliberate, and it may need some of the free interplay of my neighbor's garden design. As I reflect on the garden, I see the order and aesthetic harmony that exist when we let different plants interact with one another under only minimal controls and central direction. The composition that emerges is more complex and stimulating than a garden where everything is lined up in rows according to size and type."

"Does the focus and directedness demanded by most jobs actually encourage a certain narrowness of perception?" I ask. "Work doesn't have a high degree of tolerance for indirect and free pursuits."

"Yes. It goes with the territory of work and productivity. We have to achieve very particular outcomes. This single-mindedness needs to be complemented in some way to prevent tunnel vision and an actual loss of productivity. My most important ideas often come from inter-actions I have with people outside the workplace. I bring these in-sights to the job and try to make it more like life as a whole. We have to encourage this circulation within the entirety of our experience. It's crucial to detach for a while, go fallow, and return in a different place. Work is especially in need of this nonlinear, indirect, and subtle infu-sion of ideas and energies. This is what I try to bring to my clients."

"How?" I ask.

"My consulting practice affirms how every situation and envi-ronment is unique. I always begin by listening, observing, and doing my best to assess the particular context. Although the immediate problems are endlessly variable, people in organizations need to spend more time paying attention to one another and trying to open to the perspectives of others. I train people to look more receptively at situations while sustaining focus. It's a paradoxical skill that we see in effective leaders—the ability to be direct and indirect at the same time, to sustain a purpose while staying flexible and receptive to new relationships. Creative ideas and opportunities always emerge when considerable energy is channeled in a certain direction. But they often come unexpectedly and indirectly. The ability to embrace the opportunity and do something with it is yet another topic for discussion."

PAUL
No Letting Up

Paul is the antithesis of Karen. He is a workaholic CEO of a small corporation who is on a cell phone to his office whenever he is away, even for a rare vacation. His secretary is careful to stay close to the phone when he travels. He is likely to call at any time to check on a project or give assignments to his staff. In a sense Paul "creates with others," but the other person is always an instrument for the realization of plans that he orchestrates alone.

The one-sidedness of this work environment makes it difficult for the staff to create new things. They channel their creative energy into their relationships with one another and with people working in different parts of the organization. Their immediate work experiences are directed toward responding to the needs of Paul and carrying out his directives. Paul is kind to them and appreciative of what they do, but he has never perceived them as sources of ideas and direction. He views members of his staff as resources to be utilized in executing his plans, his sense of what has to be done.

"My operation is productive and efficient," Paul says. "The staff are well paid, and the positions are in high demand. We have very little attrition in the company. It's a rapidly growing place, and the environment is attractive.

"Not everyone is meant to lead," he continues. "There is a comfort in following and doing a good job completing tasks that are recognized by others. When we meet for evaluation sessions, the staff never ask me for more freedom."

There isn't an hour of fallow time during Paul's week. He is successful and happy and, in his own eyes, very creative.

"Hierarchy is important within organizational life," he continues. "How many people really want authority and the responsibility that goes with it? I'll bet you will find that most people like having some-one else make decisions and watch over the organization. They don't want the responsibility that goes with a larger degree of freedom at work—the headaches and the angst. They like to compartmentalize and leave the place behind at five o'clock. When they're at work, they describe how they like projects that keep them occupied. Un-certainty causes tension. Empty space can be horrifying."

Do Paul's perceptions accurately portray the workplace as you know it? Do you fit into the types he describes? Do any of your colleagues?

"Do you need to be affirmed by others?" I ask Paul.

"Not at all," he says. "I assess myself according to what gets done. The board that reviews my performance does the same. We measure profits and growth in the company's market share. It's all very objective and simple. Maybe that's the appeal—clear standards of success and failure. I rate myself according to the bottom line.

"My father was old school," Paul continues, "and maybe I am more like him than I realize, or maybe he really got to me on certain key val-ues. He used to say, 'Don't try to lead if you want to be popular. Being liked by your employees and staff should be your last concern. You want their respect, and success is what counts—theirs and yours.' "

"Is the standard of success always so clear-cut?" I ask.

"There will always be rough days and periods," Paul says, "so it is important to know how to assess overall productivity. Setbacks tell us what needs to be fixed. We've got to act as quickly as possible. I expect my staff to attack the problem once it is identified. And I have definite responsibilities in terms of leading and setting clear standards for our company's success. There are not always clear-cut, right and wrong responses to problems; but it's my job to make de-cisions and keep the enterprise moving in the right direction, toward profit, since we operate according to the universal standards of suc-cess in business. Profit is the ultimate authority in my work."

"Are there indicators that suggest that you are moving in the right direction," I ask, "even when the outcome is not clear?"

"In business," Paul asserts, "we have to respond quickly and with quality. If we do not, someone else will."

"You do not place a high value on letting things emerge in their own time," I comment.

"If I did, we'd be out of business," Paul retorts, "and hundreds of people would lose their jobs. It's a tough racket but very rewarding when we succeed."

It is clear that fallow time and space for creative regeneration do not fit into Paul's paradigm of work. In my experience, life, creativity, and work tend to include all of the aspects described in this section. Karen and Paul are universal types, and I have to admit that Paul's values and those of his workers are closer to the norm today. The acceptance of uncertainty and the responsibilities that go with creative freedom demand more from people than following directives. It is also challenging for leaders to step back and nurture the creative initiatives of others. Paul makes many valid points when he discusses his leadership style.

As we reflect upon the challenges of creating with others, it is important to avoid one-sidedness. All of the positions being discussed contribute to a larger integration of ideas that helps us respond effectively to an endless succession of new situations and problems. Paul and Karen, with their distinctly different styles, suggest that people need to find work and community situations that match their basic orientations to life.

If you feel very opposite to either Paul or Karen, do they say things that have a certain degree of relevance to your experience? How might the characteristics of their respective styles be useful to you? Destructive? Do you combine qualities from both of them? Imagine a combination of the worst of Paul's and Karen's traits. Now create an amalgamation of the best.

Have you found the right context in life for the application of your particular interests and your way of working with people? Are you able to take advantage of the opportunities offered to you? If not, what is the reason? Do you know what you want to do with your life? Are your interests and skills properly matched with your current work situation? If you are presently experiencing a mismatch between your skills and your environment, what can you do to improve the situation?

CREATIVE PRACTICE

Criticism tends to throw most of us off-balance. It can be one of the most difficult things to accept. Yet it also offers great opportunities to enhance how we interact with others.

I recall being criticized in a group. We were sitting on the floor, and I instinctively braced my back against a wall for support. When the tension starts to rise in a group or in a relationship, and when criticisms begin to come my way, I try to focus on my breathing and really work at staying open and listening. If there is validity to the criticism, it is very important to listen attentively and without defense, giving the other person the sense that they are being heard.

Stand or sit with your back to a wall. Imagine the surface as your helper, as a source of support. Envision yourself as having the same stability as the wall. Feeling the support of the wall, open your mind, senses, and heart. Center and balance your body; spread your arms; open your hands; imagine the quadrants of your body as the four sections of a mandala organized around a central point. As you find a way of feeling secure within your body and feelings, try to embed this image within your memory. Imagine yourself being criticized, and open yourself to the communications of the other person while you are in this balanced and receptive position. Call up this image as a guide, protector, and supporter the next time you are criticized or faced with a stressful situation.

I read once about a Mexican shaman who spent time every day walking on a thin board in order to maintain his sense of balance. He described how walking between worlds was frightening, personally challenging, and dangerous. Maintaining bodily balance allowed him to negotiate the difficult terrain of performing soul retrieval for others. In my studio workshops, I emphasize breath, openness, and maintaining an overall sense of equilibrium as ways to be fully present and responsive during challenging situations.

What do you do to stay open when you feel threatened and criticized? The situation always gets worse when you tighten up and try to force a shift in direction. Balance and breath exercises are helpful ways of staying open when you feel stress. When threatened, we are generally off balance. Anxiety and panic are also characterized by an interruption of relaxed breathing. Sit or stand in a balanced position and practice simple breathing exercises in which you achieve a heightened awareness of slowly taking air in and out. Reflect upon the inhaling of breath as a way of taking in the presence and communications of another person, and then exhale with the feeling of giving life and energy to the other.

Make a series of mandala drawings in your journal as a way of establishing balance and openness. A mandala, sometimes defined as a magic circle, is typically a round configuration divided into four equal parts that meet and connect in the center.

Make a mandala with images of things you find difficult to hear in each of the four quarters. Use forms, colors, figures, symbols, and, if you want, words, to express your feelings. Contemplate the mandala as a way of containing all things that you fear the most. Trust that the center and boundaries will hold whatever you need to express. The configuration is balanced, and there is no sense of being overwhelmed. Everything has its place within the overall composition. Imagine yourself as being balanced and capable of holding difficult images and communications from other people.

Create another mandala with your images of strength and balance in each quarter.

Produce a third mandala combining your strengths and weaknesses in relation to receiving criticism.

Reflect upon all three configurations as talismans, as a trinity of images that holds your different ways of dealing with challenging communications. The first image contains the difficult, or shadow, aspects related to receiving critical and threatening communications.

The mandala conveys how you are not perfect, but you are nevertheless able to hold together your overall balance and form when challenged by threats.

The second mandala contains your strengths, gathered together and amplified by their relationship to one another. Their dynamic union expresses a power that is more than a simple addition of the parts.

The third mandala expresses the inevitable relationship and partnership between strengths and weaknesses. Consider the reciprocal relationship between your weak and strong qualities when they are gathered together into a coherent whole. Imagine how the third mandala, containing your completeness, your light and dark characteristics, and your contraries, may suggest the most effective route to creative power.

⟶ Work together with a partner after making the mandalas described above. Practice giving and receiving feedback by taking turns responding to each other's mandalas. Focus completely on describing the physical qualities of what you see. Don't make value judgments of any kind. Try to be as descriptive as possible. This exercise will help you to learn how to focus comments about what another person has done on physical facts that you both agree are present.

The exercise also helps the person receiving the feedback to listen openly to what another sees. Ideas and suggestions about how things might change grow naturally from listening to what is, and is not, present. As you practice this exercise, you develop a sensitivity to how these descriptive statements differ from value judgments, personal opinions, and other forms of criticism that tend to misrepresent what is physically present.

⟶ Try to imagine yourself flowing like water, like a river, when confronted with difficult situations and criticism. Set up a pitcher and a large bowl. Fill the pitcher with water, and pour it into the bowl slowly, over and over again. Practice this ritual as a meditation. Watch the effortless way in which the water moves in relation to gravity. Listen to the sounds the water makes. Observe how water fills space within the bowl after being poured and how it establishes an effortless equilibrium.

When confronted with threats, try to imagine yourself moving over and around them like water. Envision the problems as objects making contact with you like water. A friend describes how the *Tao Te Ching* says that water "never fights / it flows around without harm." The water flows naturally to low and stable places. When faced with intense pressure, try to become fluid like water, rather than tight and stiff.

⟶   Write poetic statements in which you imagine yourself as water making contact with obstacles. What does it feel like to approach the different objects? What happens when you touch? When you pass? What do you take with you? Leave behind? Is the sensation different as you flow toward, around, over, or under the next thing in your path? Are there differences between the way the water connects with difficult things and pleasant things? Use poetic images to describe these scenarios in as much detail as possible.

Reverse the process of poetic reflection, and imagine yourself as the objects touched by the water. How does it feel to have the water flow over you? Envision criticisms and the things that threaten you as water. What happens when the water comes and goes? When it flows as a steady stream? Transfer your feelings directly into words and images. Don't worry about how they connect to one another. Just try to let the images flow like water, and trust that they will find their way to a resting place, to low ground.

⟶   Expand the creative writing practice to body movement. Imagine yourself as water moving over, around, and under obstacles. Pause and shift to moving like a branch, a stone, or an object that is touched and moved by water. Roll with the water. Reflect upon how the feelings you experience can help when you are next confronted with difficult situations. Contemplate the images and remember them. Place them in a memory sanctuary from which they can be called up when you need them for support and guidance.

Experiment with watercolors and other wet paints with which you can focus primarily on flow and fluid movement. Don't be overly concerned with the visual appearance of the image. Concentrate more on the sense of how the paint moves. Explore different kinds of movements—sweeping, fast and forceful, slow and deliberate, intermittent, constant, abrupt, smooth, and so forth. Reflect upon the different sensations you feel in response to each of the movements. Imagine yourself as the paint undergoing these different experiences, as the brush, as the paper. Practice this exercise of pure flow as an antidote to struggle and obsession. Focus on the interaction of the participating elements, and explore how they correspond to your relationships with people.

Don't be concerned with anything other than making the most authentic and mindful gestures you can. Try to be present and intrigued with every aspect of the experience, no matter what the outcome.

These mental approaches might actually help you make more aesthetically pleasing pictures, but don't be concerned with artistic outcomes as you work. Beautiful products of expression are wonderful and valued, but they come to us spontaneously like grace. When we try too hard to achieve them, we block the pure flow. "*Tout est grace,*" all is grace, said Saint Thérèse of Lisieux. Every movement is precious.

Focus on what you are doing for its own sake. Record the different sensations you experience in your journal. Try to approach criticism through the heart of Saint Thérèse—All is grace. If you can open to criticism from others and let it flow like water, it will find its way to where it needs to go; maybe it will only pass by and touch you on its way to low ground. Contemplate the correspondence between what you do in your creative practice and how you live your life.

The next time you find yourself in an emotionally challenging situation, see if you can recall some of these sensations. Imagine yourself flowing like the paint or moving like the brush or receiving everything like the paper. Reframe a difficult communication addressed to you as paint that simply needs to make its presence known on paper.

Imagine all of these critical communications and threatening emotions as gestures with paint on paper. They make contributions to the overall composition, and the surface holds them without being destroyed. The creative process moves on to yet another series of expressions. It does not have to be arrested at any one place. Yet pauses and changes in direction are welcomed. The flow is forever renewing itself. The natural movement of nature continues through even the most difficult situations; all are part of a larger and eternal movement.

⮕ Shift this practice of flow to working with a partner. Encourage your partner to make occasional and unplanned interventions in your body movement or free expression with paint on paper. Rather than resist the actions as interruptions, focus all of your energy on welcoming these actions; use them as points that stimulate a new direction.

⮕ Continue working with your partner, and experiment with the principles discussed in the sections dealing with Karen and Paul. Practice Karen's idea of creative ecology by moving back and forth from one expressive medium to another every three to five minutes. Move to body movement from painting, back to painting, and so forth, making at least three shifts in action. Do the same with movement and creative writing, or with writing and painting. To prevent confusion and fragmentation, don't introduce more than two different expressive activities as you begin this practice. As you become more accustomed to making shifts from one mode of activity to another, you might experiment with additional media. You can do these exercises alone or with your partner.

You can also experiment with taking pauses to meditate at different phases of your work with one medium. How does your expression change as a result of these breaks and shifts? Do you become more aware of what you are doing? Are there any effects upon quality?

⮕ Work with your partner, and practice Paul's approach to constant direction from a leader. Take turns leading and following. As one of you moves or paints, the other gives directions.

Express yourself only as directed by your partner. Try to really play with this process; merge yourself with the directions, welcome them, and see how they affect your expression. Is there some value in this way of working? Is it more suited to some people than others?

7

FLYING
SPARKS
Relationships
with People and Places

We Owe Everything to Those Who Shape Us

The art studio environment has taught me that we need the presence of other people to make creative energy in a particular place. We need witnesses and guides, supporters and critical helpers, motivators and traveling companions. The same thing happens in team sports, where the group generates possibilities and a creative flow that could never occur in individual competition. Magic happens in the spontaneous arrivals and new insights shaped by the give-and-take with other people.

For some reason we have not seen how these same forces of collective interplay apply to the creative process. We still largely approach creativity as an individual activity. Poets rant about thefts of "their" ideas and images, not seeing that, in creation, everything is based upon influences. It is no wonder creative people long to be admitted to excellent schools or to work with teams of similarly motivated colleagues. The great moments of civilization and the most significant artistic and scientific movements are always connected to groups of people influencing one another. We owe everything to those who shape us through relationships.

Many of my closest collaborations in the arts and therapy have been with Paolo Knill. We have been in creative discourse for thirty years. After a talk with Paolo, there is never a clear sense of who initiated or created an idea. New insights are always generated by the dialogue, which acts as a third and integrating entity. Our talks are always a source of renewal and inspiration, that I can bring to whatever I am creating at the time.

Paolo says, "The discourse is a transformative environment. Things spring forth that would never come from the individual mind. Whatever germinates in my mind afterward was something planed by the conversation, something that takes my thought further. You do something different with it than I. We cast off our individual forms from this heat, and every figure we generate is different. Our relationship affirms how creation is communal conversation, with individuals then doing their own work in response to the exchange."

Do you have a close collaborator in your life? How often do you experience truly creative and transformative conversations?

When people quickly assume that they are not creative, they are generally looking at themselves in isolation, rather than in the context of their relationships with others. They may realize that their judgments are often based on perception, but they continue to view creativity as something within themselves rather than as a quality of their families, communities, and other centers of creative action.

Have there been extended periods in your life when you were alienated from creative activity? Why did this occur? Did you doubt your creative abilities? If you had received more support from others, would this have affected your relationship to creativity? Do your feel that you are able to

put your creative resources to use in your life? What are
these resources? How have you used them?

Within my studios there are often people who have not made art
of any kind since childhood, and I take great pleasure in encouraging
them to paint and move again with a child's spontaneity. The logic of
simply picking up where you left off makes it difficult to resist. If I
am able to persuade people that their childlike gestures and compo-
sitions have aesthetic value, they discover that they are able to paint
with originality and vitality. They also see how others positively receive the expressions, and this support helps sustain their ongoing relationship with creative activity.

Can you remember people who supported your creative
expression in childhood? What did they do? Do you recall the
qualities of your expression that sparked their interest? What
was your most recent experience of being affirmed by another
person for something creative that you did? How did you feel?
When was the last time you affirmed the creative expression of
another person? How did you do it? Do you do this often?
Why do you support the creativity of others?
    Can you recall a recent situation where you missed the
opportunity to support the creativity of someone else?
Re-create that situation in your mind, and imagine how
you could have acted differently. What might have been
the results?
    Prepare yourself to be more responsive to the
opportunities you have every day to affirm the creativity of
another person. Take the focus off yourself, and imagine
your creative practice as supporting the things that others
do. What effects might this type of action have on creativity?

MARY
A Social Basis to Creativity

All too often we find ourselves in positions that do not match our
ideal expectations and desires. Mary worked her way up from modest

positions in small organizations. She describes how every group she encountered had special qualities that furthered her learning and personal development. The most unlikely people and situations were consistently her greatest teachers. What is perceived as ordinary can be the source of extraordinary experience, while our stereotypic notions of quality and value are often the greatest deterrents to imagination.

"My most satisfying creative moments," Mary says, "occur when I see the value in places where I have lived and worked that first appeared depressing or meaningless. There is no formula for making this happen. It's just a matter of dealing with each situation, staying connected to it, and not getting too far ahead of the circumstances in which you find yourself. I owe everything to the people with whom I work. Their ideas have always stimulated my own. They've always helped me make the most of every situation."

If we examine our personal histories with creativity, we will probably see that peak creative periods are characterized by affirming and inspirational relationships with other people. Sometimes these connections can be with historical figures who, by their example, stimulate us to explore new and different ideas. We look at what is possible, rather than being overly concerned with all of the things that can go wrong.

"Other people have stimulated and supported my creative expression to such a large degree," Mary says, "that maybe there is a social basis to creativity. I want to be around imaginative people and part of an organization that is committed to creative outcomes. The environment gets to me. I feel different when I enter. The creative energy is in the atmosphere in a very real way."

I ask Mary, "Can any person walk into an environment like this and immediately begin to act creatively?"

"Yes and no," she replies. "It always impresses me how accessible the creative process can be if a person is open and the environment is supportive. But there is also an element of physical and mental preparation that needs to take place to fulfill creative potential. We have to be attuned. A person cannot expect to perform physically at the most effective and satisfying levels without training. If the body is prepared, it is more apt to react effortlessly. The same thing applies to creative expression. It's both innate and practiced. It's like running or hitting a ball. Some people are born with special talents, but creative expression needs to be exercised."

In keeping with Mary's comparison to athletics, opportunities for creative expression range from solitary marathons to the quick interplay of team sports. However, even the most individual sports depend upon the participation of others. Competitors are also necessary contributors. The total field of play generates an energy that carries everyone within it. Individual actions respond to what others do. Challenges from others elevate performance. We are pushed to dig deeply into ourselves and tap new resources. Creative growth results from active collaboration with others, who incite us to instinctively reach for new levels of expression.

> *Have you experienced the social basis of creativity that Mary describes? Identify someone in your current work situation who contributes to your creative expression. What is it about that person that stimulates you? Is there somebody whose annoying or irritating actions inspire you to respond in a creative way? Make an inventory of the people and environments that have stimulated your creative expression with their positive energy. Identify which qualities in these people and environments influenced you. Do the same with the people and environments whose negative qualities activated your creative expression.*

LAURA
Different Kinds of Creative Relationships

The history of the creative process affirms the importance of close working relationships with others, as well as the varied roles people take in giving and receiving support from one another. Some of us may have received more than we have given and vice versa. Domestic relationships often break up on the basis of one-sidedness within the creative interplay. The same thing happens at work. Yet many people clearly prefer supporting the creative expressions of others.

Vincent Van Gogh relied on his brother Theo for economic, emotional, and artistic support. Theo was a literal lifeline for Vincent.

Other celebrated relationships include Gertrude Stein and Alice B. Toklas, and the threesome of Henry Miller, Lawrence Durrell, and Anaïs Nin. The Stein and Toklas companionship expanded into a group network and important Paris salon involving Hemingway, Picasso, and others. Virginia Woolf and the Bloomsbury group offer another example of a noted gathering of creative people.

In science there has been a similar history of teams of people working together in the process of discovery. Whether in a high school science lab or an art studio, whether in the most advanced centers of inquiry at the Lawrence Livermore National Labs or at the Metropolitan Opera, collaboration among participants is the basis of the creative enterprise. Prominent cooperative relationships in science and the arts underscore how people create together in every sector of life. Both in major centers of creation and simple domestic relationships, people influence one another in subtle and very direct ways. Everything in the creative process originates from the interplay of people and environments.

> *Examine your history in relation to giving and receiving creative energy. How do you think others perceive you in relation to this issue? Consider asking people how they view you. Are these perceptions accurate? Is there anything you can do to alter them?*

Most people report that it is very gratifying to give support to the creative expression of others. However, many find it difficult and even threatening to step aside and let others receive credit for creative achievements, especially when their contributions to the process are invisible and unrecognized.

Laura, an educator, describes how one person in a creative relationship can make an environment that fosters the creative expression of another. She relates how Edith Lewis, a journalist, created a supportive domestic and emotional environment for Willa Cather. Laura affirms how we need others to "feed energy" and that the dynamic of a relationship between two people can extend to a group, as with the Bloomsbury group and the Stein-Toklas salon.

"Creative relationships and groups are often tied to the collective energy of the times," Laura says. "There may be political forces that draw people together and galvanize creation. These cooperative gatherings seem to be more active at certain moments in history, and at other times people are more solitary in their creation.

As Laura speaks, I become aware of how her enthusiasm for the subject of creative relationships activates my own energy and interest in the subject. I reflect on my history with close colleagues like Paolo and recall how I have been inspired and energized by creative dialogue. I am one of those people who, if it were not for supportive and inspirational relationships, would not be involved at all in the creative process.

Laura also brings to mind how one person will often make personal sacrifices to support the creativity of another. Literary and artistic biographies are full of stories of these invisible supporters. Nora Joyce, the wife of James, is among the most famous. In the world of sports we have observed the extraordinary commitment that Richard Williams has made to the careers of his daughters Venus and Serena.

Do you serve others within close relationships? Or are you more likely to depend upon the help of others? Are you able to give unconditionally to others? To what extent do you establish a balance between giving and receiving in relationships? What might you do to correct imbalances that currently exist?

Laura says, "Sometimes the sacrifice relationship is just that; but at other times when we give to others in this way, we ourselves gain. I was close to a photographer who was very committed to his art. I helped him; and through the process, I became involved in photography. In looking at life through his eyes, appreciating his work, and seeing the world through his camera, I realized that there were things that I wanted to do."

"The medium got to you," I say. "It was a third factor in the relationship."

"Right," Laura responds. "In creative relationships everything is always unfolding into something else."

We might examine the extent to which we have the ability to

spark and cultivate the creativity of others. I know many art teachers and art therapists who have channeled all of their artistic abilities into furthering the expression of others; their greatest satisfaction comes from this role. Other artist colleagues refuse to "midwife" the expression of others, finding that they need clear boundaries between their work and what others do. They have experienced some of the pathologies of enmeshment that occur within close creative relationships, and they respond by establishing firm separations between themselves and others. This same dynamic exists in the workplace and day-to-day relationships. The patterns that we see in the artistic community extend to life as a whole.

> *Where do you stand in relation to this issue? Can you*
> *identify different types of relationships in your own creative*
> *history and your immediate environment? What factors*
> *contribute to collaboration, and which to separation?*

Many of us need very open-ended exchanges with other people. When in a dialogue with another individual or with a group, we strive to orchestrate the participating elements into a new creation of some kind. I realize that some may want a more controlled and predictable structure in their relationships with others. Needs for control may arise as a way of avoiding vulnerability or as an expression of a particular style of approaching the world and relationships. There have been great artists and creators who rigidly controlled their environments, so I cannot dismiss this way of approaching life.

Yet, if they are to succeed in the creative realm, free spirits and those who thrive on control must both find ways of getting beyond themselves. Creativity requires the ability to establish relationships with things outside of ourselves. Highly controlled people and those with more open-ended temperaments have different ways of approaching their relationships with other people and environments, but they share an ability to respond imaginatively to what the context presents to them.

> *To what extent do you rely on having a predictable*
> *environment? On having opportunities for change? Also*

look at how much you are able to surrender the need for control at work and in your personal relationships. If you have great needs for control, how does this affect others? Do your needs for safety and control create an environment where the needs of others for these conditions are sacrificed?

Look at little things in daily life in terms of control. Are you able to drop what you are doing when another person enters and needs attention? When you receive a call? Who typically ends a telephone conversation? To what extent do you allow others to take the initiative in a conversation? If you are someone who tends to control the dynamics of conversations, try to take on the role of listener. Step back and let others come forward. Make a point of letting the other person end the interaction. How does it feel? If it feels strange and new, maybe it is time to change.

Are you able to flourish in environments where you have little control? If you enjoy change, are you able to let others determine the rate of flux? Are you more creative when you initiate something, when you respond, or both?

STAN AND LEAH
Yin and Yang

Stan and Leah are a married couple. Stan is a management consultant, Leah an art teacher. They have diametrically opposed styles of working with people in groups; yet they actively support one another's work and describe how helpful the other's way of approaching a situation can be.

Stan introduces an idea or a problem and gives groups the freedom to respond as they see fit. He is a master of coordinating the spontaneous expressions of group members and channeling the varied responses into a common focus. He identifies the different threads and helps the group weave them into new forms.

Often Stan will simply encourage his groups to work freely with creative media, without goals of any kind, for a designated period of time. "Whatever needs to emerge into the group's consciousness will always surface," Stan insists. "I am reluctant to give directions and tasks, because my sense of what needs to be done might have little to with what is brewing within group members. My goal is to create an environment that responds to the needs of groups and taps into the energies of the present moment. I am in awe of what comes out of people when they are given the freedom to express themselves. The ideas and the group dynamic are always much more imaginative when I step back and let people take the lead in communicating what they are concerned about at that particular moment. I then work with the group and help them shape their interactions into a collective creation. People constantly say that these unplanned creations have an almost magical and energizing power that inspires new cycles of creation. I guess this is because they well up from inside us, without the step-by-step calculations that typically characterize human constructions."

"But there must be strategic and calculated things that you do," I say, "to establish the environment for this type of creative process."

"Yes, I need to set things up so that the energy can be released and find its way to a creation. Rumi wrote a poem about the need to keep sweeping the paths to heaven in our daily lives. I'm someone who works at keeping the paths free so that people can connect with one another and with their own creative potential. After all these years, I remain in awe of how the creative process finds its way to fulfillment within a safe and supportive, yet aesthetically stimulating environment. Safety by itself isn't enough. In order to take expressive risks and do new things, people need to be aroused and challenged."

"Most of us need coaching of some kind," I say, "especially when we lose confidence and doubt ourselves."

"I try to do this in a way that acknowledges the unique conditions a person faces," Stan replies. "People see through superficial affirmations. I work at paying attention to the particular situation, at being another set of eyes and ears for the person. When I am able to really observe what is happening and to describe what I see, I keep the other person in the driver's seat. Better yet, I keep the person's 'process' as the source of discovery. I want them to find the resolution within an individual's experience. The results are more rewarding and long-lasting when this happens. The answers always emerge from the creative process itself. As leaders and teachers, we are most effective when we actively support people in finding out for themselves."

In contrast to Stan, Leah carefully and laboriously prepares for all of her art classes. She says, "Children and adults need structure in order to freely express themselves. Materials presented in an attractive and enticing way inspire expression. One of my responsibilities as an art teacher is setting up activities and materials. I go to great lengths to plan what we use and what the goals will be. I am expected to demonstrate a range and breadth of creative expressions. Not only will parents complain if the same art materials are used all year with relatively constant results, but most children, I find, really need variety. When they work with just one medium, it is easy for them to get stuck. I remember school experiences with the same watercolor tins week after week. Children benefit from experiments with different materials that expand their imagination. I like to think that there is imagination in the materials themselves waiting to be released, like the sculpture which strives to express the spirit of the stone or the particular piece of wood."

"Leah, do you think that your way of working is a response to the needs of the context in which you work?" I ask.

"Yes and no," she replies. "The children probably need the structure, but I do too. I get frazzled when things are chaotic, whereas Stan welcomes this as a way of getting things moving. He's comfortable with chaos; I need order. We may find a way of balancing this through our relationship."

"Yes, you hate chaos, Leah," Stan agrees.

"The creative process keeps chaos at bay," she comments. "Art makes order and harmony."

"And for me art needs to break things up, so there can be a new order," Stan responds. "Nietzsche felt we have to have chaos inside in order to 'give birth to the dancing star.'"

"Stan thrives on not knowing what will happen in an art studio. I prefer to carefully orchestrate what the children do."

"I do provide a simple structure in my work," Stan says, "and then expression emerges. I'm energized by the unexpected. I need it, and I trust that something will always be there."

"When Stan gives a talk to a group," Leah adds, "he tries to connect with his spontaneous feelings."

"And Leah prepares everything carefully in advance and reads her presentations."

"I do go off on an occasional tangent," Leah admits. "But yes, I like to prepare and script my expressions. Also, in my teaching I repeat successful activities with the children year after year because their creations are always different."

"This makes me realize," Stan interjects, "that I can't be present within a group when I am reading from a script. I have to make contact with what I feel happening at that moment. I realize that this is risky because I might miss the mark completely. It's happened to me before, and I had to confront the emptiness. The audience said it was fascinating, but they might have been feeling sorry for me. It was torturous when I went blank. Even so, I still have to operate this way in order to feel present and alive and fully open to the interplay of the moment. Thank goodness Leah wasn't there."

"In spite of these major differences in styles, values, and interests," I say, "you seem to work well together. Is it the old cliché that opposites attract?"

Leah inquires: "Who's going to answer that one?"

"There is no question," Stan says, "that I am drawn to people and things that are different than me. There is something to be said for complementarity or the creative interaction between extremes."

"Stan and I have many common interests, like our commitment to creativity," Leah says. "But even in our efforts to describe what we share, we say different things."

"We both like tennis," Stan quips, "especially long volleys."

"It would probably be boring if he were just like me," Leah adds. "Too much of one thing, one type. I guess it all breaks down to being committed to creativity and to each other, and accepting and even enjoying the different ways of the other person."

"And I have often thought," Stan concludes, "that we expand each other through our differences."

Do people who have distinctly different styles than you stimulate you? Nietzsche said there is magic in extremes. Do you agree? What types of extremes are sources of creative energy for you? What extremes are destructive? Have you experienced both?

What does it take for people with significantly different perspectives to work together? The author Lawrence Durrell suggested that there is nothing more valuable than variety. Do you agree? Do you seek out variety in your life? Does it take a special openness to accept the many different kinds of people in the world? Do you think that artists and creative types are more interested in doing this than the average person? Why or why not?

Have you visited or worked in organizations where everyone is expected to act the same way? How do you feel in these environments?

Do Sam and Leah strike you as unusual people, or is it common to see people with very different styles working closely with one another? Do the common traits of Stan and Leah seem more apparent than they might think? You might say that differences are relative, and that these two people chose to focus in our conversation more on how they are different from one another than how they are the same. Do you think we do this sometimes to distinguish ourselves within creative relationships? Is personal individuation a healthy and creative thing to desire? Could the conversation between Stan and Leah have just as easily focused on how they are the same?

What is your history of relationships with similar and opposite types of people? Are common values more important than differences to you? When it comes to creative relationships, do you think that some kind of common bond or commitment is necessary?

LUCY
Affirming Others

Lucy is director of community relations for a large corporation. In a focus group conversation, she described how important it is not only to provide opportunities for feedback, but also to give serious consideration to what people say. "When an individual or members of a group," she says, "are asked to give their opinions on an issue or suggest solutions to problems, it is important to seriously consider the recommendations. Reasonable people do not expect the leader to automatically accept or use their ideas, but they feel that they should be taken into account. For example, a group of people is asked to make suggestions for an annual company outing. They meet, discuss possibilities, generate ideas, and make a recommendation. Later they learn through the grapevine (a communication network in organizations that both promotes and deflates creativity) that the CEO has decided where the event will take place. The location is not the one they recommended, and they assume that she intended to hold it there all along. They feel that their time and energy were wasted; and when future requests for suggestions are requested, they are regarded with skepticism. When people start to feel that their ideas carry no weight, they stop thinking creatively. Have you ever experienced this?"

"Yes," I reply, "and this example makes me look at myself and times when, having already determined what needed to be done, I might have requested suggestions from people. Perhaps I was hoping they would affirm what I wanted to do. This makes me realize that when I ask people for their ideas, I had better listen, take them seriously, and be prepared to change direction in response to something they say. I think that if others know their opinions are respected and taken seriously, the process of communicating ideas will always circulate fresh creative energy through a community."

"When only one person in an organization is allowed to be creative," Lucy replies, "it's like the blood stops flowing throughout the whole body. The head becomes bloated, top-heavy, and the larger corpus loses energy and weakens. Good circulation is a basic principle of health as well as creativity."

"And organizational vitality," I say.

"I'm someone who has always looked at creativity as an individual artistic activity," Lucy asserts. "I have to admit that I have seen my work in organizations as a necessity, what I have to do to make a living. If there is going to be creativity in the workplace, it is dependent on the structure of the organization and the character of the people at the top."

"Organizational culture enhances or restricts creativity," I answer.

"Absolutely," Lucy says.

"Is there one primary thing you would recommend," I ask, "for encouraging a creative culture in organizational life?"

"This may sound too simple," Lucy explains, "but I think the most important thing is taking other people seriously and respecting what they say when they generate ideas. And, even more fundamentally, we have to give people the chance to make suggestions, especially within their areas of responsibility."

"Can you give an example?"

"In my experience the most creative ideas at work come from brainstorming with my coworkers," Lucy continues. "The team of people in my department has shown me that brainstorming with others leads to heightened levels of awareness and creative problem solving. We trust each other enough to bounce ideas around, share information, and approach situations from different directions. We operate on a shared belief that there is no single, correct answer.

"Anything goes when we brainstorm; we don't judge one another. There is never a sense that one of us in the group has the right answer. We're fascinated by whatever emerges from our interplay.

"There is something special that happens when teams of people who are all familiar with the issues and problems become involved in this kind of brainstorming. Having a common body of knowledge is essential. But we can only be creative if we are allowed to freely share ideas and not be judged. The creative energies freeze abruptly when people feel threatened or attacked for what they are doing."

"It seems," I say, "that we need leaders who give us the freedom to create and the support to sustain our efforts when we run up against inevitable obstacles within ourselves and the process itself. As a rule, leaders are not aware of how much support and encouragement people need in order to act in more creative ways. Most of us have some pretty deep-seated insecurities."

"Leaders have an enormous effect on creativity within their organization," Lucy responds. "Many obstacles to creation extend from what we might see as leadership pathologies: when people only put forth ideas that fit into plans already established by leaders; when workers put more energy into protecting themselves than creating new ideas; when workers feel that it is in their best interest to act in ways that enhance the ego of the leader; when a person within an organization is willing to act as a spy and inform leaders of what others might have done or said in opposition to the positions taken by leaders."

"Sounds like the secret police are an archetypal phenomenon," I reply.

"Yes, there are immense obstacles to creative expression within the typical organization," Lucy declares. "It can probably all be traced back to the need that leaders have to control other people and make them feel that power resides outside themselves."

"Lucy, it's almost as if the typical organizational structure is designed to prevent creative expression, to guard against original ideas that threaten the status quo established by a controlling leader. Creative leaders, on the other hand, orchestrate diverse intentions into a sense of purpose that transcends individuals, including themselves."

"In these restrictive situations," she answers, "other people are used to check and prevent the release of creative power, rather than enhance it. You're right, the typical organizational structure is more liable to restrain creativity than inspire it. No wonder I have always done my creative work in isolation. But I am starting to see that I may be overlooking something in my relationships at work, something large in a creative sense." She pauses and says, "I'll keep thinking about these issues."

What makes you feel secure at work? Insecure? What conditions help you to feel self-confident?

Do you think that a sense of personal security is fundamental to creative vitality in the workplace? Do you believe that people have an inherent ability to work creatively with others when the environment is right? Do you agree with Lucy's belief that leaders have to take people

seriously and respect what they say in order to generate
creative ideas? When you function in a leadership role, can
you transcend personal attitudes and needs in order to
achieve a group goal? If a personal adversary in the group
generates a potentially valuable idea, can you give it serious
consideration?

Seeing Familiar Places for the First Time

I remember the first time I walked into an art school. People were
doing something different in each studio: painting, making objects
with steel, drawing human figures from a model, sitting together in a
circle talking about a particular work of art. Others were reading
alone in a garden area or talking with a friend. Art was everywhere,
hanging formally in the galleries and lying about the studios. The environment, its visual images, movements, smells and sounds, had a
potent expressive power. I wanted to do what they were doing. I was
responding to the community of people as a dynamic center, rather
than focusing on particular individuals. The strongest impression
was the energy conveyed by the whole environment.

I had this same reaction when I first visited school and college
campuses, churches, homes, athletic events, courts, government
buildings, hospitals, offices, and factories. I was always focused on
the overall energy and aesthetic qualities of the particular place.
Even the most depressing environments, like the state mental hospital where I once worked, generated distinct qualities and spirits.

When working on a book dealing with the spirits of things and
places, I had a meeting in the publisher's office. I was struck by the
way people arranged their office spaces with personal and aesthetic
artifacts. We humans have a natural tendency to arrange our spaces
in ways that generate creative energy; and as I walked through the
office spaces, I viewed them like galleries in a living museum featur-
ing varied office shrines and installations.

In those environments where creative energy is most apparent—
art and music studios, construction sites, classroom discussions, and
scientific laboratories—there are clear and strong images of people
doing things with one another or with the physical world. The

viewer as visitor is outside the dynamic interplay but still perceives its energy clearly. Something vital is happening in those places during the particular moments of observation.

Each of us probably gravitates toward a particular type of environment for aesthetic stimulation. Some people prefer open spaces in nature; others like the crowded conditions of cities, where people interact in close proximity. There are artists who find inspiration in travel and others who stay at home to create. My colleague Vivien describes how she begins her day walking in her neighborhood park where she can see Boston in the distance. She feels a sense of balance in her body by seeing the city where she will be going to work while experiencing the freedom of being in the country. She says, "This meditation gives me a transitional moment. Sometimes when I get to the top of the hill I sing, 'I'm sitting on top of the world.' Still I have time to prepare myself for facing traffic, people, my computer, and the challenging day. Every day I know I will be dealing with minor and major problems. I need this moment of peace before I start. I get support from the sensory connections to the trees, the light, the water, and the animals."

> What environments do you find most stimulating? Where do you do your best and most consistent creative work? In what kind of relationship is your creativity stimulated? Restricted? Is your creative style more peripatetic or still?
>
> What qualities of nature best describe your creative activity? A calm pond? A turbulent sea? Gusts of wind? A leaf falling gently to the ground? A blazing fire? Perhaps there are many faces to your creative style. What are they? Is your creative expression composed of a pantheon of different aspects? Do these different qualities always work together in the same way?

An examination of the essential operations of creative and spiritual traditions reveals a common focus on awareness of the present moment. As I have emphasized throughout this book, engagement of the particular instants of experience is the way to access the creative energy that is present within them. If our minds are occupied with something other that the immediate situation, we are disconnected from the resources that exist before us. The emphasis of contemplative traditions on mindfulness suggests that the best resources for creative transformation are our moment-to-moment actions in a given situation.

Our perceptions are generally more open when we are in new environments. The energy conveyed by fresh experiences is more likely to find its way past the perceptual barriers that we continually construct through routine behaviors. Because so much sensory detail is filtered out by our mental habits, we need to find ways to approach situations as though we are seeing them for the first time.

> *Recall your first encounters with environments that evoked strong feelings in you. What were your reactions? Have your sensitivities changed in relation to these places? When was the last time you were struck by the expressive quality of an environment or group of people? What was it about the situation that excited your interest? How do you think a new person visiting your work environment would respond? Are there environments in your life that generate more energy than others? What accounts for the differences? Are you the same in all of these places, or do you change in relation to them? What about you changes in relation to different places? What remains the same?*

MATTHEW
Different Environments Energize One Another

Matthew is a musician who works during the day as a department head in a government agency. "Some might think that my life is split," Matthew says, "because I have such different interests. I guess this way of looking assumes that a person can be only one thing. I've discovered that I need to be active in more than one environment to feel complete. In addition to my job and my music, I also have my family; and I still compete as a distance runner. I'm energized and shaped by each of these environments. They contribute different things to my life. I like to think of myself as someone who walks between worlds. What really interests me is how they influence one another."

"How does that happen?" I ask.

"There is a transfer of energy from one to the other," Matthew responds. "They feed each other. I guess I view myself as an ecological system that needs different types of energy. My music has never been just a release from the stress of work, though it definitely performs this function at times. Music is more apt to move the energy generated from work into a different form. It's all about creative transformation and how an experience in one area stimulates movement in another domain. I take experiences and feelings from work and bring them into my music and vice versa. The same thing applies to running. The older I get, the more I realize how the endurance, breath, and speed that I develop in running supports what I do in other areas. The different environments generate different energies that mix together in everything I do."

"We are amalgamations of experiences?" I suggest.

"And fragmentations of experiences," Matthew maintains. "I certainly prefer when the whole is greater than the sum of the parts, but sometimes things just don't fall together; sometimes there are difficult obstacles and chaos. These bad times also produce energy. In my life, the bad times have reinforced the need to do different things. When I am stuck in one area, I can be energized and transformed by another. My family has been the most reliable source of strength and purpose for me. If everything seems to be going wrong in work, art, and sport, all I have to do is think about my children and what they are doing with their lives; and everything comes together again."

"You step outside yourself," I say, "and think about someone else who is close to you."

"It sure works for me," Matthew says. "I read Herbert Marcuse's *One-Dimensional Man* in college and said to myself, 'I don't want to be one of those.' I love being different and having interests that might seem contradictory to some people."

"Imagination requires a mix of experiences," I say.

"And health does too," Matthew asserts. "Life itself needs a multidimensional basis. I was just reading about DNA and how when it comes to the survival of the fittest, variety is something to be desired. The author was saying that if we all had the same DNA, one parasite could eliminate human life."

"But it is challenging," I say, "to commit yourself to many different things in the world today."

"I see it as an exchange of energy," Matthew replies. "It's like running and practicing music when I am tired. The endorphins kick in, and I feel stronger and more alert afterward. If I don't do these additional things, work becomes monotonous. The different environments energize one another."

"How does that work?" I ask.

"I'm a percussionist," Matthew answers, "so perhaps it is natural that I enjoy distance running, where there is such emphasis on sustained rhythm, continuity of movement, and subtle variations. Running requires different movements and efforts; but all must be part of an overall cadence—the ability to accelerate and pass other runners; the capacity for quick bursts of speed, long and steady exertion, power uphill, and balance when running downhill; the ability to lose yourself when the mind merges with physical activity, the transcendence of monotony, the appreciation of the all-encompassing rhythm of the activity."

"It's like Henry Miller proclaiming happiness in surrender to the pulse of life," I say, "the heartbeat behind everything."

"Yes," Matthew continues, "good drumming also requires this surrender and service to the natural pulse of the music, not making too much of yourself and your skills."

"There are many clear relationships between running and your music. How do these areas relate to work?" I ask.

"I don't think the connections to work are as direct," Matthew responds, "because daily life with a community of people is complex. But I personally need a fluid and ongoing movement from one thing to another. I also hope that the disciplines I have cultivated in music and running manifest themselves in relationships with people at work. There are over three hundred people employed by my agency, many of whom I know well. We are a supportive community and we rely on each other. I have often thought about how much energy I receive when I go from one person to another in my daily engagements. The simple and seemingly superficial exchanges of communication really give me great pleasure every day: the 'Hellos' and 'How are you doings,' the smiles and simple acts of mutual recognition. These contacts can go right to the core of a person.

"I need these transfusions of energy very much. I took them for granted and completely missed their significance when I was younger, and all I could see was what I didn't like about a particular institution. I was missing the intimate face of daily life. I've learned that depth is often on the surface of experience. We don't have to go digging for it. Opportunities for deep engagement of life are always within our immediate grasp, but we are looking elsewhere. My perception of work was transformed when I began to think this way. I realized how people gave me good and creative energy through the most basic rituals of daily life. As I became more aware of these interactions and opened myself more completely to them, I received more and appreciated everything in a more complete way.

"I don't want to imply that work is always bliss and nirvana. It's usually a tough place. But the challenges are what really give us opportunities to be creative."

"How?" I ask.

"I like to solve problems, and I need the challenges that work presents to me," Matthew answers. "I've learned that I depend on this type of interaction with people to feel complete. In jobs where I was not free to work creatively with others in addressing problems, I was really frustrated. I now see that those limitations and constraints went against my basic nature.

"I try to listen to people and get them talking to one another about possible solutions to problems. I feel like the conductor of an orchestra when I do this. The energy that moves among people in dialogue is similar to the making of music in a group. I'm affected in much the same way. It's just a different medium. I thrive on the sounds, the effort, the exchange of energy, and the overall movement toward some type of harmonic pattern and a satisfying result. As with music, I have to listen in order to stay attuned."

"Your distance running and drumming experience must make you comfortable with extended dialogue," I say. "I imagine you giving people time and space to work through their ideas."

"I sure do," Matthew answers, "and I have my critics who wish that I would intervene more and get people to the point. They haven't developed the same tantric affection for the sustained pulse of dialogue. Yes, the disciplines that I practice do require patience and a gradual unfolding of experience. My way of solving problems is not much different from my drumming and running. I try to stick with whatever we are doing and keep people engaged in open and purposeful dialogue; invariably, solutions emerge from the overall effort. If we keep the energy focused and sustained, it takes us where we need to go."

"Matthew," I say, "you demonstrate how we create together with all of the different aspects of our individual lives."

"I can't live any other way," he replies. "I don't do these varied things with any intention of integrating them. Each area is pursued as an individual discipline with particular qualities that I try to master. I am not always sure how the different things come together or whether they always do. My hunch is that the connections tend to be more indirect. Vigor crosses from one area to another, and an individual's character becomes more expansive. There is more room for entertaining different realities, and there are more resources for approaching the challenges of work and life."

Can you identify different parts of your life that interact in ways similar to those described by Matthew? Have you ever had a problem in one area resolved as a result of something you did in a completely different domain? How freely does energy move across the borders of your different areas of interest?

Creative thinking and problem solving require us to spread our attention, rather than focusing on one particular way of looking at a problem. Ideas and images from one area of life provide analogical insights into completely different spheres.

Metaphor is a vehicle for transferring the resources and intelligence of one element of experience to another. The cross-fertilization builds new and more imaginative structures. The basis of this power is the transmission of creative imagination and vitality. Metaphors and analogies are conduits for the underlying transfer of energy from one domain to another.

The creative person stays open to the broad landscape of experience and the larger circulation of ideas. Fixation on one thing alone blocks the view of the whole, as well as the flow of creative energy. It drains energy without replenishing the source. As we move between worlds, as Matthew describes his commitment to multiple activities, we gather energy while expending it. We give to the environment, and it gives of itself to us.

Energizing environments are places where this flow flourishes. People like Matthew cultivate creative vitality and become conduits for transferring it to others. Matthew also demonstrates how different areas of life can stimulate one another.

> *Do the various sectors of your life complement each other in this way? How does this happen? Are there parts of your life that are alienated from one another? Is it possible to bring them into closer collaboration?*

Creating Is Conversation

Even more than support we need creative inspiration from others. The creative process thrives on the sparks we ignite in one another. You will find that the give-and-take, the charge and counter-charge, will bring things out of you that you could never have predicted. Creating is a conversation. We think through the process of talking, writing, and responding. Wonderful ideas arrive when we pass thoughts from one person to another. As with the movements of nature, everything arises from an interaction with something else.

In my office I frequently write reports on the computer with a colleague sitting next to me. We might begin by talking about what we want to do, and invariably the key ideas will emerge from the conversation. In addition to helping produce ideas, the presence of another person helps me stay focused on the completion of the task.

This collaboration propels the creative work and guards against the distractions that I often succumb to when trying alone to get something started. When working with a colleague, I am not going to read e-mail, talk on the phone, complete routine tasks, or do anything other than the task at hand. This approach to creation has been especially helpful when deadlines have to be met and when there are many other competing projects.

I have worked in similar ways with small groups and committees; we focus on the creation of text, rather than having someone take minutes that must ultimately be shaped into a proposal. We push and pull against each other in order to generate ideas. The exchange of communications within groups corresponds to how different ideas work together to make new creations within our individual expressions.

The Romantic poets referred to the "flying sparks" that ignite the imagination within relationships. When people are together in a creative community, expressions travel through the atmosphere in a contagious way. The creative process is advanced through the interplay or cross-pollination in which a new expression emerges in response to another. These experiences are part of a more general circulation of expression that characterizes the creative process.

As I have emphasized repeatedly, the sparks stirring creativity are not always pleasant. Nothing gets me going like a disturbing and unfair statement. Our irritants are vital sources of creative motivation. They upset the comfortable equilibrium and demand a response. Motivation theorists describe how people innately seek resolutions when faced with cognitive dissonances and gaps. These tensions paradoxically bring out the best in many people, especially those who thrive on adversity and challenges.

Athletes attest to how their best competitive moments occur when being pushed by a competitor. In this respect, the adversary is a necessary partner in a creative exchange that transcends individual points of view.

Competitive relationships and challenging engagements occur naturally within the creative process. We even compete with ourselves, sometimes in positive ways. At other times the internal competition, based on fears and destructive personal conflicts, undermines our creative potential. We push against others in these situations, not realizing that the real battle is taking place within ourselves. When we are immersed in these internal struggles, colleagues can bring us back to objective reality; they make it necessary for us to act in productive ways for the benefit of the group. "Come on," they say. "We need you. Let's get going together on this project."

Forces moving though our environments influence creative expression in positive and negative ways. The flow of the creative process is sometimes blissful, especially when artists feel as though they are acting as agents of a transcendent creative energy. The composer Puccini insisted that he did nothing more than transcribe what he heard from God. Puccini gives credit to the "other" moving through him. But there is always the necessity for artists to be active participants in the conversation, even if this means simply witnessing, responding, and recording what is moving through them. Receptivity is paired with initiative in every phase of the creative process.

Recall moments in your life when you were able to create and express yourself effortlessly. Duke Ellington described how he was dreaming when he played music. Has anything like this ever happened to you? If you do not view yourself as a creative person, answer these questions based on a sense of effortless flow that you experienced in sports, discussion, or work. Did it feel as though you were acting as an agent for something other than yourself? Has this happened often? What conditions enhance this kind of expression? What restricts it? Is your creative expression more responsive to environmental forces, or do you express yourself consistently in different situations?

The creative spirit is often imagined as a winged figure, because it flies in and out of our lives. Those who prefer a more controlled and predictable environment are less likely to embrace the "other" and let this force act upon them in ways that can possibly change everything.

Are you drawn to dynamic situations and places? Does a focus on forceful change and movement threaten you? Are you generally open to forces and inspirations moving

through your environment? Have you experienced
conversations with others where new ideas grew
spontaneously from the exchange? What was it about the
interaction(s) that activated the creative process?

CREATIVE PRACTICE

Just as Matthew has different interests that form a creative ecology, you no doubt have a similar circulation of varied pas-
sions and commitments flowing through your life. The following
practice suggestions give you the opportunity to become more aware
of your varied influences and capabilities. Creative activities that embody and transform your interests give them a deeper significance;
and as you concentrate upon these different aspects, they begin to influence one another and your overall consciousness in new ways.

Gather objects that represent the different areas of your life. You
might include your business card, some symbol of a sport you play
or follow, pictures of your spouse and children, something belonging
to your grandparents, an object from your childhood home, a leaf
and flower from your yard.

As one of my colleagues says in response to this practice session,
"It's like looking at who I am, all the bits and pieces that have made
me who I am today. Some things are sentimental; others are painful,
because they represent losses. The objects form a collage, but I can
change their relationship to one another. In one arrangement I
place them in a historical sequence. Then I rearrange them to get
away from this reality, to envision what *can be* as I move forward.
I want to change some of the relationships I have with other people.
As I look at the objects and what they represent and as I look
within myself, I can see what I would have done differently, what I
missed, what I want to change, and how I can respond differently
to people."

The process of working with personal objects opens a wide spectrum of creative practices for every person. The objects and symbols
hold memories and are capable of offering support, strength, and

confidence. Arranging the objects in a configuration of some kind results in a gathering of the powers they represent and an illumination of their different layers of personal significance. The process symbolizes what happens when we make use of all of our interests and abilities. The configurations are a reminder of what we are, what we can do, and how we have many different resources to use. As we reflect upon the circulation of feelings and memories aroused by the objects, we experience a corresponding activation and focusing of energy within ourselves.

⤳ This activity can be expanded to a group exercise by asking different members of a community to place something of significance to them into a collective arrangement.

⤳ Throughout time, people have carried sacred objects with them as sources of power and as a way of staying connected to others who are not present. My father, a pragmatic man of the world, was a real curator of keepsakes, things that carried memories and kept him close to people. He had a small leather pocket holder for photos and cards of loved ones and inspirational figures. His dresser and office desks similarly had places for sources of inspiration and connection to others.

All of us tend to carry things with us in this archetypal way; we fill our personal spaces with things that carry the spirits of others. Last night, leaving my office in a college building, I realized that I had forgotten to return a call. Everyone had left some time earlier, and I went behind the reception island to use the phone. Tucked under the counter of the paneled barrier, and hidden from the view of people standing on the other side, the receptionist had created a gathering of family photos and mementos. As I stood there in the dim light, the objects really came to life; I felt like I had stepped into a very personal space, pervaded by the spirits of the objects. I quickly made my call and respectfully moved back into the common space.

Perhaps you would like to experiment with the creation of inspirational office arrangements in a more mindful way. Examine what you are already doing in this area, and take some time to observe what your colleagues and friends do within their spaces to establish a circulation of creative and personal energy with objects. In addition to making your own arrangements of special things within your office space, try to appreciate and open to the expression of others as a way of establishing a sense of community with your colleagues.

        If you hope for a particular outcome in something you are doing, carry small things with you that serve as reminders and guiding images of what you hope to achieve. Sports psychology has affirmed how images guide action. Athletes focus on mental pictures and use the imagination as a way of envisioning what they need to do. Talismans, power objects, sacred pouches, and photos in our wallets are also ways of focusing energy on the objects of our desire. We take the process of visualizing outcomes into the physical dimension with these activities. Rather than feeding superstitions, these practices channel power and creative energy in the same way that athletes do with their use of the creative imagination. Russell Crowe's portrayal of the Roman General Maximus in the film *Gladiator* beautifully demonstrates how a powerful person was affirmed and guided by tiny figures, representing his wife and son, that he carried with him in a pouch.

Gather together things that you would like to carry with you in a wallet or pocket sachet. Reflect upon this collection as a way of focusing your creative energy, as a way of drawing together your varied relationships into a common focus, and as a way of accessing the energy of people and forces outside of yourself.

        One of my art therapy colleagues decided to submit to taking a certification exam that she did not ideologically support. Before the exam, she asked friends and family to give her pieces of cloth that had personal significance; she then sewed the various pieces into a cloak that she wore to the exam. The cloak brought the energies of her loved ones together into an affirmation of what really matters in her life. Through this creative act, she transformed the exam process into an art event—and passed the test with ease.

You might explore similar activities and perhaps make a banner with pieces of cloth that hold special significance or represent your interests and strengths. You can make small and inconspicuous configurations that can be carried with you all of the time or shape the material into a pouch that can hold other special things. Some may want to make bolder, more visible statements as my friend did by hanging the banner on an office wall.

This activity of sewing together pieces of cloth can make a wonderful group art activity for a team of people wanting to express and symbolize their collaboration and collective strength. Pieces of cloth representing each person and different characteristics of the group can be sewed into a large banner expressing the power and qualities of the group. Company logos and flags generally focus on one simple image that unites all. These symbols are fine, but they can be augmented by images that gather together and represent the different participants in a unified image.

8

WHAT
LEADERS
CAN AND
CANNOT DO

Control and Liberation: The Necessary Interplay

When creating together is a priority for an organization or community, the role of leaders becomes important. Because of the power they wield, leaders can either clear the path of creativity for others or obstruct it.

Considerable time and energy have been dedicated throughout history to determining how best to control, direct, form, and manage people. Those in charge decide what they want, and they create environments and plans to make sure they get it. The cultivation of creativity in communities of people is antithetical to the tendency of many leaders to control and to dominate, to make sure things are done their way. Yet a certain degree of control is unquestionably necessary in all forms of creative expression involving individuals and groups. The leader who wishes to maximize creativity within a group or organization will be constantly tested by the delicate task of maintaining balance between restraint and free expression.

The head of an enterprise may have considerable influence in declaring that creativity will be an important part of a group's culture, but mandates alone do not make a creative atmosphere. The tools of authoritarian commands and directives, useful in dealing with many life situations, simply do not apply to the cultivation of the creative imagination. Creative groups and communities are formed by what their members do on an ongoing basis. Leaders establish priorities and then work together with their communities to realize them. Our leaders can declare, "Let there be creative vitality and discovery within this community," but then they have to do everything they can to cultivate and guide the process. At times this may require them to step back and allow things to happen that are contrary to their intentions.

Letting go of the need to control people and situations can be a daunting task for many leaders. Some of us have considerable experience with controlling others and/or being controlled in relationships. The various aspects of the control process run deep in the psyche: obsession with control, dependency on external controls, resistance to any form of control. In addition to these ingrained psychological patterns, there is a necessary and complex relationship between freedom and control within the creative process. I venture to say that most people are far more comfortable in environments where everything is "under control," either by themselves or by others, than in places where there is a high degree of uncertainty.

> *Reflect back on your school experiences, and compare the emphasis placed on control versus liberation of your creative potential. Make the same assessment of your work experiences. If you are in a position of leadership and responsibility, to what extent do you either control others or encourage freedom in their expressions? Is it more difficult for you to control others or to liberate their expression?*

As someone who has spent most of his life trying to create environments that support the creativity of others, I felt a perverse delight when one of the deans at the college where I was provost said, "You're not always as liberal as you might think. Yes, you constantly encourage open discussion, but you can also be very directive." I felt that the dean saw me clearly and acknowledged the different ways in which I interact with people at work. This vignette suggests that there are few absolute principles when it comes to the process of leadership. All of us committed to creativity in groups must manage the necessary interplay between control and freedom. We have to make sure that we fulfill the responsibilities that go with our job descriptions, while also being responsive to the needs of the people with whom we work and our own desires for creative fulfillment.

Very often and quite naturally, these different commitments might appear to conflict. The absence of this tension might be perceived as a sign of imbalance and a loss of the creative force that moves us forward. Paraphrasing Walt Whitman, the leader might say, "Yes, I contradict myself. I contain the multitudes that exist within this community."

Effective leaders establish priorities and values, then do their best to maneuver within the constant interplay of forces generated by the environment. As a leader I have a responsibility to liberate the creative potential of the group and to make sure that we stay focused on our objectives; to do my best to stimulate and guide the process and to ensure that other people make contributions to the overall effort. There is an inevitable interplay between freedom and control that is not necessarily contradictory. The leader is charged with making sure that these different ways of working complement one another.

If you work as a leader, to what extent have you been personally shaped by the communities you serve? Has your style of leadership been formed by the context in which you work? Do you often feel controlled by your environment? Imagine yourself being shaped by a very different, even opposite milieu. Would you be a different person?

Although I have strayed from the ideal course on many occasions, my personal orientation to leadership has always been to support groups in finding their unique creative potential. In the early 1980s, I led a three-day studio workshop on the creative process in Gothenburg, Sweden. A colleague of mine from Amsterdam participated in the sessions. She had a far more directive style of leadership and was taken aback by my way of letting the contents and direction of the work emanate from the free expressions of group members.

We were walking on the street after the session and I said, "I'm exhausted."

"How can you be tired?" she asked. "You haven't done anything."

We laughed, and I realized how it might appear that leaders like me are not working hard, because we are not constantly intervening in what other people are doing, giving directions, or executing our own detailed plans. I assured my colleague that it takes considerable energy and focused attention to set up a creative group environment and then maintain it. Watching, waiting, and supporting the varied expressions of others involves a subtler and perhaps less visible style of leadership. I tend to give directions and orient my groups only at certain key phases of our work together; I then stand back while they work.

I feel that I am doing my best work when the structure of leadership is invisible and people say, "How did he get us to do that? What did he do?" I like it very much when people say after a session, "I don't know how I am going to describe to my husband what happened in this group. I can't put it into words. I'm just going to say, 'You had to be there.'"

I work hard to create an environment that acts upon people. My influence is more indirect. I am sure that I bring a certain degree of purpose, positive energy, confidence, and knowledge about the creative process to the work; these qualities influence people in different ways, but ideally help everyone believe in the value of what we are doing. I have also learned that leaders need to have clear goals that are explicitly stated to groups. Throughout my career I have found that if I can get groups of people working toward creative goals, there will always be surprising and significant outcomes. I am keenly aware of the potential power that groups have and I strive to arouse this force and help it move in positive directions. As a leader, I try to assure people that I will support and acknowledge them as they exert themselves in new ways.

Witnessing Others

From my first job as an art therapist in a large state hospital, to my executive positions in organizations, I have combined study of the creative process with the daily work of leadership. There are many similarities between how we cultivate creativity in art studios and in organizations. Where the observation of creativity in organizational life is often obscured by other demands, the art studio offers opportunities to experiment with the ways in which ordinary people engage in serious imaginative expression. What we have learned from these studio environments can cross over to other situations where people desire to create with one another.

For example, one of my closest colleagues at the college where I worked said to me, "So many of us have cluttered paths when it comes to creativity. Mine is full of hang-ups, inhibitions, fears, and unrealistic expectations."

I asked her, "Do you see yourself as creative?"

"Absolutely not," she replied.

This is exactly what people new to the art experience often say when they begin to work in a studio environment. They doubt their creativity simply because they have not had positive experiences with the creative process. Other people have not affirmed their creativity. Unless someone witnesses and acknowledges the creative spirit within us, it stays invisible. However, the good news is that creativity does exist in every person.

When was the last time you commented favorably on something a colleague did? Is this something you do frequently? What was the result? How did you feel when doing this? How do you think your comment was received? Were you satisfied by the outcome of your comment? Will you do something different the next time in a similar situation?

Do the things that others say to you have an impact on

your expression? What would you like to hear from others?
Is there something that you would not like to hear? What
has influenced you more—the unpleasant or the supportive
things that others have said to you?

Remember the last time you received or gave critical
feedback in a supportive way. How did it feel? Why doesn't
it happen more often?

In my studio workshops we simply start working with artistic materials; and with the proper support and guidance, every person ultimately experiences the creative energy within themselves and the studio environment as a whole. If a person makes a sincere effort, and if the space is supportive and safe, the outcomes are consistently positive. This same approach can be taken to the workplace; creative energy exists in every person and every situation at work just as it does in the art studio.

I realize that, like newcomers to the art studio, many people in every community feel that they are not creative. What is a leader to do about this? Whose responsibility is it to kindle the creative process within community life? Is it possible to foster creative expression and thinking in those workplaces where the primary emphasis is on productivity within clearly defined expectations? It might even be said that the responsibilities of leaders in organizations are often anticreative, in that deviations from the expected outcomes are considered threats to organizational stability.

In my experience as a leader, there has always been interplay between change and constancy, innovation and maintenance, imagination and routine, whimsy and discipline, exploration and containment. Successful leaders have the ability to walk gracefully between these worlds like shape-shifters, never fixed in any one place. Ineffective leaders tend to be locked into a single perspective, usually their own, and incapable of entertaining ideas that exist outside their existing frameworks. The effective leader has a natural way of embodying and moving between the different outlooks and needs that exist within communities. A defining attribute of leadership is the ability to integrate variety into a common purpose, while respecting the differences among legitimate points of view.

Recall an instance where a leader acted upon a suggestion
that you made. When was the last time you listened to the
advice of another person and changed your course of action?
Are you a person who seeks out the opinions of others?
Imagine what it must be like for a person to lead a group or
an organization without ever listening to the suggestions of
another person. What might account for such a person's way
of operating?

MIKE
There Are No Road Maps for the Deep Terrain of Creativity

In an effort to gain a more complete understanding of what lead-ers do and don't do to further creativity in others, I spoke with Mike, who works as a college professor and consultant. Mike teaches courses on leadership and has been leading creativity workshops for many years.

"Mike, how did you get started as a leader of groups? Has your style changed over the years?"

He replies, "When I finished my graduate studies, I was working at a consulting firm where there was a commitment to training new managers to be creative problem-solvers. Before graduate school, I worked in musical theater. I became the art person in the consulting company, the one who ran experiential sessions. The other trainers presented theories and case studies and essentially did a lot of talk-ing about creativity with groups. I was the one who got them work-ing outside the boundaries of words. In response to your second question, my style of leading groups has changed significantly over the years."

"How?"

"I used to have a far greater need to control what people did in my groups," Mike continues. "I have seen over and over again that whatever needs to be expressed always comes to the surface if I can get groups working together in positive ways. There is rarely one theme or particular creative activity that will tap into what each in-dividual in the group needs to express. I can't assume that my direc-tives and ideas will be right for everyone in the group."

"But isn't there a trick," I say, "to finding universal themes and structures for creativity to which every person can relate?"

"Absolutely," Mike answers. "Everyone can connect to anger, co-operation, destruction and renewal, life passages, opposites, and other universal themes. These common emotions and patterns touch us in significant ways and evoke deep concerns. When I first began to lead creativity workshops with managers, one of my routine exercises involved the building of bridges together with another person. I made building materials available, asked the group members to select partners, and then had them work as twosomes in making bridge structures."

"The theme is loaded with possibilities," I reply.

"Yes," Mike continues, "the bridge has many symbolic and practical meanings in relation to the workplace. We all have our stories about failed efforts to reach out to others, being isolated and disconnected, needing better communication with certain people, and finding common interests that transcend our differences. Bridge building is a theme that runs deep in the experience of most people both in positive and negative ways."

"So why do you question the value of this type of exercise?" I ask.

"The more experienced I become," Mike explains, "the less satisfied I am with standardized gimmicks. I could probably lead groups for the rest of my life dealing with themes related to bridging interests, different cultures, opposing emotions within ourselves. But ultimately this way of working puts too much emphasis on what the leader wants people to do."

"What's wrong with that?" I inquire.

"Control and order certainly have an important place in both creativity and leadership," Mike answers. "And I am always intrigued that so many people really like to be told exactly what to do rather than deal with anything unknown. If I tell people exactly what to do, they are less likely to be original. I would rather see the bridge emerge as something a particular person chooses to engage, while other participants might choose to make other things. This freedom of expression means a great deal to me in leading groups. I think we go deeper into the creative process when we allow individual themes to emerge. I have to admit that as I speak to you about this, I am realizing that this commitment to the freedom of individual expression might have more to do with my beliefs than with the interests of the people who attend my workshops. I have to think more about this. Am I doing this for me or for them?"

"Can you say more about how you have come to feel this way?"

"I led my first workshop groups in highly directive ways. At first it was exciting to see how people could execute my plans and improvise upon them. It was enjoyable to orchestrate the group and achieve goals. But after a while I saw that the groups were carrying out *my* ideas and plans. Also, the outcomes were relatively homogeneous. The process was tightly controlled, and there were few surprises. The groups consistently validated 'my' methods of achieving creative results. After I mastered this way of leading groups, it began to feel superficial. It had too much to do with me; there was not enough focus on what individual group members could create."

"But what happens when you give groups this freedom and then they don't work well together or produce creative results?" I ask. "Don't they challenge you and say, 'What are you going to teach us? Anybody can just let people work freely?' "

"It's always risky when you give up control," Mike replies. "But we have to make space for new expressions and ideas to come forward."

"I can imagine that an inexperienced person is more apt to insist on tight controls when leading groups."

"Yes, I surely did," Mike says. "Some leaders can never let go of this way of operating."

"Why?" I ask.

"Perhaps it's a mix of things: habit, fear of the unknown, personal insecurity, needs for order and control. When I first led groups, I was terrified of losing control."

"Did it ever happen to you?"

"Absolutely," Mike acknowledges. "And I learned from it. One of my greatest lessons came when I realized that talented and creative groups are more likely to rebel against being overly controlled. When the uprisings came during my early groups, I didn't have a clue how to work with their intensity. Concepts and techniques seemed to evaporate in relation to the powerful energy generated by the group. I instinctively tried to relax myself and the other group members when this happened."

"Sounds like your instincts told you to do what the most experienced guru might do," I remark.

"Yes," Mike replies. "Instincts can be intelligent and wise. But I didn't have a clue. I was terrified, whereas the guru is knowledgeable and relaxed in the face of fragmentation."

"The experienced person might see the purpose in the disintegration," I say, "perhaps even the necessity. But I suspect that gurus get scared too. Sometimes we need the fear to help us tune into what's happening."

"When we allow ourselves to openly accept our present circumstances in a healthy group setting," Mike emphasizes, "we always come together, and the overall momentum carries us forward in a creative way."

"After all of your experience with this process, what advice do you give to other group leaders?" I ask.

"Accept the conflict," Mike answers. "Stay open. Listen to people. Avoid rigid defensiveness, which will only encourage the group to become more ferocious. Most of all, work hard at keeping the environment safe for people. Groups really bond when they feel supported when things appear to be breaking down. They begin to trust and respect leaders who can stay focused and committed to everyone, even when they are being attacked. There is real truth to the term 'testing behavior.' People check out the thickness of new ice before they skate freely and with abandon."

"Do you concentrate on all of these things when tension begins to elevate in a group?"

"No, I just concentrate on what's happening and try not to think about too many things," Mike continues. "When people see me dealing with issues, it helps them calm down and stay open."

"People need the freedom to wrestle with the challenges, and even the risks, presented by the creative process," I answer. "If we don't allow this to happen naturally, the group is liable to go after the leader as a way of asserting its power."

"There you have it," Mike declares. "If everything is controlled and all the difficulties and choices are minimized for people, they are not being exposed to what I consider the true creative process. I want to encourage experiences in my workshops that correspond to the challenging conditions of life. My goal is to train people to engage the creative process themselves, without needing me to set up an exercise for them."

"It sounds to me," I say, "as if you too need to be challenged, to explore new dimensions of the creative process, to stretch yourself, to take risks, and to work more at the edge of conventional practice."

"I hadn't thought about it that way before," Mike acknowledges. "But this way of working certainly does have something to do with me. I take risks; but they are always calculated in relation to my sense of what people need, what the creative process needs to go further. I am always working toward the goal of maximizing creativity."

"This is probably the answer to your earlier question," I say. "You desire more. You want to go further and learn more, and this is no doubt why you are leading the group. I trust that you also model these values to your workshop groups."

"Yes," Mike agrees, "after a while I wasn't learning as much from the highly controlled groups. It felt like we were going through the same motions in session after session, and it had no aesthetic appeal to me. I felt that the creative process was not realizing its potential."

"But don't some people need structure in order to loosen up?" I question.

"Yes," Mike continues. "Going though a fixed routine can promote relaxation and concentration and help us open up to new ideas. Like athletes, many artists have their regular warm-ups and preparation rituals. Count how many times Nomar Garciaparra adjusts his gloves and taps himself while getting ready to hit a pitch. He does this routine before entering the unknown, to prepare for whatever the pitcher throws at him. His response as a batter cannot be planned in advance. It emerges from the unique conditions of the pitch, which is delivered with the goal of surprising him and catching him off guard.

"There is a big difference between highly controlled preparation procedures and an overall game plan that is arranged in advance.

When I was telling people what to do in a workshop, I felt like I was choreographing the game. This type of control doesn't apply to leadership in the creative process. There has to be room for improvisation and spontaneous responses to challenging conditions."

"How do students respond to this more open-ended approach to leadership and creation?" I ask.

"Their natural inclination is to want a formula of some kind, a 'how to do it' technique like the bridge-making exercise that we discussed," Mike answers. "At first they always resist the more open-ended approach. I tell them that their anxiety and reluctance are normal, and that they are on the verge of something good—if they are willing to take the next step. And they get madder at me."

"You've learned the hard way," I comment. "I say to people in my studios that resistance is the gateway, the sign that they are getting close."

"I have been through some ordeals with this method," Mike admits. "But it helps to know that it works. It's never easy. There is still a great deal of hard work and energy needed to cultivate and protect the creative process in a workshop group. The risks are always there. Many people have an innate desire for tight and restrictive controls when given opportunities for expressive freedom. My experience with creativity training has taught me that there is often a pervasive fear of freedom and a love of control."

I ask, "Have you answered your earlier question about why you work in this way?"

"As long as I keep doing the work," Mike ponders, "the question will never be completely answered. I have a stubborn need to keep pushing at the edges of creativity, to explore the unknown. This conversation is helping me get a better handle on why I persist in encouraging as much freedom of expression as possible, why I never select themes or tight directives for my groups and why I am compelled to give them space and opportunities to work with whatever happens to be moving through them at a particular time.

"It's all about focusing more on them and less on me, and all of us concentrating more on the creative process than on ourselves, on what is moving through an environment at a particular time rather than prescribed activities like bridges, on learning how to engage the unique internal and external forces operating within ourselves and our environments. I keep telling my students that there are no road maps for the deep terrain of creativity.

"Probably the best answer to my question is an operational one, with two major outcomes. First, I have learned that when we work in this open way, our actions correspond more closely to the creative process. And secondly, I see that my best students go on to be leaders who really understand how the creative process works in groups of people."

"Is there anything in particular that keeps you going and willing to take on the hard work involved in training?"

"I am inspired by senior executives," Mike says, beaming, "very successful and powerful people, who have the eureka experience during one of my workshops and see that they have to change their way of operating in order to facilitate creativity in others. But my greatest satisfaction comes when the student or management trainee who fights most aggressively against this way of working, winds up doing some of the best work with it later in life. I do take delight when they refer back to the 'good old days' when they tormented me with their opposition. Maybe the intensity of the struggle is directly proportional to the value of the outcome."

Have you ever experienced a situation like the one Mike describes, where the thing his students oppose most fiercely later becomes something to which they attach great value? I recall the playwright Samuel Beckett describing how he realized at the end of his life that the darkness he constantly struggled against was the purpose of his work.

As I listened to Mike speak, I recalled teachers and figures in my life who held fast to challenging and difficult principles that I was reluctant to accept. Leaders are demanding in what they expect from their communities; they accept a certain degree of conflict and discomfort, in order to push at what Mike calls the "edges" of what we are willing to do. These leaders tolerate tension and uncertainty in order to help people reach new levels of creativity, to transcend complacency. As Theodore Roethke suggests in his poem "The Waking," we learn by doing what we don't want to do, by going where we "have to go."

> *When was the last time a person or a situation pushed you to*
> *new limits? Did you embrace the challenge without*
> *hesitation? If you experienced resistance, what was its*
> *source? Do you feel that you need a challenge of some kind,*
> *a push from someone, to go beyond your usual way of*
> *responding to a situation? How do you respond to situations*
> *where there is a high degree of uncertainty and where you do*
> *not know exactly what you are supposed to do? Have you*
> *ever been in a condition like this, where you let go of the*
> *desire to control everything? Were you able to let events*
> *unfold? Were you surprised by the results? Why?*

If we turn the tables on how leaders challenge their constituents to operate in more creative ways, we will see how environments "push" leaders to take their performances to new levels of creativity. In most life situations there is an ongoing interplay among participants in the creative process. Mike clearly described how he sought out more demanding conditions in order to learn and to go deeper in understanding creativity. In this respect our creative work clearly depends upon the larger field in which we operate.

I was talking with a historian about this process of creative interplay with others, and she said, "In the study of history there is a tendency to examine the lives of 'great men' with very little recognition of how these people were shaped by their times and the people around them. Of course the great historical figures impact the world in major ways, but they don't do it in isolation."

Leadership studies have similarly focused on the styles and achievements of major figures and not as much on how they are creations of their environments. There has to be more attention given to how organizations and historical periods shape leaders.

Contemporary leaders are increasingly faced with the challenge of establishing common goals and standards while respecting the multiplicity of interests and ideas that exist within groups. The latter condition has been called a "postmodern" worldview, but it is actually an archetypal aspect of human interaction that has regained attention as we recognize the complex basis of human experience. From antiquity to the present, leaders have balanced demands for unity and order with needs for flexibility and change. Rigid orthodoxies and fixed ideas may prevail for extended periods of time, but they are ultimately replaced by systems that resonate more closely with the continual interplay of human experience. An example of this is how the command-and-control style of leadership, described earlier by John, has been replaced in many sectors of organizational life by collaborative team work.

In keeping with the workings of the creative process, successful leaders combine a clear sense of purpose with operational processes that allow individuals and groups to freely connect with one another. A certain degree of chaos is always present within creative work and in other situations where outcomes cannot be planned in advance. We work together in mutually supportive ways and learn to trust that when we open ourselves to conflicts and unexpected forces, the overall process will carry us to new and often better places.

Creative outcomes formed through this dynamic process owe their power and relevance to the fact that they have been shaped by the free interplay of the key ideas, forces, and people that constitute the overall community. As Mike described through his experiences, there is always a sensitive interplay between the leader's complementary commitments to control and liberation. Effective leaders understand and respect this subtle process of creation and apply their skills to furthering it. Sometimes the leader presents a challenging idea or a criticism with the goal of motivating others to act in different and new ways. At other times the leader coordinates others in an orchestral fashion, channeling the resources of a community toward mutual creation. When more controlling leaders tell people what to do and insist that they operate in strict accordance with directives, the creative resources and energies of the group are often sacrificed. This type of leadership fears the loss of control and perceives differences of opinion as fragmentation.

In environments focused completely on control, spontaneous interactions among participants may be perceived as harmful and chaotic. These highly controlled settings perhaps find fulfillment in carefully regulated procedures and orderly systems. There is little commitment to encouraging contrasting positions to influence one another and find their way to a new synthesis.

Tightly controlled systems have been more the rule than the exception throughout history; and they are plentiful today, attesting to the needs that groups have for order and clear procedures. As a person working in a leadership role, I take order very seriously and find it to be inseparable from creative freedom. Taking either to an extreme creates problems in group and community life.

SHIRLEY
We Need to Delegate More to the Environment

After speaking to Mike about the relationship between control and freedom in the creativity workshops he leads, I wanted to examine whether similar principles apply to leading groups of young children. Shirley, a third-grade teacher, talks about how she deals with leadership issues in her classroom and the extent to which she needs to control the environment in order to further the creative expressions of the children.

"My classroom promotes both control and liberation," Shirley says. "The students work together constantly. As a teacher, I have to establish a safe and orderly environment as the most essential condition; but the controls serve creative freedom. The children require reliable surroundings in order to naturally express themselves. I also believe that control and organization within the classroom environment help the children achieve harmony and discipline within themselves. It's my job to create this space that supports and guides them."

"The creation of a space that helps people realize their potential is something that leaders ideally achieve," I say.

"It's what I try to do every day in the third grade," Shirley says.

"We can look in lofty places for illustrations of leadership, but maybe the third grade is a good place to start," I propose.

"There are twenty-two children in my class," Shirley replies, "and I have to relate to them as a group and as individuals. I set goals for the overall achievement of the group, and in recent years I've been required to prepare the children for tests designed to assure a certain level of competence in basic subjects. But in addition to organizing the classroom to help all the children meet these objectives, I focus on finding ways to connect to the interests and talents of the individual child. We become a stronger and more interesting group when the children are able to distinguish themselves as individuals."

"Does relating to the individual take time and lots of energy?" I ask.

"I can't operate in any other way," Shirley responds. "Each child is an endless reservoir of discovery for me. The work is difficult when the channels between the individual children and me are blocked, when the children are not interacting harmoniously. When the environment is constructed properly and things are operating in an optimal way, the work seems effortless; everything falls together, and it feels as if the children teach themselves and one another. There have been times when I tried too hard with my lesson plans and teaching techniques, and these initiatives interrupted the flow of the children's learning."

"It is fascinating and challenging," I reply, "to think that the environment has more of an impact on children than teachers. Of course, teachers and leaders are responsible for creating the milieu; but it is sobering to think that the environment operates as a relatively autonomous force."

"I am very aware of this in my teaching," Shirley says. "I can't be everywhere and in constant contact with each individual child. But all of the children are potentially in a learning relationship with the classroom as a whole. Even now I need to work further on stepping back, observing more, and allowing the classroom milieu to do its work."

"Leadership," I reply, "requires a focus on the entire spectrum of action taking place within a given place."

"I agree," Shirley continues. "We teachers all too often make the mistake of concentrating on ourselves as the source of learning and feel that we have to be constantly directing the learning process. This results in a tendency to assume that all of the children are in the same place. We speak to them as a single unit and miss the individual. Teachers need to work more at designing learning environments that operate without their constant direction. We have to delegate more to the environment and learn how to step back and let it do its work."

"Teaching and all forms of leading," I answer, "are subtle art forms. We have to learn when to move forward and when to step back. The psychoanalyst D. W. Winnicott described how progress was often hindered by his interventions and clever interpretations of what a person said. He decided that it was his job to create an environment that acts upon people. 'If only we can wait,' he said, people find meaning for themselves in a more creative and pleasurable way. But we need to insert ourselves and our ideas at the right times."

"Of course I intervene, set group and individual goals, demonstrate, organize, and hold individuals accountable," Shirley continues. "Yet, honestly, I have to say that what I do is only part of the way the overall environment acts upon people. I think that the biggest mistake made by teachers, and perhaps by leaders as well, is thinking that everything depends upon what they do, that everything flows directly from their plans. I have to admit that many of the best things that happen in a classroom occur in spite of what I do or plan. Thank goodness I can see this and give the credit to the children when it happens. It's affirming to them and a source of fulfillment for me. I know that I have a part to play in it all, but it is enough that I am just a participant. I don't need more."

"Teachers and leaders who need to control everything," I say, "don't leave room for this to occur."

"That's right," Shirley says. "Everything has to fit into their playbooks and lesson plans. We still train teachers in this way, and schools place such heavy emphasis on lesson plans that it tends to be the unusual teacher who is crazy enough to do all the extra work I do with the space."

"When you speak about teachers stepping back and letting go of the controls, I think about what happened with the free schools and the open classrooms of the early 1970s. Wasn't that period characterized by chaos?"

"It was," Shirley asserts, "because there is more to creating a learning environment than simply eliminating rows of desks and letting anything happen. The chaos was the result of an absence of order and planning in the environment. The classroom has to open up the different channels of learning in individual children. A great deal of care and creativity goes into planning the environment so that it acts upon children in a positive way."

"Schools have focused almost exclusively," I say, "on the written lesson plan and very little on what the physical space does, how people interact within it, and how the total environment works."

Shirley continues: "My husband is a football coach, and I can just imagine him trying to operate without watching the game, just looking at his playbook. Teachers, on the other hand, are expected to slavishly follow lesson plans, with little or no regard for what happens in the room with the children. My husband believes in careful planning; but once the players are out on the field, he has to improvise, engaging what is happening in the moment."

"But there are so many classroom environments," I respond, "where control is an absolute value. What is that all about?"

"Unfortunately," Shirley replies, "control becomes the end and the means, rather than just one of the ingredients required to support more complete learning."

"From what you have said, there also appears to be a reluctance or inability to recognize multiple perspectives on situations," I say.

"Yes, absolutely," Shirley declares. "But there is an even greater aversion to allowing different things to happen at the same time. The traditional model of the teacher as leader has been profoundly linear. There is a constant emphasis on one thing happening at a time. My classroom is designed to encourage simultaneous action."

"It seems that the classroom environment needs to correspond in some way to what we want to teach," I say. "Is there one thing that you emphasize as a priority in your classroom?"

"Participation," Shirley answers.

"I agree with you. In my different leadership roles, the most basic task is to get people actively involved and contributing to whatever needs to be done. The organization is defined by what people do within it every day. The interplay is everything."

"More has to be done with this in our classrooms," Shirley insists. "We have to make learning reflect what is required for success in society. Three things come to mind. First, the students have to be engaged and motivated. They also have to take responsibility for their learning and realize that the outcomes of what they do or do not do will affect other people, as well as themselves. And, most importantly, they have to coordinate their actions with those of other people. We have neglected these aspects of teamwork in our classrooms."

"Teaching according to prearranged directives has a different effect I assume?"

"Whatever you do in the classroom will influence the process of the child's thinking," Shirley says.

"That's a sobering thought," I say. "The mind is shaped by what it does and what it perceives. Exclusive emphasis on standardization, direction, and control might form consciousness with little tolerance for creativity."

Shirley continues: "This is one of the reasons why I give so much attention to making the classroom into a stimulating and engaging place that arouses curiosity. I was a physics major in college. The quantum view of the world impressed me. In my third-grade classroom, I see how the action of an individual child has effects that reverberate throughout the group. The interdependence of life-forms also appealed to me as a student. When I apply these principles to my classroom, I see that we need varied and vital contributions from all members of the group in order to realize our creative potential."

"It sounds demanding."

"Yes," Shirley says, "it is a heck of a lot more work to lead an environment like this, but I can't operate in any other way. I personally need the stimulation, so I don't see myself as someone terribly altruistic. It takes huge amounts of energy from me; but when it's working well, it gives more back. It's a circulating system. Physics again. I see over and over that there is an underlying order to it all."

Can you imagine yourself running a classroom like the one Shirley describes? Can you tolerate many different things happening simultaneously in a room? How do you feel when

you are a participant in a group like this? Are you able to let
things happen spontaneously? Do you believe that human
systems are self-regulating? What is the role of the leader in
relation to control? Do participants in groups have
responsibilities in relation to control and order? Can an or-
ganization or community of people realize its collective
potential for creativity when all systems are subjected to
strict controls?

Shirley's third-grade classroom offers many lessons about the role
of leaders in furthering the creativity of others. Her descriptions of
the classroom space expand the discourse on leadership to include
the use of the physical environment as a source of motivation and
control as well as a vital contributor to the shaping of new ideas.

I was intrigued by Shirley's idea of delegating authority to the environment. Her vision of leadership includes much more than what
the person in charge does with people. My experience as an artist indicates that we are always creating with the world, never in complete
isolation. Shirley's dialogue helps me see how leaders similarly make
use of the total context in which they work.

Mike's commitment to training people to take more responsibility
for their creative discovery without relying on recipes from leaders
corresponds closely to Shirley's emphasis on children's freedom to simultaneously explore different directions in their learning. In both
cases it is assumed that participants will be initiating activities and
exploring ideas that extend beyond the immediate plans of the person
in charge of the environment. Yet the leader does carefully manage a
setting that provides both inspiration and guidance to all involved.

This type of creative space requires a new vision of leadership, one
that cultivates self-regulating forces within individuals and groups.
While maintaining the responsibilities and powers of authority, leaders simultaneously delegate them to everyone in the community. In a
creative system, people support one another both in letting things
happen spontaneously and in maintaining control. The idea of linear
leadership no longer corresponds to science, the dynamics of creativity, or group participation.

In my experience, leaders are primarily distinguished from others by the responsibility they have for viewing and running the whole field of participation in a group or organization. Yet the task of managing the complex interplay that takes place between the forces of control and liberation in a group is beyond the scope of what one person can do alone. Leaders and participants have to explore new ways of interacting with one another. The ultimate goal of this new participation will be a deep trust in the intelligence and creativity of human systems, a trust that only experience can bring.

Build a Culture that Supports the Creative Process

After three decades of training people to work with the creative process, I can say unequivocally that we learn about creativity through our own experience with it. Professional training programs preparing people to work creatively with others must make personal creative work a priority in their course of studies. It is remarkable how little attention graduate programs give to enhancing the creative expression of future leaders. Similarly, students do not realize how the cultivation of creative sensibilities will benefit their future performance.

Even if opportunities are provided for experimentation with the creative process during a person's professional training, an ongoing personal relationship with creative practice is necessary if we are to stay attuned to the dynamics of creative imagination. We will be more effective in transmitting creative energy to others and supporting their creative initiatives if we are personally involved with the process. Art teachers, creative arts therapists, editors, and others whose work is focused on furthering the creative expression of others know how personal creative expression enhances their work; but they often find it difficult to make the time or muster the energy to stay actively engaged with art making.

Has there been a relationship between your personal creative expression and your creativity at work? Does your work environment offer you opportunities for personal creative expression? Do you make time for creative activities outside of your work environment? If you are not involved in personal creative expression at work, do you know someone who is? Do you see ways that this involvement influences his or her impact on others? Do you know colleagues who are involved in creative activities outside of the workplace? Do you see their creative practice having an influence on what they do at work?

If you are not involved in personal creative activity inside or outside the workplace, why is this? Is there anything you can do to change the situation? Can you recall times in your life when you were immersed in the creative process? How did this affect your work in other areas and your relationships with others? Imagine how you will influence others if you are more involved in creative activity.

As Eleanor described earlier, the inability to find time for practice is a major obstacle when it comes to significantly advancing the place of creative expression in the workplace and in our daily lives. However, if creativity becomes a priority within organizational life, time will be made for its cultivation. This will only happen when leaders realize that providing opportunities for personal creative expression in the workplace makes it more appealing and productive. To reach this conclusion, leaders must undergo personal experiences with creativity; this process will form the basis of the new organizational culture.

Imagine the changes that will occur in the workplace if the creative vitality of organizations is viewed as a responsibility of leaders, if leaders are expected to have an understanding of the creative process as a prerequisite for the work they do. Leaders may not be capable of doing this by themselves. The people who are served by organizations and who work in them can find ways to bring this awareness to the workplace. Perhaps it also starts in training programs, where a new vision of organizational life and productivity can be put into action. Leaders, and those who aspire to leadership positions, will always do what they have to do in order to succeed. Perhaps putting creative outcomes into job descriptions and curriculum requirements will change entrenched behaviors and attitudes.

Even though leaders must have experience with the creative process in order to foster it in others, the practice of leadership can be likened more to the role of coach than that of primary player. So often organizations are constructed around the creative activities of leaders, and workers serve as instruments, simply carrying out plans from above.

The leader who cultivates the creativity of others serves as a guide and mentor for a community of people. To do this, leaders must have a personal understanding of the creative process, but they must also be able to put personal visibility aside to make space for the expression of others. The overall performance of others takes on more importance than any particular thing that the leader does. The leader's expertise with creativity is channeled into the creation of community, and the total environment of the organization becomes the object of the leader's creative effort. This focus can be a challenging one for leaders who have advanced their careers on the merits of their individual actions.

The leader who thrives on attention and adoration will have a difficult time learning that a more self-effacing style enhances the creativity of the total community. Leaders who maintain their positions through absolute control leave no room for others to create. When leaders define their role exclusively in terms of what *they* do, they forfeit the opportunity to advance the creativity of their community as a whole.

The practice of leadership offers an opportunity to advance a new post-narcissistic practice of creativity. In art, psychology, and leadership, the past century has been characterized by a one-sided emphasis on the self. In contrast, the larger perspective of history indicates that creative exuberance is a quality of communities, places, and particular epochs. We have to declare that a more creative community life is necessary, that we have concentrated too much on individuals, and that this has something to do with our social ills. Who is better positioned to do this than the leaders of our organizations? They can model a more self-effacing way of being in creative relationships with others.

John Cage, one of the leaders of twentieth-century art culture, believed that everything in life was capable of being made into art and that every person could be an artist. In advancing the ubiquitous nature of art, he suggests to a certain extent that artists might cease to exist as a separate group of people. Similar ideas about the nature of art run through the avant-garde schools of the twentieth century, beginning with Marcel Duchamp and Dada. When asked to define what art is, Picasso asked, "What isn't?"

> *What will happen if we begin to think about what we do on the job as art? How do you imagine this expansion and democratization of artistic practice would affect the art world? On a more practical level, where can artistic ideas and practices be most useful within the workplace and organizational life?*

Artists constantly describe how their most fulfilling work is done when they are part of a vital and supportive community. They are invigorated by the energy of other artists; it helps their creativity. The same applies to feelings of fulfillment at work.

> *Reflect upon a situation where you were not able to stand aside and support the expression of another. What made it difficult to let go of center stage? Do you have a need to be constantly visible? Do you think being in the limelight helps or hinders your work with others? If you are a dominating type, imagine yourself as a more invisible presence. How would this change your experience and the performance of others?*
>
> *Does your work environment enable you to support the creativity of others? Do you want to do this? What features of the environment could be changed to allow you to be more effective in supporting others? What are your personal qualities that further the creativity of others? What do you do that restricts their creative expression? What can you change to enable yourself to be more effective?*

The leaders I admire embody the best aspects of their community and represent these traits and energies to the external world. The solitary leader is an oxymoron. A person cannot lead without the participation of others. Leaders from antiquity to the present have been shaped by their relationships with the world. The best among them measured success by how much they helped others to realize their potential and do what they needed to do.

Norm
Everyone in the Organization Has to Be a Leader

I spoke with Norm, a business and psychology professor who worked for twenty years as a manager in the computer industry, about the relationship between the personal creativity of leaders and the creative vitality of their organizations.

"Their creativity is directed toward setting up environments," Norm says. "They try to empower people to take risks, and in order to do this the occasional failure is accepted. Only the heads of organizations can affect people in this way. They have the responsibility to build a culture and a reward structure that supports the creative process. They can also encourage creativity by setting up competition—whoever comes up with the best idea wins, that kind of thing. It churns up creative juices when people reach for the golden ring and then get recognized."

"So creative leaders invent systems," I reply. "I assume they make structures in response to particular needs."

"Absolutely," Norm answers. "They recognize the key skills that are required in their organizations and make sure they are supported. High tech can't do anything unless engineers are creative and turning out new products, so the skills of the engineer are valued highest in this type of organization. They are regarded even higher than management. A 'hierarchy of the professional' is created so these people don't have to manage to achieve status. The same applies to professors, medical doctors, and journalists."

"How does the personality of the leader support creativity?" I ask.

"They have to set an example. At Digital Equipment Company, Ken Olson made himself accessible to the ordinary employee. He tried to keep his office open. In many organizations, the middle management stops the flow of communication. There has to be upward and downward communication. Olson invited people into his office from all levels of the organization to create this flow of information."

"The principle of flow is often raised in conversations I have with people about creativity in organizational life," I reply. "Creativity, in the personal and collective realms alike, appears to be based on a vital and open circulation of energy. One of my students likes to quote the painter Ad Reinhardt, who said, 'Art disease is a hardening of the categories.' Your description of fluid communications involving all levels of an organization affirms the idea that creativity is based upon unfettered flow."

"Communication cannot flow in only one direction," Norm adds. "It has to move around the total environment, gather the best ideas from everybody, and then make them accessible to people. When people at the top respectfully listen to and acknowledge what comes up from below, everyone feels a sense of belonging; and this collegial atmosphere becomes one of greatest strengths of the organization. This circulation of communication is characteristic of creative environments."

"And healthy ones too." I interject.

"That quote about the hardening of the categories is on target," Norm says. "It applies to business as well as art."

"How was Ken Olson creative?" I ask. "How did he set examples?"

"He was a risk taker in many ways, and he certainly encouraged others to be bold and to take risks. That was rewarded in the organization. Leaders have to realize that they can't do everything. They have to create situations where they are unnecessary. Everyone in the organization has to be a leader, and Olson saw his job as turning them into leaders. Very often people would do upward delegation to Olson; he would pass it back and say, 'You solve it.' He could not have everyone looking to him to solve problems. All of the other bosses then start to do the same thing, emulating the leader's behavior."

"Is this a form of operant conditioning?

"It's about values rather than conditioning. It's letting people know the purpose and beliefs of an organization and expecting them to act in ways that are consistent with the belief structure. There is an old saying that applies to this: 'Believe what I do and not what I say.' If there is an inconsistency, everyone picks right up on it. People learn by watching what happens. They place more value on this than what a leader says. The leader's actions have to be consistent with the values of the organization. There are many leaders who talk about empowering people and sometimes praise them; but in the end, these leaders put themselves in the spotlight and take credit for organizational accomplishments."

"Recognition seems to mean a lot when it comes to encouraging creativity," I say.

"Yes," Norm answers, "and it is a major function of the leader to give this to people."

"The leader must cultivate a certain degree of selflessness?"

"They need to show a concern for what others do and then expect this to become essential to the culture of the organization. If leaders have ideas that inspire them, they have to surround themselves with people who share the ideas and who will communicate them to the organization."

"If I want to encourage creativity as a leader," I reply, "how I act in relation to others might have more impact than anything else I do. The leader sets the tone of an environment. We think of leaders today in terms of strategic plans and decisions that are made from afar. We don't pay enough attention to how interpersonal chemistry affects people."

Norm continues: "Olson traveled coach, even though he was running one of the most important companies in the United States. He couldn't go first-class and expect his employees to save money. He modeled the values of the organization completely. People trusted him. He encouraged people to seek him out and not be intimidated by his power. This is a problem leaders often have. They might go around talking to people, but the workers are careful what they say to them. There is a suspicion that leaders will use the information to advance their own interests rather than those of the group, and there is a fear that leaders might hurt people with the information. So they tell the emperor that he has a suit on."

"It's the old situation of telling the people in charge what they want to hear," I say.

"Organizations then set up procedures that block feedback, that thwart learning," Norm replies.

"Doesn't it all depend upon whether or not the leader is an avid learner?" I ask. "Someone who can't tolerate stereotypic behavior? Someone who takes delight in the critical and imaginative people within a community? Someone more interested in receiving fresh insights than compliments?"

"Yes," Norm answers. "They are never satisfied themselves, never at rest, and they value these qualities in others. They know that life is complex and that proposed solutions never work the way they are supposed to. They accept ambiguity and uncertainty. And while they may try to reduce uncertainty, they know they will never get rid of it. They don't want what Olson called 'MBA answers.' Leaders typically have a built-in crap detector. They know when an answer is too pat, too simple, when people are reluctant to move into the unknown and explore new possibilities. This is sounding like the way an artist thinks and acts."

"Yes," I say, "artists push at the edges of experience. If we operate exclusively within the realm of what we already know, we are not learning. You see people who can't express themselves outside an established formula. I am very sensitive to this type of stock expression, the equivalent of what you described as 'MBA answers.' I admire the artists who are always venturing into the unknown."

"The problem is how we deal with unpredictability," Norm answers.

"The poet John Keats described 'negative capability' as the ability to deal with uncertainty. It applies as much to leadership as it does to art," I propose. "This conversation is making me realize that there is a correspondence between the mind of the creative artist and that of the creative leader; a restlessness, a constant search."

"Creative leaders begin with the assumption that the existing solutions aren't adequate," Norm says. "They want to see people discussing problems and exploring different possibilities, because they know there are no easy solutions."

"As we discuss these characteristics of the creative leader, I realize that they are not common. Even people who value imagination, who consider themselves to be 'creative types,' often tend toward regularity, repetition of what works, and, most of all, ensuring that they are always in control," I say. "It's a rare person who thrives on the conditions you describe. Leaders certainly are not trained in this way. I can imagine leadership training that resembles the challenging psychological conditions that Marine platoon leaders or Navy Seals undergo. If we want to change primary instincts, we have to work directly with them. I can imagine spontaneity and creative expression exercises that will challenge people as much, or more, than a Spartan physical regime. Being able to thrive in an environment of constant change and uncertainty goes contrary to instincts of the average person. I don't know many leaders who encourage their communities to question everything and who are open to constant self-assessment. A deep commitment to the creative process is not common in leadership."

"Not everyone rises through the ranks because they are creative," Norm responds. "Many organizations are political and dominated by rigid bureaucracy, and their leaders put these values above creativity; they reward loyalty to the status quo more than questioning it and adding to the existing values. People are expected to delegate upward so the leader can solve all of the problems."

"Classic hierarchy and control," I say.

"This is welcomed in many places. The tendency in most organizations is to be uncreative. Leaders rise by manipulating the system to their advantage."

"Perhaps most organizations reward and promote people who are contra-creative," I speculate.

"All organizations have a built-in problem," Norm answers. "The tendency is to look for predictability and to value it. The manager who moves up is the one who is predictable. Someone may be destroying an organization on the way up by getting the job done in a predictable way. Leaders have to guard against destructive trends, like only turning out numbers. Most organizations are numbers-driven, thus creating conditions that limit growth and the ability of the organization to adapt to the environment."

"There is definitely a dark side to leadership," I say, "an appeal to base emotions in order to direct people. I remember my father saying to me, 'People understand fear, and they respond to it.'"

"For many managers, fear and anger are powerful tools," Norm answers. "People will work hard to escape from it. Fear drives out other emotions. It is a major part of the survival instinct. When an organization is structured around fear, it is hard to bring anything else in. It makes people move. Fear motivates and gets people to do things that they don't want to do. There are few chances to pose problems differently when an environment is ruled by fear. People act in ways that will be approved. They act quickly, often too quickly when many problems need time. You act in a shortsighted fashion and do things that you know are not the right things to do."

"Because survival is a moment-to-moment process," I say. "You act in order to live another day rather than do something that might be the best response to the problem."

"I don't think managers are aware of the extent to which they create situations where fear is the driving emotion," Norm reflects. "People are forced into the 'C.Y.A.' response, protecting themselves rather than creating. Human nature is complex, and we are motivated by many emotions."

"And yet fear is sometimes necessary," I reply. "We need all of the emotions."

"Managers can't always dwell on the positive side of human nature when the quickest and most powerful tool might be fear. The good news is that it gets things done, and there are situations where everyone's survival in an organization depends on immediate and forceful action."

"Fear certainly has its place," I say. "But environments become pathological when fear is constant and dominant, especially when there are no real threats from the outside. One of my colleagues calls it 'the power of negative thinking.' There are many leaders who provoke constant crisis as a mode of control. They create the problems and then solve them."

Norm continues: "A certain amount of fear and trembling gets the juices going, but when pervasive it causes people to act irrationally. It creates a kind of martial order and stops people from participating in the solutions."

"What you call pervasive fear in an environment shuts down creativity."

"Fear becomes a U-shaped curve," Norm replies. "Going down the 'U,' good things can happen; and then it turns backward in debilitating ways. People start getting protective, then move in coun-terproductive directions. It's hard to be creative when you are wor-ried about being fired."

"Leaders have their own fear," I say. "Some use fear as a source of personal motivation, while others pass it on to other people and let them deal with it. Fear has an important place within the creative process. The effective leader has to be able to entertain fear in much the same way that they embrace uncertainty. Bad things happen when leaders are paralyzed by fear or transfer their fears onto other people without dealing with them."

"It's the strongest of our emotions, and it can be easily manipu-lated. Does fear contribute to creative expression?" Norm asks.

"A poet friend was just speaking to me about the important place that fear has within her work," I respond. "She explained the edge that fear provides, the way it arouses deep emotions and im-ages that inform her writing. Actors also describe how they worry if they are not frightened before a performance. Nerves activate and stir up all of our resources that might otherwise go to sleep. The fear is useful if it is channeled into creative expression. Those who try to banish fear altogether are kidding themselves, and they over-look a source of creative power. When fear shuts us down or forces us to act abruptly, without making use of our other faculties, then it creates serious problems. We see these negative aspects of fear in people who are petrified when given the opportunity to express themselves in creative ways and in those who isolate themselves from other people. They lose the energy and power that comes from relationships."

"Separating people from one another," Norm interjects, "is the best way to limit their collective strength."

"Maybe we distance ourselves from our fears," I reply, "as a way of avoiding their power to bring change. Perhaps the creative leaders you describe dread complacency, and they do something positive with the fear every day. How does a person work at cultivating the qualities required for creative leadership?"

"Everything depends upon the openness a person has to learn-ing," Norm answers. "There has to be an ability to give up old pat-terns when they are no longer appropriate to new situations. Leaders can't get stuck in the paradigms that guided them in previous achievements. If they use old solutions in dealing with new problems, they will make mistakes. There needs to be constant openness to the environment. You have to respond to the problem at hand and look at how it is different rather than how it is the same."

"People describe how creative organizations have an open atmosphere," I add.

"It's essential for the creative organization to be responsive to the outside world. Most organizations aren't," Norm answers. "Their vision is turned inward. They respond to internal situations. They don't keep an eye on the outside, where nothing stands still. You can't have a successful and creative organization where the emphasis is on staying the same and where everyone focuses on how to play the game within the company. IBM had to go outside for a leader, because one could not be found inside. Everyone was too accustomed to the established way of doing things. They didn't have the ability to lead the company through a process of major change. The hardest thing that leaders do is keep their organizations externally focused; when it comes to everyday interactions with people, leaders have an essentially internal focus."

"Leaders must live in two worlds," I say, "and move between them, never being exclusively inside or outside."

"Yes," Norm continues. "It's a great challenge because leaders have to take good care of the inside of their organizations. It takes a lot to maintain this dual focus."

"The leader has to be able to see the entire field," I add. "The community needs to be grounded in itself, yet always capable of getting outside of itself."

"The critical thing is keeping an organization open to learning," Norm asserts. "You learn by trying things out and seeing what happens. We have to learn from our mistakes. It's amazing how many organizations don't even learn by aversive conditioning, the 'hot plate' lesson. An individual, a team, or the organization as a whole gets 'burned' as a result of some action, and still they take the same route, touching the 'hot plate' again."

"In many aspects of life we persist in our behaviors, even when they hurt us."

"The leader has to create an environment where this doesn't happen," Norm insists. "Investors want predictability, as do boards of directors, and this drives leaders to create predictable systems. People inside want it too. But organizations are never going to be totally predictable. If they are too predictable, bad things happen. You can only be predictable when you ignore complexity."

"The same thing happens with creative expression," I say. "Artists often feel contrary pressures. Most creative artists have to produce outcomes that satisfy people and yet avoid superficiality. The serious artist has to maintain the integrity of the search."

"Leaders encounter this challenge too," Norm replies. "They lose face when their organizations do not produce predictable results, but the world does not let itself be easily predicted; and when the focus is only on the predictable, you become maladapted to the external environment."

"The leader has to hold the tension between the extremes, balancing results with constant inquiry and innovation," I say. "There has to be respect for the different positions and an ability to make them work together. I constantly see how people who are not in leadership roles have a tendency to look at problems and issues from only one perspective, their own—actually all too many leaders do this too. The leader must be able to let go of a personal position and view the entire scene.

"This way of looking at things can be defined as the basis of the creative process, the ability to shift among various points of view and to open to new possibilities. This is what creative artists do, and scientists."

"Creative leaders have to do it too," Norm says. "They have to act. They can't get caught in the paralysis that comes from overanalyzing the different points of view. People who wait for inspiration never get anything done. It's the process of activity, moving in a particular direction, that helps you discover what the answers are."

Do you agree that leaders should serve the creativity of others by acting as "keepers" of the environment? Have you ever experienced leaders who see themselves as having this role? In relation to the issues described by Norm, how would

*you characterize your work setting? Do leaders create
environments that support the creativity of others? How do
they do this? How can they be more effective in supporting
the creativity of others?*

Norm's statement that everybody within an organization has to be a leader presents an important challenge both to official leaders and other people in the organization. Just as my group therapy supervisor said to me long ago, "Never assume that a gathering of people is a group," we cannot assume that people with high-level positions are leaders.

Leadership can occur spontaneously among peers or be formally designated through official roles. Sometimes those placed in positions of authority are poorer leaders than their subordinates. Leadership is a way of being in relationship to others. Some people find themselves functioning as leaders without ever taking on a formal role of any kind.

*Think of those people in your work environment who lead
without having a formal leadership position. What is it
about them that makes this possible? What do you admire
about them? How might leaders learn from them? What
traits do they have that leaders might adopt?
Do you agree with Norm's description of how the
personal qualities of the leader affect the creativity of others?
Are there qualities of leaders that you feel are essential to
supporting the creative expression of others?*

Norm's statements about fear evoke important issues related to creative motivation. In my work helping people to become more creative, I have generally taken the approach of trying to rid students of their fear of expression. This attempt to free the environment of one of our most powerful sources of creative energy may have negative consequences.

A colleague describes the usefulness of fear: "Fear can be great. It encourages and sometimes forces me to do things I might otherwise not want to do."

Like any other powerful tool or medicine, fear has to be engaged carefully, with an attentive eye on its positive and negative effects. From the boardroom to the studio, risk taking is universally recognized as an essential feature of every form of creative activity. Fear helps us calculate risks in a realistic way. As my colleague says, "Fear doesn't have to be frightening. It can be healthy and safe."

> *Has fear ever had a positive effect upon your creative expression? Do you believe that it has an important role in the workplace? Recall the last time you experienced fear at work. What effect did it have on you? Are you apt to do things that create fear in others? Do you do this intentionally? Are you comfortable with these actions? If not, how can you change them?*
>
> *To what extent have you taken risks in your work environment? What has been the outcome? Do you support others in taking risks? Can you do more to support others? Are you as supportive of risk takers when they take positions opposed to you?*

Like the arts, leadership is a discipline perfected through practice and direct experience. Experiential training both in leading and in being led are essential in perfecting the skills needed to lead others. Through experience we discover our personal leadership styles and learn how they resemble and differ from the styles of others. The Socratic charge to "know thyself" is a pillar of leadership. It is equally important to know others and understand what they need in order to succeed.

In preparing for leadership, it is essential to identify both positive and negative role models that will help form your own way of working with people. Don't be afraid to deviate from standard principles; cultivate your own unique interests and methods as a leader. Leaders who work from their natural way of being with people tend to be grounded and resourceful in times of change and crisis; they are not playing roles that contradict their primary responses to situations and environments.

Effective leadership also requires you to be keenly aware of your bad habits and behaviors, those that have negative effects on people. Leadership training should be a process of self-discovery. So few of the people leading today's organizations have ever experienced anything like this in their formal education.

I have always been amazed how the majority of people that I supervise have great difficulty in identifying their weaknesses as leaders. They are able to write down pages describing strengths, but an honest assessment of weaknesses often draws a blank. I tell them that they will receive much better evaluations from me if they can openly assess areas that need work.

"You will show more insight and ability to manage yourself toward change if you can do this," I say. "You need to be in charge of your own self-evaluation and learning process. I will help you with it. How can you assess and lead others if you don't practice this on yourself? What is it that you want to become? Where are you in relation to that goal? How do the people in your division view you as a leader? Can you take a 360-degree look at yourself? Are you open to criticism and willing to change behaviors that interfere with the achievement of common objectives?"

What are your innate leadership qualities? How have they been perfected through experience? What are your bad habits in relation to leading others? Have you tried in a systematic way to change them? How have you become aware of your strengths and weaknesses as a leader? Self-observation? Feedback from others?

What is your leadership ideal? What life experiences, positive and negative, have helped you shaped this vision? How close are you to achieving your ideal?

Have you ever had the opportunity to work closely with leaders who support the creativity of others? What do they do or not do to make this possible? Have you been influenced by them in a lasting way?

Can an uncreative person support the creativity of others? To what extent does the personal creativity of the leader influence others? How do leaders focused primarily on their own creative legacy affect you?

CREATIVE PRACTICE

Leaders who support the creative expressions of others have to develop the ability to let go of constant control. They need to tolerate a certain degree of chaos, be comfortable and confident when facing the unknown, and trust that significant outcomes will emerge. Try the following experiments with spontaneous expressions and performance art to increase your ability to be totally present and focused while exploring uncertainty. The activities can be done alone, with another person acting as a witness, or with a small group.

In leadership training, people can benefit greatly from direct experiences with challenging creative activities that have little direct connection to the agendas of the workplace. In this way we encounter the risks, fears, uncertainties, and formative dynamics of creativity in a more complete way. We can then learn how to apply these principles to the endless scenarios that emerge in our relations with others.

The following practice suggestions also focus on witnessing and responding to the expressions of others. Leaders who learn how to do this effectively will help people in their communities to more completely realize their potential. As a man in one of my studios described, "I was amazed at how I felt when people began to respond with interest to my expressions. We have so much unrealized potential, and we are disconnected from the creative source of life. I feel connected to this source when I am creating in a group with people who support each other. This doesn't happen in politics, and it sure doesn't happen at work."

     Meditate upon a blank sheet of paper; try to empty your mind of all thoughts. Close your eyes. Move spontaneously on the paper with the art materials (markers, pens, oil pastels), thinking only about being as aware as possible of the movements you are making.

Open your eyes, and continue to move in response to the configurations you made on the paper. Let the movements lead you. Follow them with complete attention to their qualities. This exercise will help you to initiate actions in more spontaneous, responsive, and sensitive ways.

⟶ Work with a partner, continuing the previous exercise through teamwork. One person begins by leading with a series of gestures on the paper, and the other follows by responding to them. The leader then takes on the role of following the partner, and vice versa, within the ongoing creation of the picture. Allow the artwork to emerge from the interplay of leaders and followers constantly changing roles. Reflect upon how leading and following grow out of one another and inform one another. The process requires a sustained responsiveness and sensitivity to the exchange of expression.

Practice this exercise with different materials—clay configurations, constructions with sticks and other natural materials—and experience the way different media influence the interplay.

⟶ Together with a partner, take turns doing five-minute performance-art pieces in which one person acts and the other witnesses. The performances should be focused on a simple theme, with the goal of being totally present and open to letting expressions emerge just the way they did in the previous drawing exercises. I tell participants that the only mistake they can make is to plan what they are going to do in advance.

The performers select a theme, what objects they will use, and how they will present themselves; everything else emerges organically from the event. This is a very challenging task for leaders who are used to choreographing and orchestrating what people do.

I tell participants that depth in a performance is usually tied to establishing a simple focus that furthers a sense of concentration and presence. In Chapter 6, I described the simple exercise of pouring water from a pitcher to a bowl. This activity might be enacted in a performance exploring the processes of letting go and of receiving and holding.

One of the most memorable performances I have seen involved a woman with long hair that was always tied tightly in a bun. She let down her hair in an intimate way, spent time combing the hair, and then gathered it up again in a bun. The group watching the piece was transfixed.

Another performance involved a man being taped to a metal chair with masking tape. He could have easily broken through his bonds, but in the piece he enacted the struggle of pushing to the edge of release while staying bound to the chair. Another man enacted a scene of carrying many things that he could not let go of. His continued holding of the cumbersome objects, embodying themes of tension and balance, had a strong impact on the audience.

In another performance, a woman came on stage with a bundle of sticks, arranged them in a circular configuration around her, sat quietly for a few minutes in the center, uttered a gentle chant, gathered the sticks again, and left the stage empty.

In all of these pieces the structure is simple; the performance unfolds as a way of being present within the situation, letting the expressions emerge from one another without plans of any kind. There is typically some fear aroused by doing these things in front of other people, but we find that attentive and empathetic witnessing furthers the energy of the performances. Doing things that involve a sense of uncertainty and no awareness of what the final outcome will be also heightens fear. In my work with groups, individuals do performances with all of the participants acting as a supportive audience.

Paying close attention to another person and giving feedback is an important part of the overall method. When the atmosphere is highly focused and compassionate, the giving of feedback is experienced as sustaining the energy of the performance.

We learn how to be present in a situation, how to let events emerge, and how to hold the space for the expression of others. Most important, we discover that if we are truly involved and committed, something significant always happens. The focus shifts from making things happen to letting them emerge and paying careful attention to what they convey.

It is a great and unusual luxury to receive the total attention and support of other people. When this happens, we discover how much we need this kind of interaction with others and how it contributes to building the creative environment that Norm described.

9

CREATING FROM THE HARD PLACES

The Creative Process and Healing Are Inseparable

Creative energy flows through every environment as blood courses through our bodies and sap rises in the trunks of trees. When the circulation of creative energy is blocked and diminished, the environment loses life-sustaining nourishment. When negative and harmful forces arrest the free movement of energy, the same thing happens within our bodies, relationships, families, and organizations. Traditional Chinese medicine teaches that vital energy, called *ch'i*, moves through paths or meridian lines within the body. Since obstructions to the flow are perceived as causes of illness, therapeutic treatment focuses on restoring the natural movement.

In individuals, relationships, groups, and organizations, healing occurs when the circulation of creative energy is restored. This is often achieved by transforming the negative and disturbing energy into an affirmation of life. Momentum shifts, and energy builds in a positive way. As we see so clearly in athletic events, positive momentum has considerable power. Healing environments cultivate this creative energy and help people to open themselves to it.

The creative process and healing are inseparable. They both transform problems and tensions into affirmations of life. Healing is different from curing. Whereas the latter eradicates symptoms, the former involves attitudinal changes, learning how to live with problems and even to use them in some creative way. Healing also entails accepting the conditions of our lives, appreciating what we have, letting go of complaints, realizing that we are not alone in our difficulties, and feeling connected to the whole of experience. Organizational life depends as much on the dynamics of healing as it does upon creation.

The healing process requires acceptance of what is happening at the present moment, while letting go of the need to control every aspect of our lives. In this respect, healing involves a compassionate embrace of life as it is. Compassion allows us to realize that others share our suffering. Healing emanates from the realization that we are not alone, that we are part of a larger community dealing with the challenges of life. This understanding takes us beyond ourselves and connects us to the creative energy that moves through life. In this way, the greatest threats to our existence affirm our participation in the human community and its ongoing circulation of creative energy. These vulnerabilities help us to transcend our limited individual perspective.

This assent to our condition does not mean we abandon the desire to change and transform our circumstances. Rather, acceptance of what exists is a necessary condition of creative transformation. In *The Birth of Tragedy,* Nietzsche describes how art heals by turning "nauseous thoughts about the horror or absurdity of existence into notions with which one can live" and by affirming that life is ultimately "powerful and pleasurable." Our life situations are what they are, and the creative process enables us to live with them in new ways. If we bring creative energy and a life-affirming spirit to difficult situations, this condition is contagious. Others are influenced and inspired.

The deep, healing movements of creation differ from attempts to attack symptoms and eliminate them through control and domination. Creative energy requires a complete mix of life's essential ingredients—unpleasant states as well as pleasant states, tension as well as calm. Therefore, healing approaches that embrace only the "light," in an attempt to dispel the "dark," limit the powers of creative transformation.

There is a respected place on the palette of creative expression for dark and brooding colors that take us to the essential depths of our earthly and physical experience. Be wary of those who advise reflection exclusively on the bright hues of the air and sky. We need the complete spectrum of colors and emotions in order to bring all of our resources to bear on the task at hand.

As the world's many spiritual traditions teach, the toxin is the antitoxin, problems are opportunities, breaking apart is essential to new creation, and the fall always precedes the resurrection. Darkness and light are necessary partners, and a realistic perspective on creativity welcomes all the aspects of our lives. The complete range of our life experiences is necessary to activate the transforming powers of creation.

The Power of Disturbance

Creation can be defined as an original act of imagination that brings something into existence. It is a desire and innate drive to make new connections between things, to give form, and to transform. The newness of creation may simply be a fresh perspective on a habitual or troubling situation. Creativity enables us to view every moment as new. As I have emphasized throughout this book, our perception of things is the ultimate source of creative vitality: it allows us to use every instant of experience as an opening to new ways of viewing the world. It may take a long time to realize that the person or situation that disturbs us the most might be the one that could have the greatest impact on our ability to make positive and creative changes. Nothing generates energy more effectively than tension and discomfort. The challenge of the creative process is to harness this potential power and use it to benefit others and ourselves.

The first prerequisite for transforming conflict and tension is the ability to change our perception of troubling or habitual situations. The second requirement is being able to identify the creative potential latent in these situations. The third, and formative, factor is the ability to act in a way that demonstrates that the best things about life can emerge from irritating or difficult situations. When experiential outcomes help us to see the opportunities created by problems we fight and deny, the third step may precede the first and the second. Many of us stumble upon these discoveries, realizing only afterward that difficult phases in our lives are necessary conditions of creation.

> *Have your greatest achievements come easily? Or did they emerge from adversity? In keeping with the evolutionary transformations of nature, the creative process may require conflict and tension that push us into new ways of relating to the world. Is it possible to create without a certain amount of destruction? Do you believe that something must always be let go before new life can emerge?*

When Existential Discontents Grow Out of Proportion

The simplest and most ordinary activities can offer opportunities for healing and creative transformation. I recently met with a group of colleagues and found myself immersed in discontents and thoughts about all of the things that were going wrong in my work. Immediately after this session, I made a site visit to a first-year undergraduate student who was doing an internship in the art room of a Montessori school.

I walked into a fourth-grade art class and sat down with a group of children who were engrossed in a project that the intern was leading. They were making art books by folding a long piece of paper into eight or ten overlapping pages. The intern asked the children to make a sequence of drawings in which an object is gradually transformed into something else.

I sat with three girls who were eager to show their work. The girl next to me was making a series of pictures with an accompanying text about how a wooden bridge spanning a stream gradually turns into a dolphin. The pictures were delightful, with the bridge progressively changing frame by frame into the sea creature that dives into the water and freely swims away. I felt my mood changing in the same sequential and transforming manner illustrated by the child, moving from self-absorbed negativity to wonder at what the children were doing.

The teacher and the intern milled about the room offering assistance, but otherwise the children worked completely on their own. I became part of the overall flow of the classroom and felt my discontent being lifted and replaced by appreciation and excitement. The atmosphere of the art room acted upon me.

The intern and teacher were happy that I came to see what they were doing. As I stood talking with them, a line of children formed to show me their work. I came to the school to pay attention to what other people were doing, and they healed and renewed me that day.

This simple visit manifested all of the elements of healing that I described above: becoming part of something larger than yourself, restoring the circulation of creative energy, accepting the conditions of your life and appreciating what you have, letting go of complaints, focusing on another person's situation rather than your own, and transforming negativity into an affirmation of life. In my case, the power of the transformation was augmented by the realization that the pains and discomforts largely owed to my state of mind, something that is very much subject to my control.

Existential discontents can proliferate into major problems if we do not find ways to transform them and view them from a larger and less self-centered viewpoint. Healing, like creativity, is to a great extent a matter of getting outside ourselves and realizing that we are not alone in our difficulties. When we lose this perspective, we often begin to sink under the weight of our own negativity.

Do everyday tensions and conflicts sometimes spiral out of proportion to their actual significance in your life? What is it that you do to augment their influence?

M. L. O'Connor: Art Kept Me Alive

My work with art and healing has exposed me to many situations where people create in response to the most difficult and frightening experiences. Cancer patients and others suffering from life-threatening illnesses have been my teachers with regard to the healing process. Creativity and positive attitudes won't necessarily cure illnesses, but they have potent powers to heal those who are directly and indirectly afflicted by them.

I had the good fortune to work with Mary Louise (M.L.) O'Connor, who founded the Creative Arts Program at the Dana Farber Cancer Institute in Boston. M.L. was diagnosed with metastatic melanoma and told that she had a short time to live. She was an experienced poet, and she started studying expressive arts therapy with a desire to use the arts as a way of helping herself and other cancer patients. Rather than dwelling on the negative aspects of her illness, she immersed herself in the arts and creativity research. Cancer was engaged as a way of going deeper into life and the creative process.

M.L. describes how she first brought the arts to the Dana Farber Cancer Institute: "I decided, well I've studied all this expressive arts therapy; let's see if it works. I kept up with my poetry; and although I'm not an artist, I began to draw the different treatments and how I felt about them. I accessed my unconscious process. Actually, this was not difficult, because I was mostly in unconscious process. It was pretty easy. I just kept working. I would be in the infusion room, and nurses would see me with my oil pastels coloring away as other patients watched me. And the doctors knew about what I was doing. Meanwhile, I was writing my master's thesis on how it felt to be at sea in a place where the beliefs were so completely different.

"As it turned out, my treatments were for the most part successful with a few ups and downs; but even so, the art reflected the downs and the art actually happened before the downs. You could almost go back and look at the whole history of treatment as expressed in the arts. And I put all of this into my master's thesis. When I finally had the thesis compiled, I ended up on a respirator for ten days due to treatment problems. I came out of that and got better; when I was able to speak coherently, I said to my young doctor, 'Can you believe

I earned twelve graduate credits this semester for what I went through?' He gave a big laugh."

"It is significant that your art reflected the downs before they happened. Did other things occur as a result of making art?" I ask.

"The nurses were very interested," M.L. answers. "They were the first to become involved. When I showed them the whole artistic compilation of the particular time period that they had gone through with me, it opened up another dimension. Then the physicians asked for copies, which they used in lectures they gave around the country. They wanted to show what a patient using their particular therapy accomplished while doing their protocols. They hoped to show that their particular protocols, which at that time were vaccines, were not so debilitating. I couldn't have done this if I had chemotherapy.

"Now that I am really approaching death, I can still use the arts in this way."

"You said the nurses responded first and that the arts opened another dimension. Can you describe this?" I ask.

"I don't know if the nurses could define what dimension it opened," M.L. replies. "But it gave a different feeling-tone to the experience they knew so well. It took them into the archetypal. It really brought an archetypal feeling-tone to the everyday clinical world."

"What is the archetypal dimension that you entered?"

"I'm thinking of one picture that I drew during the IL-12 treatment; I was the first human to receive this treatment. I just started fussing with the oil pastels and let something happen. Fish were in the sky and birds in the sea. There were Valkyrian figures coming to the rescue. It was bizarre. Yet it was exactly what my body was feeling.

"Then I wrote poetry when I was so desperately ill. I focused on the myth of Inanna, who goes into the underworld and suffers. The poem I wrote about this experience deeply affects people. These are certainly images that came from my unconscious. They are in psyche, the larger psyche that includes us all.

"Usually I like to write about beauty and love and all that stuff, but in this one I felt I had to write what was happening. If I was to experience this, I had to write what was true. Inanna is a myth that predates the story of Demeter and Persephone. Inanna is taken into the underworld. She goes into the underworld and is crucified. It's pretty graphic and horrible.

"When I was having a fever and aching beyond all aches, they stopped that clinical trial. It was too much for me. While I was doing that trial, I was sick and couldn't say anything; but I kept thinking of Inanna."

M.L. reads the poem:

INANNA

I cannot soar
when the sea sick sky invades
all senses, and
my stomach retches out the ill taste of everything, and
my mouth and throat are full of salivating sores, and
I cannot swallow
though I thirst
when all is gray, and
there is no horizon in the dark death cave
I cannot rise

Darting figures prod and pull, whispering
to feign dying
to endure this underworld
where I am loathe to find
nauseous and empty next to Death
no escape from pain
dreams heavy and hopeless
no light nor love
nor any memories save the wracking moment
when Death turns its face
thinking I am his

But I hold on
to nothing
   nothing calls
   nothing sings

I hold on
    a trace heart beat
    for no reason
I hold on
    barely hearing the whispers of Enki's envoys, as they
drag me through the gates

And since I am so much dead
Death does not know
I have escaped

"That's what happened to Inanna. These little figures that she made come and save her. I wrote an accompanying poem that asks where these little figures are this time. Will they come and save me? Will they drag me through the gates? They're not always there. If they're not there, it doesn't mean that I haven't tried. It's really a matter of the larger psyche."

I spoke to M.L. shortly before she died and asked: "How did art making and the creative process contribute to your treatment? People say that your energy increases when you are reading poetry and making art."

"There may have been a time in this sickness when my attitude, my mental intentions, and my art kept me alive," M.L. responds. "Now I'm in a place where I can honor what life I have, but I am no decision maker. The decision is someplace else. This is why, when you are working with patients, there is a time to encourage and there is a time to be with the moment and honor every sacred thing that is happening. There was a woman at Dana Farber whom I helped in this way. I knew the sacred space, and I knew she was going to die. I knew how to be with her. Others were saying, 'Oh, you can fight it.' The gung ho sports approach wasn't right then."

I interject, "You said, 'Art kept me alive.' "

"With art, you're in life. Art is being deeply involved in life. You're making art. You're building. You're changing. You're shaping, and you're not just a bump on a log or a zombie sitting in a clinic waiting for the doctor to see you. You're not getting absorbed in your disease and comparing how you're doing to how somebody else is doing. You're not equating yourself with the disease. When you use art, you're touching life. You're giving. You're expressing. You're part of the human world, and you're expressing the noblest part of being human."

The courage of M. L. O'Connor in celebrating life through creative expression, even as it was slipping away from her, had a significant impact on the Dana Farber environment. At a memorial service held for her at the hospital, the CEO described how she taught the doctors how "there is a difference between curing and healing; that there can be healing when curing is impossible; and that art heals."

M.L. demonstrated to the hospital community that artistic expression enables patients and their families to be actively involved in the overall treatment process, applying all of their creative and spiritual energies to the affirmation of life. The institutional environment is changed in a palpable way when creative energy circulates through it. This healthy movement of the creative process is then transmitted to patients, who open to it and in turn augment the environmental energy through their personal expression. The staff also feel the benefits of this more creative and life-affirming atmosphere; the expressions of patients give them the strength and energy needed to sustain their efforts in challenging situations.

I visited with M.L. at her deathbed to record the remarks she made above. She asked her family to withhold her morphine that morning. "I want to be clear when Shaun is here," she told them.

During the visit, she was concerned about the comfort of all of us who were present. She used humor to help us relax and open to the message that she wanted to give—that life is to be cherished, celebrated, and creatively engaged right to the last minute. I have never witnessed a more profound demonstration of how the creative process can transform the most difficult places in life.

Do the worst conditions of life have a unique ability to make us more aware of what really matters? Can there be inspiration in adversity? What accounts for this? Do you agree with M.L. that the quality and purpose of life are profoundly affected by our attitudes? Has there been a person in your life who has helped you see that there may be opportunities for creation in the most difficult conditions? Have you experienced the sense of the sacred space that she described? What is it that created the sanctity for you? Does it have something to do with relationships with other people?

What was the most challenging situation you have ever faced? How did you handle it? Did the momentum of the incident simply carry you through the process, or were you able to do creative things that altered the flow of events? Did the situation inspire creative responses from you afterward? Does it still influence you?

J. L. Moreno described his method of Psychodrama as offering people a chance to revisit difficult situations from the past and respond to them in more creative ways. Reflect upon events in your life where you would like a second chance to respond. Imagine yourself acting differently. How does it feel? Are you more effective? How do you envision other people responding to your different way of acting? Can you apply these changes to your life today?

The Transforming Role of Crisis and the Healing Power of Community

I was on the phone with Julia Kristeller of the School of Visual Arts in New York City. It was a week after the attack on the World Trade Center, located twenty blocks south of the school. Julia called me to plan a lecture we had scheduled a year earlier on "the collective imagination" and how community environments affect the process of creativity and healing. We did our business, and it was clear that she wanted to talk about what was happening in the city. I had spoken with another SVA faculty member two days after the devastating incident; still shaken, she spoke of how the entire school community stood on the street and watched with tears as the towers collapsed in lower Manhattan.

Julia says, "Your lecture topic turns out to be strangely timely. The theme of healing by being together with other people is very relevant to what we are now experiencing in New York. We are seeing how healing comes through community."

"How is it happening?" I ask.

"It's happening everywhere on the streets of New York. It is a creative act of community, with people accessing what's needed and letting go of ego. People found themselves doing things they did not think they were capable of doing. It didn't have to be written down for them. They just did it and can't explain how. Ordinary people did all of this. Nobody planned out what had to be done. In shelters people came together, and things happened spontaneously and without direction. Children were making hundreds of peanut butter sandwiches. I realized how we have an enormous capacity to be creative."

"Crisis can bring out the best in us and change our lives," I answer.

"We've always known that on smaller scales through relationships and deaths," Julia continues, "but the events of the past week brought it to a new level of creativity. People on the street needed to talk and tell their stories, to share their soul with total strangers. The Chinese word for crisis is made up of two symbols: danger and opportunity."

It seems at first glance to be a striking paradox that events can occur with greater creative spontaneity during a crisis. If we look more closely at what happens during times of crisis, we might discover that this state activates qualities characteristic of the creative process. We drop everything, let go of our habitual preoccupations, and reach beyond ourselves.

Hard places actually seem to enhance creativity. They establish priorities. People come together in crisis, and the same thing happens to our personal faculties. Vulnerability opens feelings, and we move beyond superficiality to deeper sensibilities. During a lecture that I gave in Netanya, Israel, at a particularly dangerous time, I realized how crisis can create a slipstream effect in groups of people. There is typically a flow of creative expression and an openness to others when we respond to serious threats. Crises evoke an immersion into the present moment that creativity requires.

What did you learn about the human response to crisis from the September 11, 2001 tragedy? Has your life been changed by this event? Do you have different priorities? Have you

viewed communities of people in a different way? Were you
inspired by the way people responded to the crisis? What do
you consider to be the source of the courage and resolve that
you witnessed? Do you feel that people were energized by
one another? Do environments and groups of people acting
together generate creativity and power?

In art therapy, I have observed how people express themselves
with expressive vitality and imagination when they are experiencing
personal crisis and upheaval. But when the acute phase of disturbance passes, they lose this intensity. When Heraclitus said that conflict is good, he was referring to its ability to activate, arouse, open,
and change life. Crisis breaks down all of the fixed elements that prevent us from relating to one another in new ways.

People say to me that corporations and the organizational world
have recognized the importance of a more creative life within the
workplace, but they don't know how to put this knowledge into
practice. They introduce some canned methods and practices that do
not go beneath the surface. Yet in times of crisis, when their existence
is truly threatened, people come together in new and more creative
ways. They are forced to "let go" and "embrace the unknown," processes that provide access to the deeper movements of creativity.

Does opening to more creative, less superficial relationships
require a certain degree of crisis in our lives? If so, why do
you think this is?

People create crisis and fear all the time to mobilize themselves
and other people. As Norm stated earlier, fear is a powerful source of
motivation. There are people who thrive on a daily crisis syndrome
and become addicted to it. Even if the crisis is fabricated and in many
ways illusory, it is real for the people experiencing it, especially if
someone in power creates it.

Do you ever use crisis and conflict in this way? Do you know
others who do? What does a constant state of crisis do to
people?

I personally do not respond well to environments where crisis levels are manipulated by leaders in order to influence people. Unnecessary crisis is not an effective basis of motivation for many of us. The creative process and life are always going to be reliable sources of difficulties and challenging conditions, so I don't need incitements other than what will emerge naturally from a given situation. I am inspired and motivated by the creative expressions of people who have been faced with difficult situations and the support that people give to one another.

A teacher describes to me how creativity and healing characterize her school environment because there is "a community of people looking out for each other."

"Creativity is inspired," she explained, "through models and observable examples of support, whereas threats to creativity include jealousy, negative attention, leaders who show no interest in what others do, and dominating egos."

Do you sometimes fabricate the difficulties you experience at work and in relationships? Have others done this to you? How do you react?

What kinds of work conditions motivate you most? When you are confronted with difficulties and crises, what do you need from other people? Can you recall an incident where other people and your environment helped you deal creatively with challenges? Where they hindered your responsiveness?

I was talking with an artist colleague with whom I serve on the board of an art association. She described how many of our most difficult situations in organizational life occur when "people focused on the same territory try to dominate one another rather than work together."

"Why do we do this?" I asked.

"Because power is valued over creativity, even among the creative," she answered.

Do you find that relationships with others both generate tensions and provide the basis for their transformation?

Where do you stand in relation to the use of domination in solving problems?

Prevailing over another person in the same community through the use of power, rather than reasoned understanding, will always leave bad feelings in its wake. Cooperation is the only way through a difficult situation. The community needs to cultivate its ability to hold people together, to support risks, and to generate the confidence and support needed to transform difficult situations.

LISA
Making Creative Energy as an Artist-in-Residence

Lisa is an art therapist who has shifted her emphasis from clinical practice to organizational development. She studied law before training as an art therapist, and she is now focused on integrating her interests in creativity and leadership.

"The board of a large company has invited me to work with them in cultivating a more creative work environment," Lisa says. "It is a sophisticated group, and they understand the difference between superficial commitments to innovation and the challenging work that needs to be done in order to achieve a truly creative environment. I was invited to work with this organization because my clinical work with individuals and groups involved the deeper dimensions of how we both further and obstruct creative expression. The company realizes how creativity is tied to conflict, threats, and ongoing challenges presented by external environments; they want someone who has had experience helping people deal with these dynamics. They are looking for something more than creative exercises for employees and one-shot workshops. I've essentially been asked to be an artist-in-residence."

"What are your responsibilities?" I ask.

"An artist-in-residence can stay within a creative role," Lisa responds. "This is significant in organizational life, where so many demands are placed on creative people who have other responsibilities. People are paid to watch over the fiscal and human resources, so why not pay someone to be the keeper of the creative process. I liked the idea, and I jumped at the opportunity."

"Are you expected to set up an easel and paint in public places?" I ask.

"Actually, I might do this at some point," Lisa responds. "It may not be so far-fetched. There may be benefits to making art as people work at their jobs. Maybe I can make art works focused on what I feel happening in the organizational environment. We hire consultants to make assessments based on quantitative data; why not let an artist give a qualitative interpretation of what's happening through her creative medium. There can be some real value to increasing the number of ways we investigate what's going on in a community. Thanks for the idea. I'll do it."

"I was being sarcastic," I confess.

"Yes," Lisa replies, "But just the fact that we might be reluctant to make art as a way of directly contributing to community, or that we might question the relevance of creative expression, suggests that this issue needs attention."

"Listening to you helps me realize that it makes complete sense to encourage artists to assess the creative vitality of organizations with their unique ways of interpreting experiences and expressing what they feel."

"This is a wonderful idea," Lisa responds. "But right now, they want me to move through the community and evaluate how people relate to one another, and how the company can do more to integrate the creative process into everything it does. They're interested in what I see from the perspective of creativity. I especially appreciate their suspicion of the stock approaches to creativity development."

"It's unusual," I say, "for leadership to realize that creativity is a frame of reference and that the creative eye may look from a different vantage point than the controlling or directive one."

"The senior management believes that a more creative workplace will generate a stronger sense of community that will ultimately produce better results," Lisa responds.

"Do you mean that they realize that creativity enhancement doesn't fall within the grids of a strategic plan?"

"That's right," Lisa replies. "Some things can be planned and tracked in a linear way, and other things fall outside these frameworks."

"Why is it taking so long for the organizational world to focus on the cultivation of creativity and its unique intelligence?" I ask.

"Organizations have always been governed by the most traditional hierarchical forms of leadership and power," Lisa responds. "It is only recently that work communities and leaders have been searching for something else. There is a sense that a creative environment will be more productive because it is better suited to the outcomes we expect at this point in history."

"And is there a new set of problems?" I ask.

"I think that the shifting emphasis is directed more toward a new sense of opportunity," Lisa answers. "There is a realization that work is a stressful and difficult place. There are people who see an opportunity in this. They want me to research this facet of organizational life and explore how the negative energy can be transformed and put to good use."

"What are some of the things you are doing?" I ask.

"I am learning a great deal," Lisa affirms, "and this is being encouraged by the company. They know this is new territory, and senior management is committed to ongoing learning. My main focus right now is assessing the creative energy generated by the work environment. I am looking at places where this energy is strong and places where it is not as potent."

"What do you mean by creative energy?" I ask.

"Creative energy is characterized by vitality, openness, and imagination. The energy is high powered when it circulates freely, when dynamic connections are made among participants, when there is a certain degree of chaos and openness, and most of all when creative conversions easily occur. If people block or oppose changes and the forming of new relationships between things, the environment is not going to be characterized by creative energy."

"Can creative energy be measured?"

"People can report on their feelings of creative vitality," Lisa explains. "They are also very sensitive to the creative energy of other people, groups, and areas within the company. It is quite remarkable how accurate people can be when they assess one another. The other person sometimes sees us better than we see ourselves."

"So everyone in the company becomes a coresearcher," I say.

"Yes," Lisa says. "I have also considered generating questionnaire data, but at this point I am gathering so much useful information from the self-reporting that people do. The observations people make of themselves and others seem very accurate and consistent with what I observe. Talking to people, observing what they do, asking questions, and listening to the ideas of others is in itself an activity that generates creative energy. I don't think questionnaires are able to do this. So the means becomes the end when the community begins to assess its creativity."

"What are people telling you?"

"There is remarkable consistency among many of the responses," Lisa replies. "Almost everybody describes how creativity flourishes when it becomes part of the culture of the organization and how it needs to be supported at all levels, from peers as well as the top. I constantly hear how areas within the organization that support risk and free expression are more creatively active than those where making mistakes can hurt you. There is also a spirit of generosity in the most creative sectors of the organization, where people really give time and attention to one another, where disagreements are openly discussed, and where the group brainstorms together as a way of responding to problems. They don't panic and get down on each other when something bad happens. The leader really sets the tone in making sure that people support one another when adversity hits."

"A positive and safe environment is maintained," I say.

"Absolutely," Lisa answers. "Disappointments have to be accepted, like they say, as 'part of the process.' They are unavoidable in life. Artists and creative types certainly know this. No one escapes it. We've all reached for goals that dissolve just when we thought we were there. 'The sun also rises,' and we do too after our setbacks. We have to see all of this in perspective. We can't be devastated by disappointments. We need to learn from them."

"Is this where the process of coaching enters?" I ask.

"Yes," Lisa replies, "effective leaders coach, mentor, and affirm people in their groups. Everybody needs this, even the individuals who we see as most successful and creative."

"They often need it more," I say.

"Because they are always sticking their necks out," Lisa maintains, "always taking risks and trying new things. They need the support and they deserve it."

"What else do people describe as a characteristic of creative environments?" I ask.

"There is a willingness to tackle the really difficult problems, the ones that others avoid."

"Is this unusual?" I ask.

"Yes," Lisa replies. "Many people are intimidated by problems and anything that interrupts the orderly flow of their activities. Most organizations are actually constructed to avoid anything out of the ordinary. The creative environment is able to quickly embrace a challenging situation and adapt to it. I see this as a primary attribute of creative teams, something that really distinguishes them from more conventional groups of people."

"How do the effective and creative teams respond to crisis?" I ask.

"They take it in stride," Lisa asserts. "They don't jump too quickly. I was with a director earlier today who responded to a crisis by telling her team to be present with what is happening. 'Don't rush to solutions,' she said. One of the engineers in the team saw that I was fascinated, and he said to me with a smile, 'Problems are the subject matter of our creative work. What would we do without them? They wouldn't need us here.'"

"Is there an operational lesson in these situations?" I ask.

"Creative groups accept problems with a sense of curiosity," Lisa replies. "They withhold the tendency to give instant explanations and solutions. I've observed how creative teams really immerse themselves in the problems and open to them completely. As they do this, the problem begins to lose its overwhelming nature. The team begins to see the difficulty more objectively, as a phenomenon just like anything else. Of course there are emergencies that demand immediate reactions, but we don't want to call 911 in response to every problem."

"Are there other qualities that you have observed?" I ask.

"There are many," Lisa responds, "Experimentation is crucial, together with its accompanying values: tolerance of errors and really paying attention to mistakes so that we learn from them and prevent them from happening again. Perhaps the most distinctive quality of all the creative environments I have observed is the pervasive atmosphere of honesty and directness, the sense that it is dangerous to sweep things under the rug and to avoid conflict. The creative groups welcome variety and different ways of approaching situations. They don't insist on a single way of operating. Collaboration is encouraged, even among opposing points of view. Every perspective is embraced as offering something to the collective effort, whether or not it is accepted. People energize one another the way musicians do. As D. H. Lawrence said, 'We are transmitters of life.' There is a lot of listening going on; people study what others are doing, and they show interest in one another's problems. When things get rough and challenging, the creative teams really distinguish themselves."

I say, "It sounds like they do their best work in the hardest places."

"They stay open," Lisa continues, "and they are able to ride out the process of things breaking apart because they know and trust that these events are necessary to the making of new creations. This is probably their best work, because the more conventional team is incapable of doing this."

"And what characterizes environments where there is little creative energy?" I ask.

"People are separated and isolated," Lisa answers. "As we say today, they stay inside the box; they are comfortable there, and they have little desire to change because that will require them to act in new ways. And they retreat to these enclosures when threatened or when the going gets tough."

"Have you established goals based on your experience so far?" I ask.

"At this early stage," Lisa responds, "I have a sense that the generation of creative energy needs to be a primary objective of the company. We need to establish conditions for producing and sustaining this energy, with the realization that it will always find its way to the problems and tasks that need to be addressed. From artistic practice we learn that the creative process knows the way through the most challenging situations, those that can never be resolved through analytic and strategic planning. There is a need for processes that create outside the lines, that cross over from one framework to another and make new integrations."

"I know what you mean Lisa. A farmer in Connemara once said to me, 'Can't fence anything with wings.' "

"The really difficult problems," Lisa continues, "aren't solved by step-by-step procedures. This is what we learn in the practice of art. Difficult and often opposing elements converge and shape something new on the basis of their interaction. I want to bring this understanding to organizational life. Creative integrations not only diverge from the step-by-step procedures of analytic problem solving, but they are apt to break everything apart and refashion a new synthesis from the pieces."

"Sounds Dionysian or like shamanic dismemberment," I remark, "breaking apart to create anew."

"Creativity can be a tough assignment," Lisa responds.

Do you agree with Lisa's idea that organizations need to give more attention to generating creative energy? Is it time to expand our culture's notion of what is essential to·human productivity and satisfaction? Why do you think we continue to overlook these needs? Is it because people want to stay within the box? Do you think organizations really want to cultivate the free exercise of creative expression? Is the making of creative energy a priority? Or do organizations actually want containment and complete control over people? Do they need this in order to conduct their business? If the answers are relative, where is creativity encouraged and where is it discouraged?

What do you think about the position that Lisa has been given? Does it sound realistic? Would you like to do something like this? Are you capable of committing yourself completely to cultivating the creative process? Is this commitment realistic in the organization where you work? Would the leader and/or the workforce have difficulty with it? What makes it difficult? What resources do you see that might make it possible? What needs to change? Who needs to make the changes? Are you capable of mobilizing others to change?

Make a list of things that might be done within your organization to cultivate a more creative environment.

Distinguish between actions that can be taken immediately and those that will take more time and effort. Also list the obstacles to doing these things within yourself, others, and the structure of the organization.

The creative changes that Lisa describes are demanding, and they do require a certain Dionysian deconstruction and renewal. Establish some aesthetic distance from yourself and all of the issues that we have been discussing regarding creativity. Try to take a hard and objective look at yourself and your environment. Are you comfortable inside the boxes of habit and routine? Do you really want to live a more creative life? Do you think that others do?

CREATIVE PRACTICE

The first step in working with difficult and threatening situations is to accept their presence and open to them. When we enter the crucible of a relationship with something we fear, there is little doubt that we will be changed. Creative engagement involves a partnership with the problem, rather than the more common tendency to repress, control, and keep it under wraps.

Establish a dialogue with the threats. Get to know them better. Give them feelings. Establish compassion for them. Make bridges between you and them. Take your time with them. Things get worse when you respond too quickly. An unhurried tempo is essential in dealing with threats. Learn how to stay with the image of the difficult situation, and trust that your relationship to it will change if you can sustain connection. Stay open; you need to hold the space for the process to unfold.

Identify the times in your life when bad situations, disturbances, and errors forced you to change, to move on to something different. Gather together memories and images from these times, and record them in your journal. Write a poem using these images and giving thanks to how they shaped you. Create a symbol for each of these situations; then string them together like prayer beads, each a reminder of how problems strengthen and refine our character.

Expand this exercise to working together with a partner or a group of people. If you know the people well, select a problem or crisis in your time together that forced you all to change. If you do not know each other well, identify a social crisis or a loss. Work together to make a group tribute to the problem as an agent of change. Gather small objects and images that represent outcomes generated by the problem and arrange them into a configuration. Add prose and poetic phrases, small drawings, and other things that pay tribute to the positive results that emerge from difficult and disturbing situations.

Take time to contemplate the configuration you made together. Write brief, spontaneous prose or verse responses to the arrangement and how you felt while making it. Read your responses to one another, making sure you take pauses between each reading to reflect and make the transition to the next one.

Select a problem at work that is disturbing you. Put your usual reactions to the problem aside, and bracket your feelings as described in chapter 4. Initiate an interview with the problematic situation in your journal.

Ask it to introduce itself, to tell you what it wants, and to tell you why it acts the way it does. Inquire into what it feels; what it fears; and what it thinks about you.

Respond to these statements. Stay connected to the problem, and don't be concerned about trying to know where it is going.

Ask yourself why you are threatened by this situation, what you contribute to its power, what you might do to be less consumed by it, and how feeling less annoyed and threatened by the situation might change your relationship to it. Reflect on whether or not you really want to change your relationship to the problem. What might you lose if you change?

Explore what you and the problem have in common. Imagine the bridges that exist between the two of you. Describe them in your journal. Make drawings of them. Use pictures from magazines to make collage images that convey qualities of the bridges. Use these different media to explore how you might engage the problem more productively and creatively and to represent the barriers you have to bridge, transform, or engage in new and more helpful ways.

~~~ Identify a time when you responded in a destructive or ineffective way to a threatening situation. Imagine yourself going back to that time and acting differently. It can be especially threatening to openly confront situations where we failed and acted badly.

Use your journal to rewrite your response to the threat. Describe how you acted differently this time around, how you learned from the situation, and how you have changed as a result of the experience. You might want to expand this activity and revision the problematic situation with the drawing and collage media described above. The unique qualities of the creative materials you use help to shape new perspectives on problems.

~~~ Practice deconstructing problems and fashioning new forms from the pieces. Make a drawing or magazine collage of something that threatens you, and then rip or cut the drawing into pieces like Dionysus was taken apart by the maenads. Arrange the pieces into a new configuration, a new life. "Break, break, break," as Nietzsche said, in order to create anew.

~~~ Fear of going through the process of dissolution and letting go is typically a major block and deterrent to group members and leaders when it comes to making new things. Practice "playing" with things falling apart in order to feel comfortable with how the creative process must move through cycles of construction, deconstruction, reconstruction, readjustment, and so forth. We need to experience how organizations and relationships, like Nature, are constantly moving, and that growth requires breaking up fixities. There are many cultural traditions in which beautiful art objects, like Tibetan sand mandalas, are made and then destroyed to express and honor the cycles of creative regeneration.

Children are wonderful teachers when it comes to the cycles of creation. Work like children with wooden blocks or other building materials, making constructions, breaking them apart, then making new ones. Try to focus on the overall movement of creation, and enjoy taking things apart as much as putting them together. Do these exercises alone, with a partner, or with a group. Give heightened attention and appreciation to the process of things breaking apart.

Use this creative practice as a way of helping you let go of things that trouble you. As you perform the physical process of constructing something and breaking it apart, you can experience a corresponding reaction with regard to emotions and problems that you need to move beyond. Try to let go of obsessive thoughts, just like the blocks falling apart. Welcome the open space of the present moment, and create something new in the place of the old and troublesome things to which you cling.

Spontaneous body movement offers wonderful and natural opportunities for practicing mindful and aesthetically pleasing dissolution. Work with a partner or with a group of people. Move freely for about a minute; then slowly make contact with others, and arrange your bodies into a sculptural configuration. Hold (freeze) the position for another twenty or thirty seconds without moving. As you stay in position, be aware of how you feel and how the bodies connect to one another. At the designated time, break apart from the others, with your senses focused on the aesthetic qualities of the dissolution as the climax of the piece.

We tend to focus our attention on how things go together and then disregard their breaking apart. In this activity, give as much attention as possible to the dissolution. You can practice this exercise alone. Working with witnesses can add important dimensions to these movement experiences. The witnesses not only give energy and support to those who move, but they offer valuable perspectives on what takes place.

Practice constructing and breaking apart in natural environments. Working alone or with others, make constructions in the sand on a beach, photograph your work, and leave it for the tide to destroy and return to nature.

Do the same thing in a field or wooded area, where you make

something from the materials indigenous to the site. Working as a group, fashion a construction, photograph the outcome, break the configuration apart, and return the materials to nature.

Write spontaneous responses conveying your feelings about the process, and read them to group members. Bury your poems in the earth so they become part of nature, or burn them as an expression of creating, letting go, and opening to the next opportunity for creation.

As Lisa suggests, let's see if our organizations can become places dedicated to the making of creative energy. Establishing a truly creative and life-affirming climate within the workplace and group life is one of the "really difficult problems" that Lisa feels cannot be solved through conventional plans and strategies. She is right in saying that we must commit ourselves to generating and sustaining the energy; then we have to trust that it will find its way to areas of need, as we do our best to guide one another toward successful outcomes.

Based on three decades of experience fostering the creative experience of groups, I am convinced that desiring, imagining, and taking different steps towards the realization of this goal will someday make it a reality. There is too much at stake in terms of happiness and fulfillment at work to do otherwise. There is too much to gain in terms of organizational vitality and productivity to miss this opportunity. And we know all too well how the small and large communities of the world need to be turned upside down in terms of fostering rather than restricting the creative potential of their members.

My hope is that this book will contribute to the creative teamwork that is always the basis of infusing organizations with imagination. Within the creative team, there are few restrictions upon how we influence and support one another. Maybe it will be possible for this spirit to grow from connections that readers of this book have with the creative process and with one another. It will give me great satisfaction if creative outcomes, always a step or two ahead of plans and expectations, emerge from this exchange and surprise us with their power to change our lives.

INDEX

Abbott, Shep, 138
Active imagination, 93–94, 99–114, 134
Aesthetic distance, 136, 147–149, 254
Alaya-vijnana, 75
Art as Medicine, 114
Artspace, 138
Augustine, Saint, 20
Aura of environment, 127–128
Automatic writing, 69–70

Becker, Norm, 218–227, 245
Beckett, Samuel, 205
Bigelow, John, 128–132, 207
Billy Budd, 139, 150
Bloomsbury group, 168
Bracketing, 107, 112
Brainstorming, 71, 98, 177
Buber, Martin, 102
Buddha, 80, 118, 125
Buddhism, 75

Cage, John, 50, 216–217
Cather, Willa, 168
Ch'i, 233
Chinese medicine, 233
Chodorow, Joan, 114
Cognitive dissonance, 102, 187
Command and control, 130
Communing with nature, 131–132
Creative autocrat, 76
Creative energy, 4–5, 73, 77–80, 83–88, 99–100, 109, 117–123, 127, 133–134, 137, 153, 163, 166, 168, 175–176, 179–181, 183–186, 188, 191, 198, 214, 227, 233–238, 247–254 242
Crisis, 244–245
Crowe, Russell, 191

Dada, 217
Dana-Farber Cancer Institute, 238, 241–242
Dante Alighieri, 38
Demeter, 239
Depth psychology, 113
Dickinson, Emily, 57

Digital Equipment Company, 218
Dionysian deconstruction, 253–254, 256
Disturbance, 235–236
Drucker, Peter, 127
Duchamp, Marcel, 217
Durrell, Lawrence, 168, 175

Ecclesiastes, 6
Einstein, Albert, 89–90, 99
Ellington, Duke, 188
Enki, 241

Fear, 29, 31–32, 34, 105, 108–109, 120, 125, 136–138, 142–143, 157, 187, 197, 201–202, 222–228, 230, 232, 245, 254–256
Festinger, Leon, 102
Flying sparks, 187
Free association, 69–70, 98
Freud, Sigmund, 99

Gadamer, Hans Georg, 140
Garciaparra, Nomar, 203
Genesis, 1–3
Gestalt dreamwork, 105
Goethe, Johann Wolfgang von, 69

Haiku, 111
Hart, Peter, 59–66
Healing process, 233–234
Hemingway, Ernest, 168
Heraclitus, 77, 245
Humanistic psychology, 130
Husserl, Edmund, 107

IBM, 225
IL-12 treatment, 239
Inanna, 239–241

Joyce, James, 94, 169
Joyce, Nora, 169
Jung, C. G., 8, 35, 93–94, 99–105, 113–114
Jung on Active Imagination, 113–114

Kafka, Franz, 90–91
Keats, John, 221

Knill, Paolo, 35, 164, 169
Kristeller, Julia, 243–244

Lawrence, D. H., 252
Levine, Steven, xi
Lewis, Edith, 168
Literalism, 105–106

Malchiodi, Cathy, 246
Mandala, 8, 157–158, 256
Marcuse, Herbert, 182
MBA answers, 221
Melville, Herman, 139–140, 150–151
Meta-cognition, 121
Michelangelo, 96
Miller, Henry, 168, 183
Moby Dick, 70, 139–140, 150
Mono-orgs, 76
Montessori, Maria, 23
Moreno, J. L., 243
Munch, Edvard, 91

Negative Capability, 221
Nelson, Truman, 44, 115–116
Newton, Isaac, 99
Nietzsche, Friedriche, 71, 126,
    173–174, 234, 256
Nin, Anaïs, 168

O, Mr., 94
O'Connor, Mary Louise, 238–243
Olson, Ken, 218–221
One Dimensional Man, 182

Parker, Jack, 51
Participation mystique, 84
Peale, Norman Vincent, 124
Perls, Fritz, 105
Persephone, 239
Personifying, 104–105, 112
Phenomenology, 107
Picasso, Pablo, 168, 217
Pollock, Jackson, 69
Post-Capitalist Society, 127
Psychoanalysis, 69–70
Psychodrama, 243
Puccini, Giacomo, 188

Reinhardt, Ad, 219
Relativizing the ego, 103–109, 112
Rilke, Rainer Maria, 101

Rogers, Carl, 130
Romantic poets, 187
Rossi Le, Laura, 167–169
Rumi, 14, 172

Sacrifice, relationship, 169–171
Safety first, 29
School of the Visual Arts, 243
September 11, 2001, 243–244
Shaman, 156–157
Shape-shifters, 198
Sisyphus, 37, 44, 48, 50, 52, 81
Slipstream, 45–46, 48, 50–54, 75, 83,
    244
Stein, Gertrude, 168
Storehouse consciousness, 75
Sufism, 8–9, 87
Surrealists, 69

Tao Te Ching, 159
The Birth of Tragedy, 126, 234
The Genealogy of Morals, 71
Thérèse of Lisieux, Saint, 160
Toklas, Alice, B., 168
Toute est grace, 160
Towner, Mark, 48–49
Trickster, 109

You Can't Go Home Again, 39

Ulysses, 94
Unconscious, 58, 75, 78, 99, 238–
    239

Van Gogh, Vincent, 91, 167
Van Gogh, Theo, 167

Weil, Simone, 118
Whitman, Walt, 195
Wilde, Oscar, 41
Williams, Richard, 169
Williams, Serena, 169
Williams, Venus, 169
Winnicott, D. W., 210
Witnessing, 23, 52, 65, 113, 163, 188,
    197–199, 230, 232, 257
Wolfe, Thomas, 39
Woolf, Virgina, 168
World Trade Center, 243–244

Zen stick, 121